Too Much Sea for Their Decks

Also by Michael Schumacher
Published by the University of Minnesota Press

Mighty Fitz: The Sinking of the Edmund Fitzgerald

November's Fury: The Deadly Great Lakes Hurricane of 1913

Torn in Two: The Sinking of the Daniel J. Morrell
and One Man's Survival on the Open Sea

The Trial of the Edmund Fitzgerald:
Eyewitness Accounts from the U.S. Coast Guard Hearings

Too Much Sea for Their Decks

SHIPWRECKS OF MINNESOTA'S
NORTH SHORE AND ISLE ROYALE

**Michael
Schumacher**

University of Minnesota Press
Minneapolis
London

Published by the University of Minnesota Press
111 Third Avenue South, Suite 290
Minneapolis, MN 55401-2520
http://www.upress.umn.edu

ISBN 978-1-5179-1284-0 (hc)
ISBN 978-1-5179-1610-7 (pb)

A Cataloging-in-Publication record for this book is available from the Library of Congress.

Printed in the United States of America on acid-free paper

The University of Minnesota is an equal-opportunity educator and employer.

32 31 30 29 28 27 26 25 24 23   10 9 8 7 6 5 4 3 2 1

To all those who worked, lived,
and died on the Great Lakes waters

"We ran into a little more sea than she could take."
—Captain Albert Stiglin of the *Henry Steinbrenner,*
interviewed by the *Detroit Free Press*

Contents

Introduction

THE TRAGIC MYSTERIES OF LAKE SUPERIOR

~~~

On the right day, when the sun is hitting the Earth at the perfect angle, when warm air is just enough to ruffle stray leaves scattered on the ground, when tiny waves are small enough to make you squint to see them, the northern shore of Lake Superior feels like magic. Old, battered bluffs rise on the horizon behind you, witness to the countless millennia that created this place. The lake runs on for as far as the eye can see, and the frigid water does not invite the casual swimmer, but for those brave and sturdy enough to test it, the depths can go from shallow to very deep in just a few strokes.

Lake Superior feels like the soul of North America. Its 31,700 square miles of surface area make it the largest freshwater lake in the world, and at its deepest point of 1,333 feet it is one of the deepest bodies of water in North America. Huge glaciers carved out the enormous areas occupied by the Great Lakes today; when time and moderate temperatures melted the glaciers, the ice, now water, filled the cavernous areas gouged out by the glaciers.

The dramatically uneven lake bottom, with its high and low spots often in proximity, contributed to the formation of numerous islands, including the cluster known as the Apostle Islands, and off Minnesota's northern shore an archipelago of islands that include, notably, Isle Royale. These islands presented all kinds of navigational hazards after commercial shipping had become predominant in the mid- to late-nineteenth century.

The Ojibwe and other Native people understood the lake's temperamental nature, especially in the fall, when the conditions around and on the lake can change in minutes. Rarely straying far from the shore, the Native people traveled in canoes that moved easily across the water and could swiftly head back to land if winds whipped up the water. Trade items included furs, food and provisions, and the minerals plentiful in the region.

The French were the first Europeans to explore the lake, called Gichigami by the Ojibwe, and the shores around it, but following their victory in the French and Indian War, the English renamed the lake Superior and controlled traffic on the water. Oddly enough, given the enormity of the lake and its access to the large stretches of land in the United States and Canada, commercial shipping was slow to develop on Lake Superior. Settlements on the lake's shores were small. The frigid climate did not encourage major development. That changed with the building of larger cities, not only around Lake Superior but near the shores of other Great Lakes. By the early years of the nineteenth century, there was a spike in the need for commercial shipping, which competed with growing rail systems.

The first commercial steam-driven vessel hit Lake Superior in 1847. By the time the rich iron ore deposits were discovered nearly a half century later, demands for shipping on Lake Superior had reached unprecedented heights. The port at Duluth could boast of being one of the largest in the United States.

This demand necessitated the designing and building of larger, stronger vessels. Schooners and wooden freighters, once dominant in shipping, gave way to steel boats, which at the time of their launching seemed indestructible. The occasionally violent weather, churning up gigantic seas, turned out to be a serious challenge, especially in the month of November, when blasts of cold Arctic air collided with water yet to be cooled from summer. Some of the lake had yet to be charted, and groundings were not uncommon. As lake traffic increased, so did the number of accidents.

The lake, as those who sailed it learned, could be both welcoming and hazardous.

〜〜〜

This is my sixth book about Great Lakes shipwrecks.

Mighty Fitz is an account of the loss of the *Edmund Fitzgerald,* and *The Trial of the* Edmund Fitzgerald, a companion volume, contains documents related to the sinking, plus a lengthy oral history drawn from the Coast Guard hearings conducted immediately following the loss.

Wreck of the Carl D. tells the story of the *Carl D. Bradley,* a gigantic limestone carrier that broke in two during a fierce November storm on Lake Michigan in 1958. Four men managed to escape to a life raft. Two survived the night, braving heavy seas and hypothermia-inducing conditions.

The *Daniel J. Morrell,* an ore carrier, broke in two and sank on Lake Huron under similar circumstances in 1966. *Torn in Two* is an account of the tragedy in which four men climbed aboard a life raft and tried to survive frigid and stormy weather. One man survived, but only after clinging to the raft wearing just a peacoat and undershorts for thirty-seven hours.

November's Fury, the story of the great hurricane hitting the lakes in 1913, involved many boats on all five lakes, all battling what is universally agreed to be the worst storm to ever hit the lakes, claiming more lives and vessels than seemed possible. Each tale of an individual boat is self-contained, yet each is part of a much larger story.

Each of these books has an essential individual theme that I hadn't considered when I embarked on my research—a theme that acted like the keel of a vessel, the backbone on which everything else was built. *Mighty Fitz,* for instance, is a Great Lakes mystery. No one will ever know for certain why or how she went down. This became evident as can be in *The Trial of the* Edmund Fitzgerald. *Wreck of the* Carl D. is a heartbreaking account of the small town of Rogers City, Michigan, which bore incredible suffering and loss; it seemed that everyone in the town was related to, or knew, one or more of the shipwreck's victims. *Torn in Two* is about survival under impossible circumstances and the price exacted from a sole survivor. Finally, *November's Fury* addresses more than a single storm: it studies the destructive forces of nature and how it possesses the ability, to quote Gordon Lightfoot, to "turn minutes to hours." Anyone who has ever been in a wreck and survived will tell you that time freezes when you are struggling to live.

To me, those themes had the power to drive the story forward. I didn't plan it that way; they simply presented themselves as the research and writing advanced.

This book is different. There is no single major undercurrent of a theme. Perhaps I subconsciously included the important aspects of shipwrecks in the other books—and they are important here—or maybe a theme hasn't yet occurred to me. I don't know.

Maybe the city of Duluth is the undercurrent in this book. Once second to only New York in handling commercial shipping traffic, Duluth figures, one way or another, in many of the accidents described here. Its harbor entrance, one of the most beautiful you will find anywhere, could be a challenge to vessels sailing in heavy weather, but, as the *Thomas Wilson*, a whaleback broadsided by another boat, learned at the beginning of the twentieth century, it didn't have to be storming for a tragedy to occur.

But it isn't just the shipwrecks that make Duluth memorable. Commercial shipping contributed to the city's exponential growth near the turn of the twentieth century, and the shores of western Lake Superior, acting as foreground to the hilly northern Minnesota terrain, into which so many homes seemed to have been carved, have given Duluth a beauty that needs to be seen and experienced by anyone journeying through the area. I have been to Duluth many times, and all this was certainly on my mind when I was working on this book.

Or perhaps the history of commercial shipping acts as the keel of this book. The topic is far too large and general to be adequately addressed in a volume of this size, but it was on my mind throughout my writing. I hope to give the reader a taste, a flavor of the extraordinary history of Great Lakes shipping, whether that entails the discovery and development of the materials shipped, the boats carrying them, the passenger services, or the ways that weather services affected shipping. I consciously tried to include the many types of vessels plying their trades for more than a century, including schooners, wooden freighters, early steel-hulled steamers, whalebacks, and bulk carriers, as they increased in size and the amount of freight that they hauled.

An evolution was at work here. This history, in turn, greatly influenced the growth of an entire region of this country.

~~~

From the beginning, I envisioned a three-pronged approach to this book's contents: the shipwrecks of Minnesota, particularly the state's northern coastline; the wrecks in proximity of Isle Royale; and three storms of different character, all having a bearing on Minnesota and Lake Superior. Each of these three sections would be presented in chronological order, but each decade of the better part of a century is represented.

I originally planned to open with the storms. All were dramatic, plus we have a tendency to see storms as the main culprits behind ship sinkings. The storms chosen carry special significance in Great Lakes history. The 1905 storm (also known as "the *Mataafa* storm," after the best-known vessel affected by it) exacted the greatest toll, in lives and material loss, in Lake Superior history; the tales of bravery and heroism in that storm are legendary in Great Lakes lore.

The storm of 1913 was indisputably the worst in the annals of shipping. Minnesota and Lake Superior were spared the worst—that horrible distinction goes to Lake Huron—but the impact on the area merited inclusion in the book.

The "Armistice Day Storm" of 1940 deserved inclusion not for its impact on Lake Superior (it was minimal, in comparison to other storms) but because of what it taught us about vicious storms and how quickly they could pop up, with devastating consequences. This was arguably the worst snowstorm to hit Minnesota, and the consequences, especially for duck hunters caught out in it, were lethal.

I ultimately decided that it might be best to present the storms last, to move from the specific to the general. This was mostly a matter of preparing the reader by offering history first, presenting the details about western Lake Superior and Isle Royale in the individual vessels' stories rather than in accounts focused on a larger area.

Part 2, on Isle Royale shipwrecks, demonstrates my point. Although the island is large (45 by 9 miles), even combined with the tiny islands nearby it is still fairly small in the grand scheme of things. In a way, it is symbolic of nature, neither benevolent or malevolent, just consistent over the millennia, stamping its wonder on humans. It has been lethal at times. The topography of the lake floor surrounding the island rises and falls, leading to groundings described in this book. The island can be welcoming, violent, peaceful, unforgiving, relentless—as the unfortunate souls on the *Kamloops* determined, after escaping the clutches of a savage storm on a lifeboat and finding their way to Isle Royale, only to perish after they were isolated and exposed to the bitter cold.

Encounters with hostile nature are part of a sailor's job, an absolute they would prefer to avoid, one they usually conquer, but one in which they are occasionally defeated, as the thousands of shipwrecks littering the floors of the Great Lakes will attest.

The stories included here are the stories of loss.

～～～

Four of my previous books, about the losses of the *Carl D. Bradley,* the *Daniel J. Morrell,* and the *Edmund Fitzgerald,* examined founderings. All three sank in storms, though all on different lakes, and all three wrecks lie in two pieces hundreds of feet beneath the surface. The *Fitzgerald* was loaded with taconite pellets; the others were sailing light. All three vessels, the largest to sink in fresh water, provide varying perspectives on foundering.

This book, like *November's Fury,* includes a mixture of sinking types, though the great percentage of losses in the 1913 storm involved capsizing, and this book, due to so many accidents occurring in shallow water near Isle Royale, reports largely on groundings. The reasons for the groundings varied, and I recognized during my research that this type of loss had a way of addressing human failings that preceded the losses. When examining the photographs of the boats aground, one can't help but wonder how this sort of thing is possible. This book provides answers.

Although the shipwrecks in this and my other books are different and similar in many ways, one thing unites the sinkings: water. This is almost grotesquely obvious, but all you have to do is spend time around or on the lakes to feel the profundity in something so basic. I can walk from my house to Lake Michigan in a matter of minutes, and I visit the lake almost every day. I have also visited the other four Great Lakes many times. I am constantly reminded, especially during stormy times, of the sheer power of the water. I am also reminded, far more often, of the incredible beauty of the water, whether it is a clear, crystalline blue, or tinged light brown after the shallows have been stirred up by a recent storm, or is slate gray. And it goes on as far as the eye can see.

This is the mystique that brought so many sailors to their jobs. It's not just the work and the money. One doesn't have to work on a freighter for those. It's *something else.*

Sometimes it's soothing.

And sometimes it destroys.

PART I
Minnesota

Stranger

~~~

There was a time, back in the nineteenth century, when one could stand on shore and look out over one of the Great Lakes and see schooners punctuating the horizon. The wind would be hitting the enormous sails of these slender wooden boats and pushing them forward toward ports happily receiving commercial trade. A crewman, screened from the sun by the billowing sails, might be situated on deck, his watch consisting of keeping a well-trained eye on the other boats in the area, the work and respite intersecting at that comfortable point that reminded him of why he originally signed up for the duty.

Schooners dominated commercial traffic on the Great Lakes in the nineteenth century. The early schooners were small, roughly 60 to 100 feet in length, with minimal crews of three or four. The boats were two masted and carried modest cargoes of package goods, fish, lumber, salt, grain, and other easily managed and transported fare. The vessels evolved in length, design, and usage as directed by basic supply, demand, and geography.

The Welland canals in Ontario had much to say about the boats' dimensions. The first canal (1832) had about 15-foot locks, permitting passage of small vessels. The second (1845), at 150 by 26 feet, was better but not by much. This led to the development of flat-bottomed vessels, which became the standard of the Great Lakes. The flat-bottomed boats required less draft, which was good not only in locks but in the shallower waters of rivers leading to and from the lakes.

The *Stranger* was typical of the smaller schooners plying their trade on Lake Superior in the late nineteenth century.

The development of the steam-driven engine spelled the beginning of the end for the schooner. The big advantage of the steamer, of course, was its power and lack of dependency on the wind and the elements, but as the nineteenth century wound down, the iron ore hauling by commercial interests turned eyes on the more productive, larger steel-hulled vessels, with the schooner being relegated to barge status.

Walter Havighurst, author of *The Long Ships Passing,* an essential summation of Great Lakes history, commented on the end of the schooner era on the lakes. "When the whalebacks were being built in Duluth," he wrote, "and the long freighters were growing longer in the yards at Detroit and Cleveland, the end of the schooners was at hand."

~~~~

The story of the *Stranger* offers the best and worst elements of the schooner trade. The diminutive, two-masted, 60-foot wooden boat was an ideal fit for the ports along the Minnesota coastline before the explosive expansion of Duluth and the growth of such towns as Two Harbors and Grand Marais. Constructed and operated by P. E. Bradshaw and Company in Superior, Wisconsin, the *Stranger,* with the right wind, could shoot up the coast, visit a port, drop off essential cargoes supplying a town, and move on. The bigger, bulkier steel-hulled vessels handled the larger freights.

The *Stranger*'s duties all but assured her of hazards later in any given shipping season: because she supplied needed cargoes to the towns on her route, the *Stranger* operated later in the year than some of her larger counterparts. The schooner struggled against the winds and high seas, and operated when ice was beginning to cover Lake Superior in late November and December; under these circumstances, the *Stranger* would duck into safe harbor and wait.

The weather was seasonal on the evening of December 11, 1875, when the *Stranger* left Duluth to deliver supplies to Grand Marais. The captain, with his three-man crew, expected an uneventful but chilly sail, to the extent that the *Stranger* left Duluth without an anchor. It was a short trip, and Ike Clark, the *Stranger*'s skipper, believed the brisk but favorable wind would push the schooner along the 108-mile trip in good time. Captain Alfred Marcott of the *Handy,* a small schooner already laid up in Duluth for the winter, offered Clark the use of his anchor for the Grand Marais trip, but Clark declined—a decision he would regret.

At twenty-four, Clark was inexperienced in commercial shipping, although he had grown up on area fishing boats, and according to the *Superior Times,* "he was considered one of the best sailors at the head of the lake." Joe Cadotte, the sole married man of the three-man crew, was old enough to be Clark's father and was a veteran of vessels of all sizes. The other two crewmen, George Coburn and James Lefave, were younger. This jaunt to Grand Marais was Lefave's initial trip on the *Stranger.*

The *Stranger* pulled out of Duluth harbor on the evening of December 11, with a strong southwest wind assisting, as hoped, on the quick, easy trip. The wind shifted as the schooner neared Grand Marais, blowing with "hurricane" force. Clark was not concerned about the welfare of his boat. He navigated the *Stranger* into the harbor without incident, but the wind was going to make the unloading difficult. Grand Marais offered docks on two different bays, and Clark reasoned that the unloading would be easier on the other bay, which provided better lee from the prevailing wind. It was about two o'clock in the afternoon, with good visibility.

The transfer went smoothly, but Clark wasn't satisfied with the *Stranger*'s positioning for unloading. He turned the schooner around and headed back to the harbor entrance, where he figured to turn and reposition the vessel. For the *Stranger*, this spelled the beginning of a series of events that doomed her.

On her way back to open water and a turn to reenter the harbor, the *Stranger*, buffeted by the heavy wind, grounded on a rocky shelf. The schooner was deposited back into deeper water, with water flooding into her hold. Captain Clark might have had the chance to rush his vessel back to shore, or at least save it by grounding her again, but he was thwarted by wind driving him back toward open water. The boat's sails, frozen and breaking apart in the maelstrom, became entangled. The crew ran out onto the deck—a perilous task in seas rocking the boat.

While witnesses onshore watched in horror, the *Stranger* rolled onto her side. Two of the crewmen on deck hung on, but George Coburn dropped in the water and drowned. The two left received a reprieve when the *Stranger* popped back upright, but this was only temporary. Without an anchor to hold her in place, the wind would blow the vessel out into the lake's deep water. The crewmen grabbed axes and chopped away at the masts. All the while, the boat continued to roll, knocking the men off their feet.

A small fishing craft near shore, holding five men witnessing the *Stranger*'s predicament, disregarded the obvious danger and lit out after the badly damaged schooner. Written accounts differ on what happened next. One version has the fishing boat pulling alongside the *Stranger* and tossing up a line, which those aboard the *Stranger* were too cold and exhausted to hang onto. The other account is similar, but in this version, the men on the smaller boat were unable to reach the men on the *Stranger* with a line. The wind, the rolling boat, the cold—all conspired to make the rescue impossible. The men on the fishing boat gave up when they concluded that their safety would be seriously compromised if they didn't return to port. They reluctantly left the *Stranger* to her fate.

The Superior Times.

SUPERIOR, THURSDAY, DEC. 23, 1875.

WRECKED.

The Schooner Stranger Wrecked at Grand Marais.

All on Board Supposed to be Lost.

Full Particulars of the Sad Affair.

We have seldom seen so deep a gloom cast over a place or a community so saddened as was this on receipt of the sad and startling intelligence Monday afternoon of the loss of the schooner Stranger, of this place, with all on board.

THE FIRST INFORMATION

arrived here early in the afternoon, and the news spreading like wild-fire, soon small knots of people gathered here and there to converse upon the all-absorbing topic, eager to learn the particulars of the sad affair, and to express their sorrow for the lost ones and sympathy for the bereaved.

THE DISASTER

occurred at Grand Marais, Minn., 108 miles down the north shore of Lake Superior, on Sunday, Dec. 12, but owing to the fact that there is no telegraph connecting that region with this, and only one mail a week,

the news of the sad accident did not reach here until eight days after its occurrence. No tidings then, of course, up to that time, had been received of the Stranger since her departure, but still no anxiety was felt on that account, or fears entertained for her safety, as it was supposed by everyone that she had arrived at her destination all right; hence, the intelligence fell like a thunderbolt upon the unsuspecting relatives and friends of the unfortunate crew.

The accounts of the sad affair, at best, are very meagre and also conflicting.

The Stranger left Superior a week ago last Saturday afternoon, with a crew of four men—Ike N. Clark, George Coburn, Joe Cadotte and Jimmie LaFave—and after going to Duluth to make some addition to her cargo, left that place at 10 o'clock in the evening, bound for Grand Marais, the wind at the time blowing very strong, but in a favorable direction, being nearly behind her. According to best accounts, she arrived at Grand Marais the following day (Sunday) at 2 P. M., having thus made the 108 miles in the quick time (for her) of sixteen hours—an average of seven miles an hour.

At

GRAND MARAIS

there are two bays, and in order to assist the reader to a better understanding of the information which follows, we have prepared a

MAP OF THE BAYS AND CONTIGUOUS COAST

North

West

East

Superior (Distance between S. and G. M., 108 miles) Grand Marais   Eagle River, on Kewee-

The loss of the *Stranger* received great attention in the Duluth–Superior area, where an increase in commercial shipping was becoming a growing interest.

In all likelihood, the three men on the *Stranger* saw the futility of their position. They were sinking in the lake, with water entering the boat at will, the schooner losing its freeboard, and the wild seas rushing over the sides of the boat. Screaming wind continued to move the *Stranger* farther from shore. Daylight disappeared, and the obscured view assured the crew of a certain loss.

No one would know the moment the *Stranger* succumbed to the forces working against her, but the lake swallowed her, and none of the sailors' bodies were recovered. The wreckage of the boat was never found, making the *Stranger* one of the many Great Lakes ghost ships.

~~~

The loss of the *Stranger*, unfortunately, was not an uncommon end to a schooner. As Walter Havighurst noted, the *Stranger*'s sinking was typical of the violent conclusions of schooners' lives:

> Few sailing vessels were broken up or moored in retirement. Some were converted into steamers, their topmasts sheared off and engines braced in their framing. Others had their masts yanked out and were used as barges. But most of the 1800s windjammers . . . were lost on the lakes. They were beautiful ships and they went the hard way.

But this did not diminish the almost romantic aura enveloping the schooner. They were hard-working vessels with a style. Again, as Havighurst commented, "They continued to carry lumber while the big ore carriers grew to five hundred and then six hundred feet. In the 1920s an occasional topsail schooner could be seen on the upper lakes. So the crew of a big freighter lined the rail to watch an old-timer with the wind in her sails. Sometimes they watched her out of sight."

Thomas Wilson

~~~

The last two decades of the nineteenth century saw a continuation of the rapid evolution of freighter design and engineering, all as a result of the explosive convergence of iron ore, lumber, and grain commerce on the Great Lakes. Two recently discovered iron ranges, the Vermilion in Minnesota and the Gogebic in Michigan's Upper Peninsula, added to existing, productive ranges and the constant demand from eastern steel mills. The railways grew enormously, which made transporting iron ore much faster and easier, transforming small, sleepy cities like Duluth and Two Harbors into hubs of shipping activity.

The freighters were getting longer and carrying more. Wooden schooners, once the pride of the shipping industry, had faded in importance: by the end of the century, it was common to see schooners used as barges, their holds packed with cargo while they were being pulled by large freighters, as a cost-effective means of hauling more freight per trip. Wooden steamers became a thing of the past. The notion of moving as much as possible, as quickly as possible remained constant; how to accomplish this was changing.

The numbers supported the changes in business. Between 1880 and 1890, grain shipping increased sixfold, lumber ninefold. The Soo Locks, one of the measuring sticks of the shipping business, tripled the number of passing vessels in the 1880–1890 decade. Historian Jules F. Wolff Jr. referred to the decade as "the Momentous Eighties." The growth moved on at an astonishing rate. The 1890s topped the previous decade, with no letup in sight. It was a good time to be a shipping company.

~~~

Alexander McDougall, a former captain on the Great Lakes, had a radical idea for ship design. The vessel would be relatively inexpensive to build and almost unsinkable. And nothing in the business would look anything like it.

When it came to shipbuilding and design, McDougall was a wunderkind. Born in Scotland in 1845, McDougall and his parents emigrated to Canada in 1854. Seven years later, he was out of school and working as a deckhand on a schooner. He rose through the ranks at lightning-fast speed, and by 1870, at the age of twenty-five, he was in command of the *Thomas A. Scott,* a package freighter. In 1878, he caught his first big break when he captained the *Hiawatha,* a 236-foot wooden bulk carrier owned by Captain Thomas Wilson of the Wilson Transit Company. Freighters towing barges had been a practice on the lakes since the 1860s, but Wilson made it a major part of his business operations. Barges, both men knew from experience, could be temperamental tows, especially in stormy weather, and over the next few years, McDougall worked at designing a better barge. He retired from commanding boats in 1881 and devoted all his time to his newfound obsession.

The result was a long, narrow, cigar-shaped hull that curved upward at either end. The vessel possessed a deep single cargo hold and a pilothouse mounted on turrets. Fully loaded, the boat settled until the deck was barely out of the water, making the boat, with its rounded decks, a foil to rough waters, which would wash over the boat rather than gathering, as they did on the standard sharp-edged freighters. The rounded stem permitted the boat to cut through water more quickly than vessels that came to a point.

The new boat was nicknamed "whaleback" because, when loaded, with limited freeboard, it reminded observers of the back of a whale swimming near the surface. It was also given the derisive nickname by those who disliked the design—and there were many—"pigboat" because looked at head-on, the front of the boat, with its rounded stem, reminded people of a giant pig's snout.

The first whaleback, named simply *101,* was constructed in Duluth, McDougall's adopted hometown, and launched to great fanfare on

Alexander McDougall, designer of the boats known as the whalebacks, dominated the design of Great Lakes vessels from the late 1880s to the early 1900s. His success was short-lived due to the construction of larger, stronger boats capable of carrying greater cargoes.

June 13, 1883. The *Duluth Evening Herald,* gushing with no attempt to temper its enthusiasm, called the 131-foot whaleboat "a vessel unsinkable, easy to handle, comparatively inexpensive, and costing but little for repairs."

McDougall accompanied the *101* on her maiden voyage. The barge was towed to Two Harbors, loaded with iron ore, and from there it was on to Cleveland. The passage went without a hitch.

The *101,* informally known as "McDougall's Dream," was used strictly as a barge. The *Colgate Hoyt,* the first whaleback to sail under her own power, was launched in 1890, and the next decade represented the heyday of the McDougall design, forty whaleboats built by McDougall, who added a facility in West Superior, Wisconsin, to boost construction. Cash-strapped after sinking all his money into the *101,* McDougall had sought financial backing for future projects, and he found it in John D. Rockefeller, the oil tycoon now interested in getting involved in the iron ore business on the Great Lakes. McDougall struck an agreement with Rockefeller, in which he sold the patents to the whaleback in exchange for cash, part ownership in the newly structured company, a position on its board of directors, and the freedom to oversee the shipyard. The new company was called the American Steel Barge Company.

McDougall might have ushered in a new type of work vessel, but his most interesting, ambitious project was a passenger whaleback capable of transporting five thousand passengers. The *Christopher*

Columbus came about because the organizers of the 1893 World's Fair in Chicago sought a means to shuttle attendees from downtown Chicago to the Columbian Exposition. McDougall was awarded a contract to build the vessel after a lively competition for the honors, though it was not the whaleback that McDougall originally proposed to build. McDougall offered to construct a 500-foot monstrosity—by far, the longest vessel on the Great Lakes at the time—and equip it with luxurious amenities and eyebrow-raising safety standards. The contract called for something much smaller, but that didn't stop McDougall from designing a craft worthy of its World's Fair status.

At a length of 362 feet, the *Christopher Columbus* was the largest vessel of any type on the Great Lakes, earning her the unofficial but coveted sobriquet "Queen of the Lakes." Constructed in a mere three months and launched on December 3, 1892, in a highly publicized and attended ceremony, the *Columbus* was McDougall's crowning achievement, as strange to look at as she was efficient. Perched on a whaleback hull, the two passenger decks resembled the decks of a standard passenger boat, except the decks were mounted on a series of turrets that gave them the appearance of being suspended over the hull. A 287-foot promenade deck bathed the vessel in an aura of luxury. The entire exterior, including the smokestack, was painted white.

The passenger vessel *Christopher Columbus,* with her trademark whaleback snout, briefly enjoyed "Queen of the Lakes" status as the longest boat on the Great Lakes.

But the decor of the *Columbus* was matched by her many safety features, beginning with a double bottom and thirty-two watertight compartments that stood up to her reputation of being unsinkable, the perfect fit for the fair's White City. It didn't hurt, either, that the vessel, powered by a triple expansion engine, sailed at nearly 20 miles per hour, a speed unmatched by lake vessels.

During the fair's six-month run, the *Christopher Columbus* shuttled more than two million passengers, but her service did not end with the fair's closing. A passenger ship company purchased the *Columbus* and used her to ferry people between Chicago and Milwaukee. By the time she went out of service, the *Christopher Columbus* had taken on more passengers than any vessel in Great Lakes history.

~~~

For all of its positive features, the whaleback was cursed by negatives that doomed it to a brief life span in popularity. Its unique design, a plus in many ways, was a negative in others. The curved decks, so efficient at keeping water from the decks in rough weather, affected the whaleback's watertight capacities. The hatch covers, placed flush over the hatch openings, had a way of warping or being damaged because of the curved decks. In addition, the curvature made loading and unloading difficult. Due to the curved decks, the hatch openings were smaller than the conventional hatches, disturbing the loading process.

Although whalebacks proved to be excellent barges, their position lower in the water made them harder for other vessels to see. This was best illustrated by a tragic collision just outside the Duluth harbor on June 7, 1902, when the whaleback *Thomas Wilson* sank after colliding with the freighter *George G. Hadley* in an accident that never should have occurred.

At 308 feet in length and 38 feet in beam, with conoidal ends and a flat bottom, the *Wilson,* built during the winter of 1891–92 in the American Steel Barge Company shipyard and named after McDougall's old friend Captain Thomas Wilson, fit the description of the long, narrow whalebacks produced by McDougall at the height of the design's popularity. Self-propelled, with a triple expansion engine and twin coal-fueled Scotch boilers driving a single propeller, the *Wilson* had plenty of power for a busy life on the lakes. Twelve hatches fed a cargo hold 24 feet deep—not the largest capacity for freight but sufficient for the whaleback's purpose. Significantly, the *Wilson* was the last whaleback constructed without hatch coamings.

The *Wilson* was launched on April 30, 1892. On her maiden voyage, she hauled grain to Buffalo, New York; she carried coal on her return trip. Just over two months later, she suffered her first serious accident when she grounded, necessitating the replacement of her propeller. The following season, in May 1893, she plowed into a barge being towed by another whaleback, damaging the barge's hull and requiring her own repairs the following month.

In June 1901, the *Wilson* was sold to the Pittsburgh Steamship Company, marking its second sale in two years. Pittsburgh Steamship would own the *Wilson* until her final voyage.

Saturday, June 7, 1902, was an ideal day for sailing, sunny and warm, with calm seas. Still, the *Wilson*'s skipper, M. C. Cameron, was concerned. The Duluth loading docks were busy, and by midmorning

The *Thomas Wilson*, unloaded, aside a loaded whaleback in the Duluth harbor.

The crew of the *Thomas Wilson.*

the *Wilson* was running behind schedule. Cameron, hoping to overcome any further delays, ordered his crew to cast off as soon as the loading had been completed, as opposed to falling further behind during the tedious process of placing and fastening the hatch covers. The fair weather left plenty of time for this after the *Wilson* was well under way.

With Milo Baker at the wheel, the *Wilson* made her way down the canal and onto Lake Superior without a hint of trouble. A tug, the *Annie L. Smith,* chugged a short distance ahead, headed toward a freighter destined for the harbor. Under ordinary circumstances, this involved a simple passing maneuver. But these were not the usual circumstances. The *Smith* had been given instructions to deliver a message to the freighter: there was no room for the boat at the Duluth coal docks, and she was to divert her entry to the harbor and turn to the docks in Superior.

The freighter, the *George G. Hadley,* a 296-foot wooden steamer built in 1888, was loaded with 2,900 tons of coal destined for the Duluth coal docks. Captain Mike Fitzgerald of the *Hadley* received the new instructions and ordered his wheelsman to turn the vessel. He apparently gave no serious consideration to the *Wilson,* even though the two vessels were closing the distance between them. In fact, while he was talking to the *Smith,* he was on the other side of the boat, out of view of the *Wilson.* As he would later recall, "The watchman said nothing about it, the second mate did not blow any whistles or call my attention, and I was watching the tug when we turned and struck. I forgot all about the other boat."

Those witnessing the collision, happening so close to the harbor, were incredulous in relating the accident to the press. "One moment the two boats were plowing through the water two hundred yards apart," one witness recalled, "and when I looked again through marine glasses the crew of the *Wilson* could be seen throwing off their clothing and jumping into the water."

The sequence of events leading to and immediately following the collision occurred very quickly—all in less than a few minutes. When those in the *Wilson* pilothouse saw the *Hadley* go into her turn, Captain Cameron had to make an immediate decision. He had two choices. He could order a starboard turn, which might lead to the whaleback's grounding in shallow water, or he could make a tight turn in the same direction that the *Hadley* was turning and hope there was enough room to avoid a collision. He chose the latter.

Both vessels were sailing at full ahead when they collided. The *Hadley* broadsided the *Wilson,* her bow driving deep into the *Wilson* near the farthest aft hatch. The *Wilson* shuddered from the impact, rolled to the port side, and returned to its upright position. Water flooded in from the gash in her side and the open hatches, and filled the boat, similar in effect to running a glass through a sink of dishwater. Water gushed into the *Hadley* as well.

Pandemonium followed. The *Wilson* crew, certain that the whaleback would sink in short order, rushed to the deck, pulling off their boots and heavy clothing, knowing full well that they needed freedom of movement once they were in the water. Those aboard the *Hadley,* some heading for lifeboats, wondered how long the freighter, her bow badly damaged at the stem, might stay afloat. The air was filled with the sounds of shouting. Crewmen from the *Wilson* leaped into the water, one of the boat's crewmen tossing life rings in after them. In its annual report, the U.S. Life-Saving Service offered a stark, yet telling, description of the scene: "While some tried to launch the [life] boats, others quickly jumped overboard, and others, gathering on the uplifted stern, unwisely waited longer."

Second Mate Neil McGilvray recalled an unnerving, almost surreal moment occurring during the *Wilson*'s final struggle. "Just before she sank, there was quite an explosion from the boiler house, I suppose when the water reached the boilers," he said. "Gas and steam came out in a cloud, which enveloped some man standing near that part of the boat. I did not see the man emerge from the steam, and do not know what became of him."

The *Wilson* sank suddenly and with very little warning. Her stern rose high in the air and she went down, bow first, her propeller driving her to the bottom of the lake. She settled upright in about 70 feet of water. Nine of the *Wilson*'s twenty-man crew drowned, either by going down with the ship, being sucked under during the sinking, or because they could not stay afloat until rescued.

On the surface, men grasped at anything they could find, from life rings to debris. Arthur Dagget had been sleeping when the *Hadley* tore into the *Wilson*, and he scrambled for the deck, arriving moments before the *Wilson* sank. He and cook Adron Tripp jumped off the stern, only to be caught up in churning waters stirred up by the suction of the sinking vessel and the spinning of her propeller. Both men were pulled under but managed to fight their way back to the surface. When they were driven under a second time, only Dagget made it back successfully. An exceptional swimmer, Dagget tread water until rescued.

Captain Cameron, the last to abandon the *Wilson*, had a similar experience of being sucked under by the sinking whaleback. "When I went down, I don't know how far underwater I went," he explained, "but I remember thinking that I never would reach the top again. I was striking out with my hands to try to get to the surface, and as I was coming up my hands struck someone else down there. He was coming up and apparently just a little ahead of me. Of course I could not see who it was, I felt him for a moment, then we were parted. When I got to the surface, I did not see anyone near me."

The *Hadley* and *Smith* remained in the area, pulling survivors from the lake and supplying half-naked men with whatever dry clothes were available. Other vessels streamed to the location and helped with the search for survivors, but after only a few minutes, it became apparent that there weren't any more.

Captain Cameron and Second Mate Neil McGilvray wound up on the *Wilson*'s life raft, which broke free during the sinking. Both men jumped overboard at the last instant, and McGilvray found the raft by chance. Cameron flailed about in the water, struggling to stay afloat. Someone on the *Hadley* saw Cameron's stress, tossed McGilvray an oar, and shouted for him to save the man thrashing in the water. The whale-back's second mate thrust the oar in Cameron's direction, the captain grabbed onto it, and McGilvray pulled him to the raft. They were rescued by the men on the *Smith*, who turned them over to the *Hadley*.

And so it went. One by one, the *Wilson* crewmen were pulled onto the *Hadley* or *Smith*. To those in the water, the rescue probably seemed to have taken hours to accomplish, but in real time it happened rather quickly. After everyone in the water had been collected, Captain Fitzgerald reasoned it was time to take his own boat to safety.

Doing so became a trial. At first, Fitzgerald figured that the *Hadley* was still strong enough to sail to Superior, but that turned out to be a miscalculation. Torrents of lake water gushed into the boat and threatened to sink her before she reached safety. At one point, while she was still in deep water, not much more than the *Hadley*'s fore and aft superstructures appeared to be above surface. The chief engineer, fearing an explosion when the cold water met the boilers, ordered everyone in the engine room to head to the deck. It was now a race against very little time. The *Hadley* aimed at the shallow water and sandy beach south of the Duluth harbor, and was sinking fast when she arrived. She settled in 24 feet of water, almost all of her stern below water, the pilothouse well above it. The *Wilson* survivors narrowly avoided what would have been their second shipwreck in a single day.

The *Thomas Wilson* became the Pittsburgh Steamship Company's first shipwreck with fatalities. Her loss in relatively shallow water presented a shipping hazard for boats entering or leaving the Duluth harbor. In the weeks ahead, a tugboat would stand guard near the

The *George G. Hadley* collided with the *Thomas Wilson* in bright, mild sailing conditions not far from the Duluth harbor. The *Wilson* sank in minutes, but the *Hadley* successfully made a mad rush to safety.

wreckage site, warning vessels of the hazard. A diver was lowered to the remains of the *Wilson*, but even in the dark, murky water he could determine that the damage to the whaleback was too extensive for any hope of salvaging it. Others surveyed the wreck and reached the same conclusion. The smokestack and other portions of the superstructure were subsequently destroyed, and rest of the wreckage remained where it was, eventually becoming a popular diving site.

The U.S. Steamboat Inspection Service investigated the accident, and the *Wilson* and *Hadley* masters were penalized for their responsibilities in the collision. Captain Cameron had his master's certification revoked for sixty days, while Captain Fitzgerald's was permanently suspended. Fitzgerald, at seventy-three, serving as a skipper for four decades with a good record, saw his suspension lifted when he passed a master's exam.

~~~

The days of the whaleback were almost over. They would be used in the decades to come, but the construction of new behemoth freighters made the whaleback, with its much smaller cargo capacity and design flaws, obsolete.

Alexander McDougall died on May 27, 1923, at the age of seventy-eight. He built forty whalebacks during his career. The *Frank Rockefeller*, constructed in 1896, renamed the *Meteor*, was the last of the whalebacks, serving until 1969. She was bought by the city of Superior in 1972 and still acts as a museum ship—and is the only whaleback still in existence.

Benjamin Noble

~~~

Was the *Benjamin Noble* overloaded when she met her demise during a vicious spring storm in 1914? It's a question that would have no definitive answer.

The *Noble* was a compact vessel, ideal (and constructed by the Detroit Shipbuilding company specifically) for transporting iron rails. At 239 feet in length and 40 feet in beam, the *Noble* lacked the size necessary to make hauling iron ore profitable. This posed no concern to the Capitol Transportation Company, the boat's owner, which counted the *Noble* as its sole Great Lakes vessel. The interest in rails was strong, and supplying the market was good for the company's coffers. Boasting of a triple expansion engine, the small freighter had plenty of power to make frequent trips to Great Lakes ports, especially Duluth and Superior, both expanding the railways leading to and from their docks. Throughout the 1913–14 winter, Capitol Transportation stayed busy taking orders for the following shipping season. The list grew until the *Benjamin Noble* was assured of remaining active.

A mild winter lifted the spirits of company officials throughout the Great Lakes region. With good sailing weather and little ice to battle, better than average profits, achieved through the early shipping season, seemed possible. In a business that found shipping companies fattening a season's profits by extending the season in November, the same applied to earlier than normal runs. Rather than spoil the possibilities by devoting the late off-season to fitting out their boats, some companies skipped the process and sent their vessels out instead.

The launching of the 239-foot freighter *Benjamin Noble*.

There was little reason to suspect any harm to steamers that had performed well the previous season.

Captain John Eisenhardt, the thirty-one-year-old master of the
Noble, quibbled with the notion. After spending five years as first mate
on other vessels, Eisenhardt was in charge of his first vessel, and he
was about to embark on his initial voyage of the season. He was the
youngest master on the lakes and had grown up around the water. His
father and grandfather had worked on the freighters, and when he
was a boy growing up in Milwaukee, he was a familiar figure around
the docks. He earned his master's certification when he was only
twenty-six, and while working as first mate on a bulk carrier, he had
been the sole survivor after his vessel wrecked near Manitou Island;
he had managed to drift on the boat's life raft until he was rescued.
Now, only a few years later, the man known as "Captain Johnny" had
command of his own vessel.

Eisenhardt had reason to be concerned about the size of the load
that Capitol Transportation president J. A. Francombe had scheduled
for the trip, originating in Conneaut, Ohio. When fully loaded with
such heavy cargo, the *Noble* settled in the water until she had minimal
freeboard. The long trip to Duluth had the potential to be difficult. In

Eisenhardt's view, his boat might have been better served if the cargo had been divided into two loads. This was not going to happen: it was neither cost effective nor competitive. Larger freighters could easily handle the cargo, and Capitol Transportation had to stay competitive. Further, Francombe had placed a rush on the shipment. The Great Northern Railroad eagerly anticipated the rails.

Eisenhardt supervised the loading of the *Noble* until he had seen enough. Two more rail cars loaded with iron rails awaited loading, but after six days of painstaking slow loading, Eisenhardt was ready to shove off. He had no intention of registering any objection to over-loading to his company, despite the *Noble*'s position in the water, which might have found the boat deeper than the load line markings recommended. Others on the dock commented about it to one another: "Hell, he ain't goin' to get very far up the lakes," one dock worker stated. Another was so alarmed that he photographed the *Noble* before she departed.

Captain Eisenhardt kept his thoughts to himself. He was in no position to protest—not if he hoped to hold the position he had worked so diligently to achieve. The *Noble* would be sailing very slowly on her journey, but if all the necessary precautions were taken, she would reach her destination with no problem.

She left the Conneaut dock on the morning of April 22.

~~~

The crew of the *Noble* had no idea what was in store for them. Their trip would take days, especially at the lower speeds commanded by the freighter's heavy load. They took a familiar route, one that placed them on Lakes Erie (briefly) and Huron before traversing the mighty expanse of Lake Superior. When they left Conneaut, the weather was fine, and it continued the pattern of exceptionally warm weather the region had been enjoying during the spring of 1914. Nothing hinted that before the *Noble* reached western Lake Superior, captain and crew would be up against what the *Duluth Herald* described as "one of the worst storms that have visited the lake regions . . . carrying with the destruction of property, loss of life, and causing the greatest anxiety in the marine circles for the vessels, crews and cargoes on the lakes."

Forecasts for stormy weather were beginning to reach the Soo Locks while the *Noble* was waiting in line to lock through, but gale warnings were not posted until the *Noble* was already on Lake Superior. The weather system was coming from the northeast, but rather than behaving like the typical nor'easter, this storm added an unusual wrinkle in the way it affected vessels sailing in it.

In the early portion of the storm, the *Noble* encountered mist, rain, and fog. The rain fell harder, and the waves built over the ensuing hours, the *Noble* all but sucked into the vortex of the fierce maelstrom. Following seas, some swelling well above the *Noble*'s decks, pushed the boat forward, swamped the decks of the overloaded vessel, and lifted her stern out of the water, causing Chief Engineer A. C. Coger to struggle to maintain level revolutions per minute, checking down when the boat's stern rose, turning it up when the stern was slammed back down. No one dared imagine what might transpire if all the pitching in the violent seas caused the cargo to shift.

The wind lashed the eastern coast of Minnesota, on land and sea alike. Glass shattered, small structures blew down. Trees were uprooted. The Duluth weather station reported steady winds exceeding 60 miles per hour. In neighboring Superior, wind buckled two coal dock trestles, sending a coal-loading machine toppling down on a boat

The *Benjamin Noble*, perhaps overloaded with steel rails, disappeared in a heavy storm in April 1914. The entire crew was lost. Wreckage was recovered, but the vessel was never found.

below. At the entrance to the Duluth canal, wind and waves disabled the southern light and foghorn, sending a man to his death when he made a run to repair the light and was swept off the canal pier.

Captains kept their boats in, tied to the docks or anchored nearby, and those who decided to take their chances quickly discovered how rough conditions really were. Two boats, the *John Lambert* and the *Minneapolis,* turned back to the shelter of Duluth and were shocked to find one of the channel lights out. The *Minneapolis,* loaded with lumber and shingles, lost its shingles, piled on deck, to water boarding the freighter and sweeping over it. By the time the boat had turned broadside into the storm and limped its way back to Duluth, her master was unprepared for guesswork. Which light, north or south, was out? An incorrect guess could bring around a reprisal of the *Mata-afa* of nearly nine years earlier, when the giant bulk carrier had hit one of the piers, grounded, and broke apart, at the cost of nine lives. Fortunately for the *Minneapolis,* the captain made a last-second—and correct—choice.

What happened to the *Noble* is impossible to determine for certain, though several vessels spotted her in the final leg of her journey. The 209-foot *Norwalk,* a small lumber vessel, sailed a short distance behind the *Noble* from April 25 through the afternoon of April 27, when she caught up to and passed the *Noble.* The two boats remained within sight of each other through the early morning hours of April 28, when both were near Knife Island, trying to remain upright and make it to Duluth Harbor. The *Daniel J. Morrell,* a massive 580-foot ore carrier, was in the area, and Captain Millen of the *Morrell* later reported seeing the two boats barely holding their own in the storm, sailing in proximity of each other until suddenly, with no warning, the lights on the trailing vessel disappeared. Millen thought nothing of it, given the conditions and the poor visibility, and only mentioned it when the *Noble* was reported long overdue in Duluth. By then, the master of the *Norwalk* had also expressed concern. Another captain, of the steamer *Lakeport,* said he had seen what had to be the *Noble* sailing about 5 miles behind him, near Two Harbors, and though the boat's lights disappeared, the captain held out hope that the boat had reached safe harbor.

She had been close. There was speculation that she could not enter the Duluth canal—not in her overloaded state and the light not functioning. The idea was supported by a Duluth woman who lived close to the harbor. The "well-known" woman, who offered her story to the *Duluth Herald* on the condition that she remain anonymous, had been standing in a darkened room, watching the storm, when a freighter's lights came into view. The boat was obviously in great distress, but she was near the harbor. The boat's lights disappeared while the woman was watching. She called her daughter, telling her that she thought her eyes were playing tricks on her, that no boat would be out in such conditions. Her daughter, who thought she had heard a faint whistle a few moments earlier, believed her mother might have actually witnessed a vessel foundering.

Despite all the differing stories, there was no doubt that the *Noble* had sunk. Duluth officials wired the Capitol Transportation Company with a message that "all hope of favorable news had been abandoned."

Wreckage drifted to shore. A patrolman with the U.S. Life-Saving Service found hatch covers on the beach near Minnesota Point. Oars, clothing, pieces of the pilothouse, life belts, and other flotsam washed ashore. Patrols of volunteers walked up and down the coastline, searching for bodies and more wreckage. No signs of the *Noble* itself turned up. There was now a mystery enveloping the boat's crew members. Captain Eisenhardt had not filed a crew manifest, so there was uncertainty about how many perished in the sinking, with most estimates saying between sixteen and twenty, and the majority set at twenty. No victims were recovered, although years later an immigrant fisherman confessed that he had snagged a body in a net. Unwilling to deal with authorities or immigration officials, he returned the body to the water and said nothing.

People were left with the empty-handed speculation that offered conversation but no certainty. What had the boat's final moments entailed? Had it been a sudden wall of inescapable water? Had there been desperate attempts to abandon ship? Had there been time to consider the end? Had there been a moment for the slightest thought? How do sailors die? And what of those left behind?

On April 25, while waiting at the Soo, John Eisenhardt sent a letter to his sister. In the letter, he expressed fear—the fear of overloading his boat.

~~~

For ninety years, the *Benjamin Noble* was relegated to ghost ship status. There were newspaper and magazine pieces written about her from time to time, and brief accounts appeared in books, but nothing substantive could be reported. No one could agree on where the boat sank. Aside from the recovered wreckage—and there was very little, at that—the hints of the canaller's location was a mystery. The men were never returned home. The *Noble* had sailed off into a storm, never to be seen again. The water she rested in was, in all likelihood, very deep—far too deep for early-twentieth-century diving technology.

In 1987, James Marshall, a Duluth maritime publisher, editor, and writer, offered a reward of $1,000 to whoever discovered the *Noble*. Marshall had been intrigued by the wreck for years, and the reward money, he reasoned, might offer incentive to the growing number of shipwreck hunters scouring the Great Lakes for lost vessels.

Still nothing. Then, at the end of October 2004, ninety years after the loss of the *Noble*, divers/shipwreck hunters, on their last run of the season, late in the afternoon, with the sun setting, spotted something with their side-scan sonar—something large enough to merit further exploration. It was in about 360 feet of water, almost exactly where, nine decades earlier, the *Daniel J. Morrell* had reported seeing a boat's lights disappearing in the storm. The only known undiscovered wreck in the area was the *Benjamin Noble*, and though it was getting late in the season to be diving in the northern waters of Lake Superior, the men decided to see if they could positively identify the wreck before calling it quits until the following spring.

Ken Merryman, part of a team including Jerry Eliason, Kraig Smith, and Randy Beebe, could only chuckle when he remembered the coincidence of finding the *Noble*. Merryman said that even though locating the *Noble* ranked "near the top of my list" of wrecks to hunt down, the group was really searching for the *Robert Wallace*, a 209-foot, four-masted wooden steamer that sprung a leak on November 17, 1902, while loaded with iron ore and towing the *Ashland*, a 218-foot schooner barge also loaded with iron ore. The *Ashland* was able to transport the *Wallace* crew to Two Harbors, but the *Wallace* had disappeared. According to Merryman, the shipwreck hunters had been looking for the *Wallace* for five years, covering a large search area. "It was like trying to find a needle in a haystack," he said.

Lake Superior's underwater topography made the process even more difficult. The lake's bottom near Minnesota's north shore could be very rocky or soft, and shallow or deep. The sonar worked most efficiently when looking at a soft lake floor.

The men identified the *Noble* on their first attempt. They already knew from the sonar's images that the wreck was not the *Robert Wallace*. The images indicated that the wreck had a steel hull; the *Wallace* was constructed from wood. The team eventually lowered a camera to the site, and it captured photos of the cargo hold and the iron rails.

The *Noble*'s end had been a violent one. It plowed into the lake bottom with tremendous force, the bow carving out a swath about 60 feet deep, stopping only when the vessel hit bedrock. The bow, completely buried in mud, pointed in the general direction of Two Harbors. The aft cabin had imploded, and there was widespread wreckage scattered around the boat.

No conclusions, however, could be drawn from the evidence about what sank the *Noble*. Merryman believed that overloading, reducing freeboard in the storm, contributed significantly to the sinking, but the underwater wreckage, along with the mysterious, contradictory speculation given by so-called witnesses, defied a final explanation. The *Benjamin Noble* and the unfortunate souls aboard her left questions that would never be answered.

Onoko

~~~

The day was clear and the waters calm when the *Onoko,* a 302-foot, thirty-three-year-old bulk carrier, sank on September 15, 1915, near Knife Island, not long after departing from Duluth with a cargo of wheat. Although everyone onboard was rescued, the monetary loss of vessel and crew was substantial.

Money lost, however, was only a fragment of the story. Few Great Lakes vessels, to that point in time, could match the *Onoko*'s colorful history, shipping record, and significance to the industry. When she was launched on February 16, 1882, she was a study in superlatives: she was the first, the longest, and the most capable of a new design of freighters that would dominate Great Lakes shipping for the next century. She was a leviathan, an eye-catching example of what could be done in moving mass tonnage of bulk cargo around the lakes.

But it wasn't always accepted. In the beginning, changing any production could be risky. No one in the business had ever seen anything like this. The *Onoko* was huge, constructed out of iron (rather than wood, still the industry standard), and perhaps strangest of all, had a deckhouse fore and aft, a total retooling of every bulk carrier on the Great Lakes. Between the two structures rising out of the front and back of the boat was a long, wooden spar deck covering a large cargo hold.

Critics of the newfangled design were quick to express their disapproval. "A monstrosity," sniffed one critic. "An eye-sore," wrote another, who piled on by adding that "for a new vessel, she is the worst looking sight that ever appeared on our inland waters."

The 302-foot *Onoko,* seen here circa 1895, was constructed with four masts, which were later removed.

Some wondered whether a boat of this nature—the longest freighter on the Great Lakes at the time of her launching—would float when fully loaded. The *Onoko* was not the first iron-hulled boat to sail on the lakes. The U.S. Navy had tested the 163-foot *Michigan*, launched in 1843 and the first iron naval vessel of any sort. Eighteen years later, in 1861, the 200-foot *Merchant*, a passenger boat, was launched by the Erie and Western Transit Company's Anchor Line as a passenger shuttle between Buffalo and Chicago.

So iron wasn't rejected outright as a building material. In fact, one shipbuilder, the Detroit Dry Dock Company, constructed an assortment of iron-hulled vessels, including passenger boats, two car ferries, a tugboat, and package freighters. In 1881, less than a year before the launching of the *Onoko*, Detroit Dry Dock produced the 235-foot *Brunswick*, technically the first iron bulk carrier on the lakes. Her life was very brief: in November, less than six months into her career, the *Brunswick* collided with a schooner near Dunkirk, New York, and sank. Four men lost their lives, and the *Brunswick* was rarely mentioned again.

One of the first steel freighters on the Great Lakes, the *Onoko* enjoyed a long career in shipping before suffering a hull fracture in good weather and sinking. Fortunately, the crew was saved.

The design, more than the material used in construction, set the *Onoko* apart from the competition. Philip Minch, the freighter's owner, favored practicality when he contracted John H. Smith of Globe Iron Works in Cleveland to build his bulk carrier. Smith, experienced in constructing iron vessels while working in Scotland, designed a steam-driven boat, whose power could be boosted by three masts mounted equidistant on the deck. Eight hatches led into a cargo hull capable of holding record amounts of iron ore. With her white-painted wooden deckhouses mounted on a black hull, the *Onoko* might have been a strange sight to the five thousand gathered to watch her slide into the water on that cold, blustery February afternoon, but there was little doubt of her purpose. The *Onoko* was created to work.

~~~~

The *Onoko* wasted no time in establishing her superiority. On her maiden voyage on April 19, 1882, she moved 2,536 tons of coal from Cleveland to Chicago in a tidy fifteen hours. According to her skipper, Captain W. H. Pringle, she steered like a yacht. The *Onoko* registered substantial profits from the beginning, regardless of her cargo. She set cargo records—and then proceeded to break her own records—in her early years of service on the lakes, prompting the *Cleveland Herald* to state, on August 22, 1884, that the "*Onoko* has proven even more successful than her owners hoped for."

The shipping industry took notice, and the new vessels followed the *Onoko*'s basic design, initially scorned by critics. The new freighters, steel in construction, grew in length every year, and the hope of finding an inexpensive means of hauling large volumes of bulk cargoes, particularly iron, was realized.

Philip Minch enjoyed the vindication of his boat's design and effectiveness prior to his death in 1887. His son, Peter G. Minch, a former skipper, and respected and popular figure around the lakes, assumed control of the Minch Transportation Company, and he, too, was enthusiastic about the new ship design and construction. Two new vessels, the *Western Reserve* and *W. H. Gilcher*, hit the water in 1890, giving Minch, between the *Onoko* and the *Western Reserve*, two of the biggest boats in the business. Although they worked for different companies, the two new freighters were so similar in construction and design that they were referred to as sister ships. Both were made of steel, rather than iron. Both met similar and tragic ends.

The 301-foot *Western Reserve*, built by the Cleveland Shipbuilding Company, focused mainly on hauling iron ore. Companies preferred the new steel boats, which they judged to be more rugged than the older, wooden bulk carriers. Peter Minch kept close watch on the performance of the *Western Reserve*, which established new cargo records in wheat and iron ore. Minch felt confident in her ability to handle whatever came up during the course of any given trip, and toward the end of August 1882 he decided to take family members on the *Western Reserve* on their way to a group vacation.

On August 30, the boat, sailing light, left Cleveland for the ore docks of Two Harbors, Minnesota. On board as passengers were Minch, his wife, Anna, son Charlie and daughter Florence, sister-in-law Mrs. Jacob Englebry, and her daughter, Bertha. It was to be a long passage, as Great Lakes journeys went, but Minch considered it a cruise to be enjoyed.

The *Western Reserve*, under the guidance of Captain Albert Myers, who hailed from Minch's hometown of Vermilion, Ohio, ran into a vicious late-summer storm and, with no water in her ballast tanks, took a severe beating. Myers dropped anchor near Whitefish Point, Michigan, and waited. He ordered the boat to sail again when he judged his two-year-old vessel capable of sailing in such adverse, but not life- or vessel-threatening conditions.

At roughly nine o'clock in the evening, while confronting a storm that had vigorously renewed itself, Myers heard a loud bang coming from the stern of the *Western Reserve*. The main mast had broken off and fallen to the deck, and a large crack split the deck and was running down the starboard and port sides of the hull. The boat was breaking in two. All crew and passengers quickly boarded lifeboats and launched them before the boat sank. The sinking took only ten minutes, and the lifeboats faced heavy seas. They had no provisions on board, including lights, which might have been used to signal any boats in the area.

"While we were in the yawl," wheelsman Harry Stewart would recall, "a steamer passed us, which I think was the *Neshoto*. We could see her red light, but they could not see us. We were to the westward of them. We shouted and screamed for half an hour, but in the roar of the storm they could not hear us. As a final resort we tried to burn one of the women's shawls, but it was too wet and would not light."

Water poured into the boats, and their passengers baled desperately. Waves swamped the boat holding the Minch family, and it capsized. All but two perished, and the survivors were picked up by the other, already overloaded lifeboat.

The survivors could only watch as the *Western Reserve*, one of the strongest and newest freighters on the lake a few hours before, broke apart and sank, sending off a powerful explosion when cold water hit the hot boilers, the boat's propeller still turning as she sank.

Several days after the boat's loss, wheelsman Harry W. Stewart offered an explicit account of the horrors the survivors faced on Lake Superior. "The sea was so heavy that it was simply impossible to do anything but to head our boat right before wind and seas. We tried to keep her up but could not do it. The water was coming over his side so we had to bale constantly, even while running before it. We did this for ten hours, making about thirty miles when, at seven o'clock in the morning of the thirty-first, when perhaps a mile off the beach, a succession of heavy seas caught our boat, lifting her nearly on end, filled her as she came down, and capsized her, throwing all into the water."

Over the next few minutes, the air was filled with the horrible sounds of screams and people crying out for help. Stewart grabbed a life preserver from the sinking lifeboat, fit it around him, and set off for shore. No one else survived. Stewart, an excellent swimmer, fought the waves and finally found his way to land and collapsed from exhaustion. He eventually crawled and walked along the waterfront, hoping to find help. In time, he located a lifesaving station.

Bodies of victims washed onto the shore, where over the following days they were retrieved by beach patrols. Peter Minch was identified by his engraved watch; Stewart helped identify others. Some were buried in Minnesota. Minch and his family were returned to Ohio. Twenty-six people lost their lives in the sinking.

The loss of the *Western Reserve* reignited the debate over the use of steel in the construction of bulk carriers, and the discussion intensified when the *W. H. Gilcher,* a 301-footer, sank on Lake Michigan without a trace on October 28, less than two months after the *Western Reserve.* The weather conditions were similar enough that the authorities reasoned that the *Gilcher* was the victim of hull failure. Others contended that the *Gilcher,* loaded with three thousand tons of coal, would have been more stable in the water than the *Western Reserve,* which was sailing light.

There were no definitive answers. Ship architects, without wreckage—or even the location of the wreckage—to examine, could offer theories but little more. Harry Stewart, the only survivor from either sinking, had seen the damage to the *Western Reserve* when he had jumped over the crack in the deck while racing to the lifeboats in the back of the boat, but he admitted that he had no idea about what caused the split. One seasoned freighter captain suggested that a wooden boat might have sprung a leak whereas a steel vessel split because its rivets might have been susceptible to shearing off in rough seas, causing the hull failure.

The debate continued. Shipyards continued to build steel vessels. And the *Onoko,* the model of the modern steel freighter, continued to sail on.

〰️

The 1915 shipping season was one of the most profitable in the annals of the Great Lakes. Predicting success depended on many variables to be reliable. Shipping profits had been fluctuating for two decades, which made the 1915 season, the third highest in shipping history, especially noteworthy.

At thirty-three, the *Onoko* was aging gracefully. She was still strong, sailing regularly, and despite a length far shorter than most of the new freighters, profitable. One estimate claimed she had earned twelve times what it cost to build her. Improvements over the years included the installation of two new Scotch boilers; redecking, moving from wood to steel; the razing of the masts; and the construction of a deckhouse for additional crew members. Her owners came and went without disturbing service. When Peter G. Minch, son of Philip Minch and a Great Lakes captain, died five years after his father in a tragic shipping accident, Philip's son-in-law, Henry Steinbrenner, and his son, George Steinbrenner, assumed control of the fleet.

Contrary to the speculations of her early critics, the *Onoko* established a safety history much better than her contemporaries. The only notable blemish, however, was a serious one. On May 16, 1896, while sailing on Lake Michigan in thick fog near Racine, Wisconsin, the *Onoko* rammed a schooner, the *Mary D. Byer.* The schooner sank, and five men were killed in the collision.

She grounded on two occasions, one in a snowstorm on December 1, 1910, and then on October 7, 1912, when she was intentionally beached following the discovery of a leak. In both cases, refloating and repair costs were minimal.

The *Onoko*'s life on the lakes came to a conclusion on the afternoon of September 15, 1915. Loaded with 109,600 bushels of wheat, the *Onoko* left the Duluth harbor, bound for Toledo. The waters were calm, and Captain W. R. Dunn saw nothing but smooth sailing ahead. Things changed dramatically about an hour into the trip when the *Onoko* was about 9 miles off Knife Island. Engineer J. J. Higgins detected a large volume of water entering the engine room at an alarming rate. He and his crew left immediately, and they were waist-deep in water by the time they were climbing the stairs leading to the deck. Higgins rushed to alert Dunn, and the captain only needed to glance at the water gushing into his boat's stern to realize that the *Onoko* had suffered some kind of fatal failure in her hull. The stern was sinking fast. There would be little time before it sank; the bow filled with water, and the *Onoko* slipped beneath the lake's surface.

The captain issued the abandon ship order, and the lifeboats, carrying everyone aboard the *Onoko,* were lowered. "The crew testified that despite the suddenness of the affair, there was no panic," reported the *Duluth Herald* the next day. "The boats were lowered in an orderly way and nobody had any difficulty in putting off from the abandoned vessel."

The escape from the sinking boat might have been eased by the presence of another vessel closing in on the scene. The *Renown,* an

The last moments of the *Onoko,* in a photograph taken from the *Renown,* a Standard Oil tanker that rescued her crew.

oil tanker owned by Standard Oil, had been close behind the *Onoko* and, seeing that something was wrong, moved in to pluck everyone from the lifeboats. The crews from both vessels were back in Duluth by three thirty that afternoon, with no reported injuries. The *Onoko,* once the most expensive freighter on the lakes, was now its costliest loss.

Henry Steinbrenner

~~~

Mishaps trail some bulk carriers more than others. History clearly illustrates this. Boats survive a long list of indignities, the kind of bumps and bruises that leave their owners reaching for their checkbooks and cursing, and many a captain has been relieved of his job following a mishap that sent a vessel to dry dock for an extended period of time. Salvagers are not cheap, and neither are repairs. Still, it is almost expected that a boat, over a Great Lakes career spanning forty, fifty years, or more—in conditions rife with storms, fog, great wind, blinding snow, miscommunication, and human errors and failings—will run into serious difficulties.

But for a small percentage of boats, such as the *Henry Steinbrenner*, accidents occurred with a frequency that prompted superstitious sailors to wonder if the freighter was jinxed. The *Steinbrenner*'s early years were marked by incidents, including a sinking, that might have been cause for suspicion.

The *Steinbrenner* had not been christened when the first incident threatened its existence. The yet-to-be-named boat, known only as hull number fourteen, was in the shipbuilding yard of the Jenks Ship Building Company in Port Huron, Michigan, when a fire broke out on March 19, 1901. Firefighters battled the blaze, which was barely contained. The partially constructed hull was spared when firemen hosed it with a constant stream of cold water, preventing warping of the metal. The boat, named the *Henry Steinbrenner*, was launched on September 28, 1902.

The vessel's namesake was part of a successful Cleveland-based shipping family. Henry's father built his fortune in the Great Lakes shipping business; he constructed and owned a fleet of boats. Henry was reluctant to become involved in the business and instead studied law and went into real estate, in which he excelled. Fate had other designs. Henry met and married Sophia Minch, whose family owned a fleet of freighters. Henry assisted the family with the financial affairs of their enterprise, and in 1901, he and his brother-in-law, Philip Minch, founded the Kinsman Transit Company, which commissioned the construction of the freighter to be called the *Henry Steinbrenner.*

The *Steinbrenner* had a familiar look to her, typical of a boat designed to haul iron, grain, and coal to ports throughout the Great Lakes. She had the look of the conventional straight-decker constructed at the turn of the century: layered deck housing on either side of the boat, with a long, flat midsection covering the cargo hold. Her lone propeller was driven by a triple expansion engine and Scotch boilers. She was, in almost every way, the twin of the *Captain Thomas Wilson,* constructed by Jenks Ship Building the previous year.

Henry Steinbrenner.

After seven full seasons of routine shipping, the *Steinbrenner* received her first major setback on December 5, 1909. A late-season run, a perennial challenge, was violently interrupted in the lower St. Marys River. Visibility was near zero in a blinding snowfall when the 532-foot *Henry A. Berwind* broadsided the *Steinbrenner,* ripping a 25-foot hole in her midships. Water washed in, and *Steinbrenner* Captain Loher sent out the abandon ship signal. All officers and crew with the exception of the captain, third mate, and wheelsman left the boat without a problem. The *Steinbrenner* sank, coming to rest in shallow water that engulfed the spar deck but left the forward deck housing above water and in good condition. The three remaining on the boat were picked up by a *Berwind* lifeboat. Luckily, no other boats rammed into the *Steinbrenner,* dead in the water in a shipping lane. Cold weather encased the boat in ice, and after examining the boat, salvager Tom Reid decided to delay refloating her until the following spring.

The *Steinbrenner* was involved in her second costly collision on October 11, 1923. As before, poor visibility was largely to blame, this

The raising of the *Henry Steinbrenner,* which sank in shallow water. Bad luck plagued the vessel from the time of her construction, when she was nearly destroyed by fire.

time caused by fog and heavy smoke from a forest fire near Whitefish Bay. The *John McCartney Kennedy,* a 354-footer two years newer than the *Steinbrenner,* hit the *Steinbrenner's* bow, one of her bow's anchors gauging a 4-foot hole in the *Steinbrenner.* The hole was above the waterline, and the *Steinbrenner* sailed safely to harbor.

The final accident of note occurred in October 1941, when the freighter plowed into a lock wall at the Soo, damaging her port bow at a cost of $24,500. The *Steinbrenner* continued a dozen more years without event.

～～～

Captain Albert Stiglin, the forty-six-year-old master of the *Steinbrenner,* waited in his shirt sleeves while the boat finished loading. The *Steinbrenner* was a new charge for him, but he knew the lakes well. Like so many of his fellow captains, he had climbed the ladder of positions until he had reached the top seven years previous. He had spent fifteen of his twenty-seven years of experience with Kinsman, the past four years on the *Philip Minch,* a 480-foot freighter.

First Mate Andrew Kraft watched the deck crew tighten the twenty-eight clamps on each of the *Steinbrenner's* twelve hatches. The weather report called for stormy conditions later in the day but nothing too serious. This led to a decision that Stiglin would later regret. If really bad weather was anticipated, the hatch covers, which were the old telescoping type and not all that watertight, would be covered by tarps and fastened down, offering added protection from the elements. On this day, however, the tarps were not deemed necessary. Other openings on the boat were covered, but Stiglin felt the boat's heavy hatch covers would suffice.

When the *Steinbrenner,* loaded with 6,800 tons of iron ore, departed the Great Northern Railway dock near Superior, Wisconsin, at 6:00 a.m. on May 10, 1953, bound for Lake Erie and Bethlehem Steel, the air temperature was near seventy degrees—an absolutely balmy spring day on the northern Great Lakes. As predicted, these conditions did not last. The early hours of the *Steinbrenner's* trip went smoothly, enough to encourage crew members to walk leisurely in the open air, but by midafternoon, the freighter was running into the projected

The *Steinbrenner* docked.

cold front. The wind freshened, torrential rain fell, and the sea began to build. According to one individual sailing at the time, the motion of sailing in the storm was like "going up and down in an elevator."

Stiglin, opting to take no chances in conditions that were still manageable, ordered the deck crew to check the hatch covers and hook up a lifeline from the front to the back of the boat. The *Steinbrenner* was not equipped with the underdeck tunnels that had become the standard in shipping, so all movement from front to back of the boat in inclement weather involved moving across a slippery and windy open deck. A lifeline became a necessity.

Not that it mattered in this case: the first seas broke over the deck about 4:30 p.m., and when dinner was served a short time later, only about one-fourth of the thirty men onboard were able to find their way to the galley. The wind blew at gale force throughout Lake Superior. Duluth recorded winds of 72 miles per hour at 6:30 p.m. This had become much more than a typical spring blow.

Concerned about the growing intensity of the storm, Captain Stiglin sent the deck crew out to check the hatch covers. Three hours later, they were at it again, with Third Mate George Wiseman and three deck crewmen examining the number eleven hatch with a loosened leaf. It was miserable work. The men were drenched by boarding water continuously washing over the deck, making the footing treacherous. They gripped their lifelines to maintain their balance. Such protection, however, was not fail-safe. Deck watch Thomas Wells was knocked into the opening of a hatch, falling into the maw. "The wave hit us and then it knocked me in the cargo hold," Wells would recall. "I had hold of the lifeline. The other three guys pulled me out and helped me to the galley."

Watchman Norman Bragg was one of the men who pulled Wells from the hold. "We pulled him out and he complained of his hip and hand. The leaf I would say was open some two feet. To be knocked in there he couldn't have gotten in there without being banged up a bit. He couldn't walk when we got him out. We carried him into the galley." Luckily, Wells was not badly injured.

The storm mounted. What had begun as heavy rain and wind had evolved into a maelstrom threatening life and vessel. Water poured over the deck from both port and starboard, rolling up the deck and assaulting the already weakened hatch covers. It was no longer conceivable to move across the deck; doing so would have been suicidal. Waves were estimated at 20 to 35 feet. It grew more fearsome as the night went on. The wind, raging out of the east-northeast, topped out with gusts of 80 miles per hour. Water entered any opening it could find, including the *Steinbrenner*'s smokestack. Roiling water crashed against doors.

Captain Stiglin attempted everything he could think of to keep his freighter ahead of the storm's clutches. He had the engine room cut the engine's speed. When the number eleven hatch leaf gave way again at 4:30 a.m., he ordered the boat's pumps to be deployed full-time, to pump out water pouring into the *Steinbrenner.*

The pumps could not keep up with the inrushing water. In a desperate effort to buy time, Stiglin ordered his wheelsman to turn the ship around, and then called his chief engineer and ordered full power for the turn. If successful, the boat might reach Passage Island near Isle Royale and hide in the lee of the storm. At the very least, the boat might find some protection for the stern. "I thought we could get some shelter back there so the men could get out and get the leaf back in place," Stiglin explained later.

In the *Steinbrenner*'s stern, men had gathered in the galley. They initially felt they had little to worry about: they had experience with rough seas. But as daylight approached and water flooded into what seemed like every room on the boat, their concerns grew.

Bernard Oberoski, the *Steinbrenner*'s second cook, similar to most stewards and galley workers on the Great Lakes, who knew the crewmen and appeared to know everything going on about their boat, watched as unconcern turned into anxiety among those now grouping in the galley. "Everybody was scared," he recalled. "A lot of the guys were praying. A lot of water was in the galley. It seeped through the cracks in the door. We had coffee. Somebody came up from the engine room and says, 'Somebody told me the captain is going to turn and see what he can do.' We got secured so we wouldn't fall. He turned but I guess it didn't do any good. He turned back again."

The hopelessness of the plight of vessel and crew, probably on Stiglin's mind for a couple hours, was reinforced when a massive wave hit the boat and blew away three hatch covers. "They were scattered," Stiglin would say of the covers. "I then knew that that was it."

Over the ensuing minutes, the three men with the captain in the pilothouse—First Mate Andrew Kraft, wheelsman Leo Thomas, and wheelsman Earl Hemmingson, in the wheelhouse though not working—saw Albert Stiglin at his most vulnerable and at his most authoritative. After seeing the loss of the three hatch covers, Stiglin transmitted a radio message seeking assistance from any boats in the area. He then called the *Steinbrenner*'s engine room and asked any available personnel to head upstairs and alert everyone in the stern of the urgent possibilities ahead; the men were to don their life jackets and proceed to the deck for further instructions.

The men occupying the bow received similar notice. "The watchman came down and said, 'Get dressed quick,'" said deckhand Ken Kumm, who was in bed at the time. "As I was getting dressed, the alarm went off. I got my preserver and ran out in the hallway and up on the deck. The captain was hollering, 'Get onto the raft.' A wave came around and washed me overboard."

Captain Stiglin's last actions before sounding the abandon ship whistle were to make a final distress call and place the Chadburn on stop. This distress call was picked up by the master of the *Hochelaga*, a 623-foot freighter. All hands were going to abandon ship, Stiglin said, and he asked that the *Hochelaga* continue to pass word about his boat's plight to other vessels, in the event that the *Steinbrenner* ceased transmissions. Stiglin gave the *Steinbrenner*'s current position and signed off.

The *Steinbrenner* was sinking quickly. Within a few minutes of Stiglin's issuing the general alarm, the stern settled low in the water, listing slightly to the starboard side. Water had flooded the cargo hold and was pouring freely into the engine room, measuring about 4 feet deep when the crew left for the deck. Cold water crept closer to the white-hot boilers. An explosion was unavoidable; all that was uncertain was when that would occur. The men on the stern wanted to avoid that at any cost.

Oddly enough, the mood on the deck was almost calm. Some of the men froze with fear; others decided to go down with the freighter. An engine room crewman took a fatalistic but humorous approach to the prospects of sinking. "I was frightened, of course, but I didn't see any emotional actions of any kind," porter David Autin said of the men assembled on the stern. "I think an oiler by the name of Frank kidded about it. He said, 'If we are going to go, let's all go happy.' Nobody made any remarks about this. Everybody was very calm."

The bow situation was similar. All the men from that portion of the boat, including Captain Stiglin, gathered at the life raft and waited. The 6-by-12-foot raft, built to hold fifteen men, was essentially a wooden platform mounted on two metal air tanks. It was designed to float free when the vessel sank. The crewmen took places on the raft and waited, mostly in silence.

The men on the stern struggled with releasing the lifeboats while they contended with hazardous waves. The two lifeboats mounted in the back of the stern carried twenty men each, so there was more than enough capacity to handle the crewmen there. The boats were equipped with oars and flares. Between the swollen seas and the *Steinbrenner* sinking lower and lower in the water, the lifeboats had little distance to travel when they were lowered.

"We had difficulty," David Autin would recall. "I don't know what the trouble was, but with the wind and the rain, it seemed that we had trouble trying to raise the boat on the port side. Someone said, 'We better go to the starboard.' I didn't hesitate at all and went to the starboard side. I think there were seven or eight there. We cleared the boat. We released it and she went out quite a ways after we released it. The wind blew it out several feet. When she came back, I got ahold of it and almost went overboard."

The mood on the stern darkened as the back of the boat continued to sink and it became clear that the end was approaching. Neither lifeboat had been launched; crewmen strained to board them and move them as far away as possible before the suction from the sinking boat brought them down. They were only marginally successful. When the *Steinbrenner* shuddered moments before taking her plunge beneath the lake's surface, the port lifeboat was hurled, empty, into the water; two men jumped into the water and boarded it.

The starboard lifeboat had been launched just before the sinking but not without difficulty. The boat was still secured to a painter when it was being lowered. Arthur Morse, the *Steinbrenner*'s third assistant engineer, had a knife and cut the rope holding the lifeboat. Instead of jumping into the boat, he waved to the seven men being lowered. "So long, boys," he shouted. "Good luck." His lifeless body would be discovered, floating in the lake, several days later.

Others refused to abandon ship as well. Oiler Frank Jozapaitis tried to talk a fellow engine room crewman into leaving, but it didn't work. "I was trying to get one coal passer in the boat, but he was standing there froze. He was scared when he couldn't find his life preserver. He stood there shaking and he said he could not see it. I grabbed him. I grabbed his life preserver and helped him put it on. I held him with one hand and got him out on the boat deck. He froze and I couldn't get him in the boat. I saw the boat going down and I made a jump for it."

The men on the raft had other problems. While it was in the process of sinking, the *Steinbrenner* tossed the men and raft overboard. The men were close to the *Steinbrenner* when she took her stern-first dive. The suction pulled them down. Stiglin went under a short distance, fought his way to the surface, and came up beneath the raft. He found a way to board the raft and joined others who had done the same. Four of the men originally on the raft did not return and were presumed dead.

Others elsewhere on the boat experienced the sensation of the *Steinbrenner*'s pulling them under. "The suction took me down," Bernard Oberoski recalled, claiming that he felt a flash of heat from the explosion caused by the cold water hitting the boilers. "I felt something eventually hit me and seen my life in front of me. Somehow the suction let me go. I swallowed water and everything. Every time I opened my mouth I got a mouthful."

Kenneth Kumm, already in the water after being swept overboard by what he described as a 30-foot wave, was swimming for his life. "It was cold," he would eventually tell a Coast Guard panel investigating the loss of the *Steinbrenner*. "I swam away from the boat because I was afraid of the suction. I swam to the lifeboat [but] I couldn't climb into the lifeboat. I happened to see where the water was rolling in the boat and I worked around to that side. [I] let the water roll me in the boat."

Oberoski swam furiously after surfacing from the suction. He was dismayed by what he saw—the flotsam from the sunken vessel and the bodies of fellow shipmates. "I looked around. One man had his head all smashed. You couldn't help yourself. The water was freezing. . . . I seen the lifeboat with Tomczak in it. I saw the fellow climb in. I tried to swim. The boat drifted into me. I couldn't have made it myself. I grabbed hold as much as I could. I tipped it sideways, and I was lucky and I could get a better hold. Then I got my right heel in and forced myself up. I lay there about ten minutes. Everybody was screaming. Frank was foaming from the mouth and vomiting. You could see he was going right away."

The survivors flopped in the three lifesaving vessels, exhausted from the ordeal, separated from each other by considerable distance, freezing, bobbing wildly in water estimated to be about thirty-five degrees. Injuries varied. "Our wheelsman had a broken leg and broken arm," Stiglin said. He tended to him on a raft not equipped with any medical supplies. "I straightened out his leg and told him he would have to lie quietly because of the broken leg."

Wheelsman Joe Radzewicz had been seriously injured when a wave lifted the life raft while it was still on the deck. The raft slammed Radzewicz into the pilothouse wall, breaking his left arm and left leg before tossing him overboard. Radzewicz had been a crewman on an earlier sinking when, in 1943, while on the *George M. Humphrey,* he was part of a collision in the Straits of Mackinac. The *Humphrey* sank, but Radzewicz escaped. Now, prone on the raft, in agonizing pain and bone-numbing cold, he could only hold onto the belief that he would survive again.

Sailors were accustomed to relying on faith—in their boat, their captain, their work, and each other. Now, floating on Lake Superior, hanging on as the storm dissipated, each man had to hold on to the faith that someone would come to his rescue, with the uncertainty whether that might happen before exposure took him down.

~~~

There was no shortage of steamers in the area. Of course, in waters as vast as Lake Superior, with vessels that crept along at much less than 20 miles per hour, in sailing conditions on the edge of a diminishing storm, *in the area* could mean hours away. For those trying to survive in wet clothing and freezing air temperatures, a couple of hours could be the difference between life and death.

A number of boats heard Captain Stiglin's call for help. The 714-foot *Joseph H. Thompson,* at one time a troopship and currently the largest boat on the Great Lakes, set off to assist the *Steinbrenner,* as did the *Wilfred Sykes,* a 678-foot behemoth that ranked as the biggest freighter on the lakes from 1949 until 1952, and the 580-foot *D. M. Clemson.* Other vessels on the move included the *Hochelaga,* the last boat in contact with the *Steinbrenner,* and the *Kerr,* the *William E. Carey,* and the *Ontadoc.* The Coast Guard from Duluth, Grand Marais, and Portage chipped in smaller vessels to join the search. All told, the search and rescue operations formed one of the largest efforts in Great Lakes history.

It was not relished work. Thoughts of a freighter's delaying or postponing a scheduled trip, of not rescuing survivors but digging for heavy, waterlogged bodies with nets and grappling hooks, of seeing

The 580-foot *Clemson* joined the search and rescue operations for the *Henry Steinbrenner* early on.

what remained of a freighter—these put sailors in touch with what could happen to them under the wrong circumstances. Still, there was an unwritten rule requiring a boat to help another vessel in trouble—unless doing so imperiled the rescue boat.

While hurrying toward the site provided by Captain Stiglin during his last radio transmission, the different vessels' commanders conferred and agreed to fan out in an attempt to cover as much of the area as possible. The *Thompson, Clemson,* and *Sykes* arrived ahead of the others, at nearly the same time, about four and a half hours after the sinking. Their timing was crucial. Hypothermia had already claimed victims. Frank Tomczak, one of the three crewmen aboard a lifeboat, had died about an hour prior to the freighters' arrival. First Mate Andrew Kraft had lost consciousness on the raft and died just as the rescue boats found them.

Picking up the survivors was an arduous task for the three huge freighters. Maneuvering into a position where they could transfer the men onto a vessel, tough under any circumstances, became more stressful due to the poor condition of the survivors. Many were too

The 678-foot freighter *Wilfred Sykes,* an instrumental vessel in the search for *Steinbrenner* survivors, enters the Duluth harbor.

weakened from their ordeal to climb a ladder or even stand up. The wheelsman with the broken leg and arm required a stretcher.

The *Thompson* came to the aid of those on the raft, with help from the *Sykes,* which formed a lee by lining up perpendicular to the *Thompson*'s stern. As Stiglin remembered, the sight of the vessels was more than welcome, but the process of boarding the *Thompson* was time-consuming. "He was coming from Superior. He sighted us and made a turn.... [He] got us on the starboard side." The *Thompson* tossed a line to the raft, which secured the raft to the freighter. A ladder was lowered, but the survivors were too weak to use it without assistance. "We informed them that we had a stretcher case, and they lowered a stretcher. We raised the stretcher case first." The others tied lines around themselves as insurance and slowly hobbled up the Jacob's ladder. They made it aboard the *Thompson* without problems. Warm baths, dry clothing, food, and coffee followed.

Crewmen aboard the *Steinbrenner* life raft, awaiting rescue by the 714-foot freighter *Joseph H. Thompson*.

The *Thompson* pulled alongside the crowded life raft and pulled the cold, tired men onboard to safety. Other freighters joined the intensive search and rescue operation.

The lifeboat cases were similar. Norman Bragg watched the *Clemson* pass and turn around, repositioning herself to line up with the lifeboat. On her first pass of the lifeboat, the *Clemson* came dangerously close: the propeller and the wake it created could have swamped the lifeboat. "I was afraid to use the [lifeboat's] oars," Bragg said about the prospects of trying to row away from the *Clemson,* "because the men were inexperienced. I am inexperienced with oars myself. I was afraid we would get in the way of the ship and they would swamp us. The *Clemson* backed up; then she came close enough to throw a heaving line. We were unable to stand up. We were bailing water all the time. . . . They threw us a line then, to which we attached ourselves. We tied it around our waists and they hauled us aboard by line."

Of the three big boats, the *Sykes* might have had the most difficulty with the fewest crewmen (two living and one dead) to bring onboard. The *Sykes* had retrieved Ken Kumm, who had clung desperately to a ladder lowered by the *Sykes.* While this transpired, the line tying the lifeboat to the *Sykes* broke free, and the lifeboat drifted away. The waves quickly pushed it out of reach. Captain George Fisher had his wheelsman turn the boat in a broad maneuver, but it became clear that Bernard Oberoski, the sailor on the lifeboat, was in no condition

Men aboard a *Steinbrenner* lifeboat.

to catch or hold on to a line, and the *Sykes*'s third mate and nine other crew members climbed into one of their own lifeboats, lowered it, and rowed through turbulent waters to the *Steinbrenner* lifeboat. They picked up Oberoski and Frank Tomczak, the dead sailor, and rowed them back to the *Sykes.*

The freighters remained in the area for hours, searching for victims and survivors. Other vessels arrived and joined the search. The *Steinbrenner*'s toll offered depressing numbers: fourteen of the *Steinbrenner*'s crew were saved; seventeen perished.

Interviewed by the *Detroit Free Press,* Captain Albert Stiglin offered a terse, understated, yet ultimately accurate summation of the forces that destroyed his boat and claimed so many lives: "We ran into a little more sea than she could take."

〰〰

After being separated, tortured, and, in too many cases, killed by nature's power and design, the *Steinbrenner* sailors, or at least her survivors, were now separated by their fellow humans. Their rescuers had places to be, and they took the survivors with them. The *Sykes* sailed on to Superior, the *Thompson* and *Clemson* to the Soo. From there, the men would be flown to Detroit, where they would testify about the shipwreck to a panel of Coast Guard officers gathering information for an official report.

The *Steinbrenner* story became national news. The most interest, as one might imagine, originated in the Midwest, in shipping communities, but the *Steinbrenner* story, from the boat's background to sinking to immense search attempts, captured the imaginations of people everywhere, including readers of the *New York Times.* Reporters clamored for interviews, which the surviving crewmen were happy to provide. The *Detroit Free Press* talked to Albert Stiglin first, beating the newspaper competition by interviewing him via radiophone.

A touch of hyperbole spiced some of the interviews. The crewmen had little, if any, experience with the press, and their responses to questions were probably offered to provide an air of solemnity to their accounts. One crewman confirmed that some of the waves hitting the *Steinbrenner* were 60 feet high—which you might encounter on the ocean but not on the Great Lakes. Another told a reporter that the pilothouse had been pounded so relentlessly that it had been pushed forward 3 feet. There were complaints about the condition of the vessel, most against the *Steinbrenner*'s stripped hatch clamps.

Watchman Norman Bragg, one of those sent out to secure hatch number eleven, criticized the boat's overall condition, saying that "nothing worked as it should aboard the ship. We were taking water something awful for nearly twelve hours before she went down." Thomas Wells, helped by Bragg when he fell through a hatch opening, agreed. The *Steinbrenner,* he declared, was "just too old."

Stiglin took a rather benevolent approach in his statements to the press—and the *Steinbrenner*'s owners. The boat had been seaworthy— she had passed her inspections, after all—and the storm, while imposing, had not been the equal of others she had negotiated in the past. The crewmen, he made a point of adding, had responded admirably in dealing with the sinking.

The *Steinbrenner* survivors barely had time to settle in their hotel rooms when they were summoned to contribute their memories to a Coast Guard inquiry into the foundering. By 1953, the Coast Guard was thoroughly examining all accidents involving loss of life, and though no one argued about what precisely had caused the *Steinbrenner* to founder, the Coast Guard wondered if anything could have been done to prevent it. Should tarps have been utilized after the boat had been loaded and the hatch clamps were battened down? Were the hatch clamps defective, as some of the reports suggested? Had appropriate measures been taken when the first hatch cover failed? Had Captain Stiglin taken the correct measures when addressing the demands of the storm and the dangers it imposed on man and vessel?

All but one of the surviving *Steinbrenner* personnel, including Captain Stiglin, appeared before the Board of Investigation. (The sole exception was the injured wheelsman, still in the hospital for treatment.) The line of questioning was firm but cordial, with board members taking turns posing questions, many answers being jotted down while someone else was posing queries. Stiglin, who testified first and longest, was called back to testify twice after his initial lengthy appearance.

After Stiglin completed his initial turn before the board, proceedings moved to Cleveland. At the beginning of each new interview, a crewman was asked a series of questions covering the basics, such as the person's name, home address, background in shipping, and position on the *Steinbrenner* at the time of the accident. A small number of respondents were represented by attorneys; most declined the offer.

A mosaic of the *Steinbrenner* and her last voyage began to form. The men ranged in the effectiveness of their recollections, but their memories of the trip, the storm, the last minutes aboard, the foundering, immediate aftermath, and rescue—all having occurred within days of their testimony—were fresh and riveting. The hearings wrapped up a week to the day after the *Steinbrenner* sinking.

The Board of Investigation pondered the testimony and on July 10, one day shy of the two-month anniversary of the *Steinbrenner* loss, submitted its report. The report offered an in-depth account of the *Steinbrenner* story, concluding that "the adverse weather conditions with mountainous seas combined [with the loss of hatch covers] to make this foundering an act of God." The report went on to say that the *Steinbrenner* was seaworthy when she left port on her final voyage.

The report exonerated Captain Stiglin of any blame for the boat's loss. In the board's judgment, tarpaulins placed over the hatch covers would have helped in keeping the water from entering the cargo hold, but the board absolved Stiglin of blame in not ordering the use of tarps. "The board concluded that any prudent master could have used the same judgment under the same conditions with erroneous weather forecasts and the favorable weather conditions prevailing at the start of the voyage," the report stated.

The report addressed the issue of stripped hatch cover clamps, admitting that there was no question that such clamps existed but also saying, first, that the number of faulty clamps was minor, and, second, that there was no telling if the defective clamps were used on the three hatch covers lost in the storm.

Despite the report's conclusion that the *Steinbrenner* was the victim of nature's fury, the Coast Guard board did make a few safety recommendations:

1. The board recommends that in addition of the life preservers presently required for this type of Great Lakes vessel that the following be required:
   a. At least three (3) life preservers to be carried in an overhead rack in the pilothouse.
   b. At least four (4) life preservers to be carried in a watertight box in the engine room.
   c. At least six (6) life preservers to be carried in a watertight box on the boat deck.

2. The board recommends that tarpaulins be required to be used at all times except during the mid-summer period, 15 May through 15 September.

Besides recommending new safety precautions, the board recommended that letters of appreciation be sent to the family of the third engineer, who gave his life to save his fellow *Steinbrenner* crewman, and to the captains of the three boats who had assisted in saving the survivors of the wreck.

~~~

But all was not over. P. A. Ovenden, leader of the merchant vessel inspection division of the Coast Guard but not a member of the Board of Investigation, voiced his dissent from the board's conclusions. At the very least, he said, Captain Stiglin was guilty of dereliction of duty; Stiglin was well versed on the practice of utilizing tarpaulins. The weather, as noted by the board, was pleasant at the time of the *Steinbrenner*'s departure, but rainy, perhaps even stormy weather had been projected for the hours ahead, and Stiglin should have considered this and ordered the placement of tarps. Ovenden had no interest in excuses. A vessel had been destroyed and men lost when the *Steinbrenner* encountered the storm and the hatch covers gave way. Stiglin, he insisted, should be stripped of his license.

He wasn't finished. Ovenden sent copies of the Coast Guard hearings to the U.S. attorney for further consideration, "Such record contains evidence of probable criminal liability on the part of the master of the *Henry Steinbrenner*," Ovenden wrote in his cover letter.

Vice Admiral and Coast Guard Commandant Merlin O'Neill endorsed Ovenden's conclusions, declaring that the Coast Guard had regulations governing the closing of hatch covers, and that Stiglin's failure to follow these regulations "very largely contributed to the foundering of the Steinbrenner." O'Neill rejected the board's findings and supported the challenge to Stiglin's master's license.

Nothing came of these protests other than their eliciting strong reactions from the shipping community. Voices from owners to masters alike tended to oppose regulations that could not guarantee positive results. Applying tarps took a lot of time, and lost time on the docks translated into revenue. Crews grumbled about the work of applying tarps, especially when the weather offered no threat.

The concerns over the use of tarps were tested four months after the loss of the *Steinbrenner* when the *Maryland,* a 530-foot bulk carrier owned by Bethlehem Transportation Company, was caught up in a freak storm on Lake Superior. The boat was sailing without the added tarp protection when heavy seas tore off two hatch covers. A daring maneuver by crewmen saw the hatch covers secured again, but the damage had been done. Tons of water sloshed around the freighter's cargo hold. The *Maryland,* commanded by A. P. Goodrow, was in grave peril. Unable to steer properly and trapped in troughs, Goodrow ordered a run for the safety of Marquette, Michigan. He was able to ground the boat in a sandy section of reef about 8 miles east of Marquette. The Coast Guard, alerted well in advance of the *Maryland*'s troubles, was nearby, and twenty-one of the boat's thirty-two member crew were helped off the vessel by use of a breeches buoy. When wind and heavy sea snapped the buoy's line, the others were brought off the boat via helicopter, believed to be the first helicopter rescue in Lake Superior history.

~~~~~

The wreck of the *Steinbrenner* was never found, though it was searched for on numerous occasions. The failure to locate it was mystifying, since so many people, including Captain Stiglin and the crews of the rescue vessels, believed they knew the location of the boat's sinking. Side-scan sonar was used to search for the wreck, but nothing was found, at least at the provided coordinates. Some speculated that the boat had disappeared in very deep water, making it more difficult to locate. Others felt that Stiglin had mistakenly transmitted the wrong location when he radioed for help while sinking.

It ultimately didn't matter. The *Steinbrenner* had become a ghost ship—one of the most recent sinkings to litter the bottom of Lake Superior, and further proof, if such was necessary, of the fatal perils of sailing the lake's stormy waters.

PART II
Isle Royale

Cumberland

~~~

The first thing you notice is the green: every shade of green imaginable, coloring leaves, needles, and stalks of every type of plant that comes to mind, from trees to grass. The thick vegetation covers the island like a living picture postcard, teasing the senses with sights and smells that cannot be dismissed. Then you remember that it has been this way since the glaciers retreated and plants began to grow.

Isle Royale, the grand dame of an archipelago of islands located roughly 17 miles southeast of Grand Portage, Minnesota, is 45 miles long and 9 miles wide, its length running from southwest to northeast. It is, by far, the largest island on the inland seas.

Its large and varied population of fur-bearing animals came to the island from Canada, arriving after moving over an ice-covered Lake Superior. They ate whatever was available, mated, and established a presence unaltered by predators. Gray wolves eventually arrived in the early twentieth century, by most estimations. Guesswork is also required to date the arrival of the moose. It has been a chicken-or-egg debate, since both were observed occupying the island at the same time. To this day, scientists study the predator–prey relationship of the wolf and moose populations.

The sparse human population on Isle Royale has been more accurately dated. Pottery and rudimentary tools discovered on the island date back 4,500 years, and more recently tools and weapons fashioned out of copper were attributed to Native people, particularly the Ojibwe, who continue to honor the island's history.

Copper, plentiful on the island and through the western Lake Superior environs, contributed heavily to the island's history. The Native Americans mined copper on Isle Royale, going as far as naming the island "Minong," which, by one translation, means "a good place to get copper." (French missionaries renamed it Isle Royale in the mid-seventeenth century.) Commercial copper mining reached its zenith in the eighteenth century.

Few people occupy the island year round, although Isle Royale is a tourist attraction when the weather is moderate. Automobiles are not permitted on the island. Food and lodging, although available on parts of the island, are minimal. Camping is popular. Boats bring tourists to boat landings, and vacationers are on their own. Fishing, boating, and kayaking, as one might expect in an area surrounded by water and laced with rivers and streams, head the list of activities.

For many years before tourism arrived on the island, commercial shipping was almost nonexistent. An occasional package freighter might drop off supplies, but there was no need for bigger boats to drop by. In fact, larger vessels did their best to avoid the area. Isle Royale and the network of islands surrounding it were a dangerous place to navigate in the autumn, when vicious Lake Superior storms strongly affected steering. The islands, by their very nature, feature very deep and very shallow waters, often in tight proximity. Over the years, the area near Isle Royale became the site of numerous shipwrecks, many resulting in loss of life. The island could be as dangerous as it was beautiful and historically significant.

The arrival of vessels signaled not only the arrival of urgently needed supplies: it also heralded the beginning of social festivities on the isolated island.

Seven miles off the western coast of Isle Royale lies Cumberland Point, site of the island's first significant shipwreck. The *Cumberland,* a 214-foot Canadian side-wheeler, had run aground on a reef near the Rock of Ages in 1877, ending the vessel's six-year career of delivering passengers and freight to northern Minnesota and southern Canada.

Boats like the *Cumberland,* with their sleek designs and sporting circular paddle wheels on either side of the vessel, were popular in the mid-nineteenth century, known for their pleasing appearances and appreciated for their efficiency. Along with the schooners, the side-wheelers did a hefty business at a time when wooden-hulled vessels dotted the horizon while delivering livestock and dry goods to areas otherwise deprived of badly needed provisions.

The *Cumberland* was built in 1871 by Melancthon Simpson in Port Robinson, Ontario. Detailed notes and records of the construction were not kept at that time, but it is known that the *Cumberland*'s engine had been previously used on the Canadian *Cataract,* a vessel built in 1846. Photographs of the *Cumberland* and other side-wheelers of the period indicate great similarity between the *Cumberland* and other vessels.

The 214-foot side-wheeler *Cumberland* frequently delivered supplies to Duluth. The vessel grounded on the Rock of Ages reef on July 24, 1877.

The boat was named in honor of Fred W. Cumberland, the general manager of Northern Railway, which, through the Toronto and Lake Superior Navigation Company, controlled much of the commercial shipping in southern Canada and northern Lake Superior. The railroads were still developing and nowhere near what they would become over the next fifty years, so transporting passengers by water served a valuable function. The *Cumberland* was built to move passengers between Duluth and Collinwood and Owen Sound in Canada on Lake Huron's Georgian Bay. She would also transport goods to railroad stations.

The *Cumberland* was launched on August 9, 1871, and her first abbreviated season was uneventful. That would not be the case for the rest of her brief service on Lake Superior. On a foggy day in July 1872, the *Cumberland*'s crew noticed another steamer, the Canadian *Manitou*, stranded on a reef near Michipicoten Island on the eastern part of Lake Superior near Canada. The *Manitou* had been built in the same city, at the same time, as the *Cumberland*, though the two vessels sailed for competing companies. The *Cumberland* went to the grounded freighter's assistance and remained at the site until the *Manitou* was freed about thirty hours later. Such assistance, wrote Frederick Stonehouse in his book *Isle Royale Shipwrecks*, was "commonplace."

Then, in September, sailing in a vicious storm, the *Cumberland* spotted the crew of a schooner, the *Maple Leaf*, stranded on an island near Isle Royale. The *Maple Leaf*, overwhelmed by the storm, had capsized, but not before her crew had abandoned ship and escaped to shore. The *Cumberland* was deadlocked in her own battle with the storm and was unable to reach the island.

Two months later, near the end of the shipping season while sailing near the St. Marys River in extremely cold weather, the *Cumberland* suffered her first notable setback when she became encased in ice and could not be freed. She was, literally, frozen in place. Leaving his first mate in command of the boat, the captain, his chief engineer, and three crewmen set out on foot to find help. They reached Collinwood, and the rest of the *Cumberland* crew joined them the following day. All were frostbitten but otherwise in good shape. By all indications, the *Cumberland* remained frozen in ice until the following spring.

Two years after the ice fiasco, in November 1874, while carrying passengers and a heavy load of cargo, the *Cumberland* encountered a hellacious storm so severe that the twisting of the vessel loosened her caulking, causing a serious leak that her pumps could not handle. The captain ordered the livestock penned on deck to be thrown overboard. According to reports, hogs, sheep, and between 75 to 150 cattle were dumped into Lake Superior while the *Cumberland* sped to the nearest port. Dry goods were jettisoned as well. When the *Cumberland* reached Port Arthur, Ontario (Prince Arthur's Landing, which eventually became part of Thunder Bay), she had 6 feet of water in her cargo hold. She sank in the shallow water of the harbor, but the passengers, crew, and, ultimately, the boat were saved.

Misfortune followed the *Cumberland*. She was again tossed about in a November storm in 1875, when she ran into blinding snow and heavy winds and came aground. Damage was minimal, and she was pulled off the rocks with little difficulty. This story repeated the following year, although serious injury was involved in this instance, when a towing line employed to extricate the *Cumberland* snapped, breaking both of the captain's legs. The mate took over, and the boat was refloated.

~~~

Although considered "a trim, staunch, and fast-sailing craft," the *Cumberland* suffered more than the average number of indignities in her brief life in commercial shipping. It is probably appropriate that she met her demise under strange circumstances, in ideal sailing conditions.

The trouble began on July 20, 1877, when the *Cumberland* grounded on a reef near Nipigon Harbor in northern Lake Superior. Tugs freed the boat three days later, but she had sustained enough damage to take 4 to 6 feet of water into her hold. The *Cumberland* transferred her passengers to another vessel, and rather than stop for repairs, she relied on her pumps to carry her through to Duluth, her intended destination.

She must have been sailing at full speed or near it, because when she hit a reef near the Rock of Ages, the boat was pushed onto the reef to her midsection. The day was clear and the water calm, but it was later determined that the *Cumberland* would have missed the reef entirely if she had sailed 100 feet to either her port or starboard side. Instead, the boat sailed into water only 6 feet deep.

The cause of the accident was easy to ascertain. Captain J. G. Parsons was using a Canadian chart that did not include the reef, which was indicated on American charts. This, of course, made sense, since the *Cumberland* was a Canadian boat sailing for a Canadian company. Parsons, in his haste to reach Duluth as quickly as possible, might have chosen a course that shaved off time but brought him closer to Isle Royale than usual. Now he and his crew were stranded on a reef, and pulling the boat back into water was going to involve a lot of work.

Efforts to free the boat were doomed. Two freighters, the *Francis Smith* and the *Quebec,* labored unsuccessfully to remove the *Cumberland* from the reef; a portion of the cargo from the stranded boat was loaded onto the *Smith.* Other tugs and heavy equipment made attempts, but nothing worked. Bad weather and the work exacted their tolls; the *Cumberland,* although in no immediate danger of sinking, started to fall apart. On August 12, all efforts were abandoned, and within two weeks, the *Cumberland* was declared a total loss.

Controversy accompanied the declaration. The *Cumberland* was insured for a good portion of her value, and with business taking a dip during the season, a rumor circulated accusing the *Cumberland*'s owners of dragging their feet in trying to save the boat and of cutting attempts to refloat the disintegrating boat in favor of collecting insurance money. The rumor, like so many, withered over time.

By early September, the *Cumberland* had broken apart and sunk.

～～～

What becomes of a vessel's remains after sinking has been of interest to divers and historians since the invention of equipment permitting deeper and longer shipwreck explorations. New wreck sites, often of vessels lost and undiscovered for a century or more, and the creation of a relatively new underwater archaeology have offered shipwreck enthusiasts and historians insights into vessel construction, the cause

A diver at the *Cumberland* wreckage.

of accidents, Great Lakes commerce, and human error previously only imagined. The ribs of old freighters, the lost engines and boilers, even dishes from the galleys . . . all speak of loss, yet, at the same time, speak volumes of a time when commercial shipping was an essential component of economic and social progress.

The *Cumberland* wreckage contributed a twist of mystery. Salvage divers visited the site within days of the *Cumberland*'s demise, and their recovery of items, along with items taken when the boat was still stranded but afloat, and the wreckage that drifted to shore, led to an auction on September 5, 1877. In an advertisement for the auction, among many items listed for sale were lifeboats, anchors, life preservers, and assorted furniture. The sale netted approximately $3,000.

One of the mysteries to emerge involved the boat's engine and boilers. They had not been recovered in time for the sale, but they were not found in the wreckage either. One line of thought focused on salvagers having removed these heavy machines, but no one came forward with any solid claims, and they were never found and identified even after more than a century of diving the wreck.

Another series of uncertainties arrived with the loss of a vessel in the same area, this one occurring in 1898, twenty-one years after the sinking of the *Cumberland*. The *Henry Chisholm*, a 257-foot wooden bulk carrier, launched in 1880. Admired for her superb craftsmanship, the *Chisholm* was towing a 220-foot schooner, the *John Martin*, with a cargo of 92,000 bushels of barley, when she ran into a powerful autumnal storm after leaving Duluth on October 16, 1898. The storm knocked the two boats around until, on October 17, Captain James Lawless of the *Martin* decided, for the sake of both vessels, to drop the towline connecting his vessel to the *Chisholm* and seek shelter separately. The *Chisholm* sailed for two more days, hanging on in the teeth of the storm until it dissipated.

With the storm behind him, Captain P. H. Smith, taking time off only to refuel, turned the *Chisholm* around and set out to find the *Martin*. Smith figured the *Martin* had sought shelter somewhere along Minnesota's northern shore, or possibly in Duluth, or in the vicinity of Isle Royale. (He learned later that the barge had been towed to safety by a passing vessel.) His boat met her demise in the treacherous waters near Isle Royale. The *Chisholm* plowed into a reef near the Rock of Ages, in the same area that had claimed the *Cumberland*. Smith and his crew abandoned the *Chisholm* without a problem, but the boat, like the *Cumberland* before it, was out in the open, exposed on all sides to the elements.

The *Chisholm* broke apart in a late October storm and sank, scattering wreckage among *Cumberland* wreckage. Salvagers were able to recover the *Chisholm*'s boilers but little else. There was no difficulty in identifying the larger pieces of wreckage of the two vessels: the two vessels were different in appearance. The smaller wreckage washed to shore in ensuing years, creating some confusion. It was of no consequence, of course, except to purists and historians: what mattered was two vessels—and youthful ones—were lost in an area that came to be known as Cumberland Point.

Algoma

NOVEMBER 7, 1885

~~~

"She is certainly the finest boat that has ever sailed upon these great inland seas, and her superiority over all other lake craft in every particular is at once apparent."

These words, a tad hyperbolic, described the *Algoma*, a 262-foot passenger steamer built by Aitken & Mansel for the Canadian Pacific Railway Company. The *Algoma* was exceptional, but she was hardly unique. In fact, she was part of a three-boat mini-fleet, all constructed by the same Scottish yard for Canadian Pacific Railway, all identical in every way, all sailing the same waters, all launched in July 1883. The other two vessels, *Athabasca* and *Alberta,* were operating before the *Algoma*.

Still, there was little debating that the *Algoma* was special in the ranks of boats operating on the Great Lakes. She was one of the first steel-hulled vessels on the lakes. She and her sister ships were the first to use electricity for lighting, and they were among the first to use Plimsoll marking to assist in determining how much a vessel could load without dropping her too deeply in the water. She possessed some of the finest fire and safety features of the time.

Passenger accommodations excelled as well. The *Algoma* was constructed to carry 180 first-class passengers and an additional 200 in steerage, with the capacity to expand to 1,000 passengers. The beautiful wood-paneled rooms were nicely furnished and well lit, with enough deck space for those wanting to spend time outdoors, prompting the *Thunder Bay Sentinel* to remark that the accommodations were "of the highest class."

The *Algoma*, a 262-foot vessel built in Scotland and owned by the Canadian Pacific Railway, is shown here at the Port Arthur dock.

Getting the *Algoma* to Lake Superior required a costly, time-consuming process. The three Aitken & Mansel vessels were too large for the Welland and other canals, so rather than constructing smaller vessels, which would have defeated the buyer's purposes, Aitken & Mansel built the boats to cross the ocean, only to be cut in two pieces that could pass through the canals. The two sections were then rejoined, the rest of the boat was fitted out, and it moved on. This changed the planning and building in Glasgow but made everything possible on the Great Lakes.

The *Algoma*, carrying a cargo of coal, sailed for North America on September 25, 1883, arriving in Montreal thirteen days later. The boat had been constructed for speed and comfort, and the trip provided plenty of both. The *Algoma* was cut down and brought, via tugboat, to the lower dry dock in Cleveland. She was reassembled and fitted out, and subsequently spent the winter in Buffalo.

The cabins were built, and work on the *Algoma* was completed in mid-March 1884. The approaching spring signaled the beginning of what her owners hoped would be a long, successful service on the lakes.

~~~

Could a vessel ever be too fast for its own good? This topic was bandied about during the *Algoma*'s service. Much to the delight of her passengers, the *Algoma* was quick. She demonstrated that repeatedly during her first year of service, setting a number of records along the way. The officials at Canadian Pacific Railway drew criticism for approving their boats' speed, the most severe of the complaints being that the company was disregarding safety to push its boats to higher speeds.

The criticism seemed validated when, on July 27, 1884, the *Alberta* collided with the *J. M. Osborne*, a wooden freighter towing two barges. Thick fog enveloped the area at the mouth of the St. Marys River. Neither boat reduced speed, despite the conditions. The *Osborne* sank, and three crewmen lost their lives. The *Alberta*, sustaining $12,000 in damage to her bow, continued on.

The press expressed its outrage, underscoring previous condemnation of the speeds taken by Canadian Pacific vessels. "There is a screw loose somewhere in the management of these steamers and the railroad company had best find out where it is before their boats are all smashed to pieces," the *Duluth Tribune* fumed.

Ironically, the *Algoma* was docked when involved in her only accident during her first year. Another freighter, the *Sovereign*, hit the *Algoma*'s starboard side, damaging one of her plates, while she was tied up at the Government Dock. The accident occurred at almost precisely the same time as the *Alberta* collision.

The 1885 season, though profitable for Canadian Pacific, was not a good one overall. Competition cut into earnings, and the year recorded some of the worst earnings in years. Ship owners were relieved to see the season draw to a close.

The *Algoma*, carrying the smallest passenger list in her two-year service, departed Owen Sound on Lake Huron for Port Arthur on Thursday, November 5, 1885. Her light load of passengers was offset by a substantial cargo of package goods and railway supplies. The boat passed through the Soo Locks at noon the following day and reached Whitefish Point about four hours later. The sky was dark, and a strong wind was blowing when the *Algoma* entered Lake Superior.

Captain John Moore, the *Algoma's* pilot, trained his eyes on what looked to be a gathering storm. As a member of a seafaring family, he had heard the stories. His father, William, had sailed in Ireland before moving to Ontario, where John and his brother, William Jr., also a sailor, were born. On the Great Lakes, changing weather was the norm.

John's experience as a skipper was limited. Bright and practical, he had spent ten years on the lakes, advancing through the ranks, earning his master's license in Toronto on April 16, 1884. He commanded the *Quebec,* a liner based in Sarnia, Ontario, very briefly before taking the top job on the *Algoma.*

The conditions on Lake Superior deteriorated as the *Algoma* made her way in a diagonal course across the lake. The wind increased steadily and temperatures fell. Wind that had begun as a strong, fresh breeze had, by the time the *Algoma* was halfway across the lake, reached gale force and was threatening to blow her off course. The boat made her customary good time throughout the night, with the wind shifting to the northeast, pushing the westward-bound *Algoma.* Rain and, eventually, snow squalls fell on the vessel. The boat pitched and rolled in increasingly violent seas. Most of the crew, whether experienced or not, were too nauseated to sleep. As those on the lake that night would remember, the storm was the worst they had ever encountered.

At one point during the night, thirty-one-year-old First Mate Joseph Hastings, who, like Moore, had emigrated from the UK to Ontario, ordered the auxiliary sails hoisted on the *Algoma's* fore and aft masts, with the purpose of stabilizing the rolling boat. It worked, and the *Algoma's* speed was bolstered by the heavy wind hitting the sails. Unfortunately, the maneuver affected the vessel's holding course.

By 4:00 a.m., Captain Moore knew the *Algoma* was in proximity of Isle Royale. He ordered a lookout posted to watch for lights, and he asked his engineer to shut down the engines while the sails were lowered. Knowing that his boat was near the treacherous reefs near the island, he ordered his wheelsman to turn toward the open water.

He miscalculated the *Algoma's* position. The boat, "tossed around like a cork" in the storm, had been blown off-course, and as the wheelsman turned, the vessel ran aground near the southeast shore of the island. It was about 4:40 a.m., with only the slightest hint of daylight in the air. Mountainous waves pounded the *Algoma* until she grounded a second time. The boat immediately started to break apart.

Pandemonium and confusion ensued. Lightly clad passengers, asleep before the loud reports of the groundings, hurried to the deck, unaware of what had happened. Waves beating down on the boat washed many overboard before they were able to get a foothold. Shouts and screams joined the cacophony of the storm. The bow, looking as if it would break away from the stern, was no longer a refuge for anyone. Crew members rushed to the back of the boat; three were swept overboard before they reached it. Water boarding the *Algoma* extinguished the engine room fires and disabled the electricity, throwing the vessel into total darkness.

Captain Moore behaved heroically amid the bedlam. He tried, with little success, to assure passengers that they were near land and would safely reach it. He set up a lifeline to assist movement from the front to the back of the stricken vessel. "The captain alone remained cool and steady," William R. McCarter, a fifty-two-year-old passenger and survivor, would tell the *Saginaw Courier-Herald*. "He showed what a man he really was just then, and did his duty like a man. When it seemed a certain death to run a lifeline along the deck, he seized a rope and strung the line, telling the excited people to hold on to the rope and not become panic stricken."

The powerful waves dismantled the boat in short order. Pieces fell to the deck and into the water. The deckhouse collapsed on Moore; he somehow managed to survive being buried in the rubble but was badly injured. Although he could barely stand or walk, he was not deterred from his efforts to help those still onboard.

The hysteria increased as the boat broke apart. More people leaped into the water, convinced it was now just a matter of time before the vessel sank. Several men reasoned that their only chance was to swim to shore; wearing life preservers, they jumped into the roiling water and swam toward the island's boulder-strewn beach. The bow finally separated from the rest of the *Algoma,* and those caught on the bow were swept to their deaths. Crewmen on the stern worked frantically at releasing the lifeboats, but when they attempted to lower them, the remnants of the boat slid off the reef, hurling men and women into the water. Most perished.

The precise number of those lost on the *Algoma* would never be known. Exact passenger lists were not kept by Canadian Pacific, and estimations were the best that could be done. The numbers reported fluctuated wildly, from thirty to just over fifty, including crew members. One overheated newspaper account reported that a hundred had died.

One fact could not be disputed: more lives were lost on the *Algoma* than in any single wreck in Lake Superior history. The record stands today.

~~~

The survivor accounts were almost as harrowing. After slipping back into the water, the stern remained afloat—but just barely. Watertight bulkheads kept the stern from totally flooding, and while waves did their best to destroy what remained of the *Algoma*, the vessel hung on.

Eleven men, including Captain Moore, were trapped on the stern, unable to escape. Moore clung to a lifeline, holding out hope that they might be rescued by a passing vessel. Moore, brought down by his injuries and no longer able to function, remained in command. Without heat, the stern was frigid; survivors had to contend with the prospects of frostbite or hypothermia claiming life or limb after they had managed to avoid death immediately following the wreck. Captain Moore offered as much encouragement as he could dredge up, even leading the group in prayer. They held on that entire Saturday. "We all owe our lives to the exertions made by the captain," John McLean, one of two surviving *Algoma* waiters, declared. "If it had not been for his coolness and prompt action we could not have gone through the first night."

Although no one on the stern had a way of knowing it, help was on the way. Three men from the *Algoma*, aided by fishermen, reached land, and the group created a makeshift raft to bring in those still trapped on the boat. The stern, listing heavily, had come to rest near shore, but though the wind was dying down, the seas were too choppy

Only two years old at the time of her November 1885 grounding near Isle Royale, the *Algoma* broke apart. Accurate passenger records were not kept in the early days of Great Lakes shipping, but it is estimated that between thirty-seven and forty-eight passengers perished in the lake's frigid waters.

to risk anything but a raft rescue. The men on the *Algoma* tossed a 40-to-50-foot rope to those onshore; the line was fixed to the raft; and the survivors, beginning with the injured captain and a crewman to hold him on the raft, were pulled to land. The fishermen took the tired, hungry, half-frozen survivors to their homes and took care of them.

Meanwhile, elsewhere on dry land, concern over the *Algoma* was growing. The vessel's arrival at Port Arthur was overdue. Vessels often took shelter where they could during violent storms, but no one reported seeing the boat. A search tug was dispatched to look for signs of the *Algoma*.

The fishermen were already working on behalf of the survivors. Captain Moore advised them that the *Athabasca* might be in the area and might be intercepted. They set out in a boat. They located the *Athabasca* and guided her to where the survivors were waiting.

News of the wreck inspired a hurricane of newspaper reporting. Newspapers from as far away as the *New York Times* published accounts largely based on testimony of survivors given in Port Arthur. Only two passengers had been saved; thirteen crewmen, including the captain, survived. Captain Moore, disabled by his injuries, was initially incapacitated and unable to speak to the press, but that did not prevent the papers from quoting him, either by words provided by those hearing him during the accident or, in one incredible case, in a totally fabricated interview that Moore took measures to disclaim.

The search for victims began shortly after the survivors were picked up. Tugs searched 20 miles of shoreline, but no other survivors were found. Victims appeared here and there, some mutilated or dismembered, crushed against the rocks, left where the raging seas had pushed them. Some reports claimed that those found on the beach had their pockets ransacked. Searchers located very few possessions— two mailbags and a couple of trunks. Pieces of the *Algoma,* torn off by the storm, washed ashore. The body of the wheelsman was located on land, buried beneath a portion of the pilothouse. The *Algoma*'s wrecked stern section still floated, but no one bothered to go through it in the aftermath of the rescue of those imprisoned on it.

Canadian Pacific, although interested in salvaging the boat's engines or boilers, discontinued searching. Instead, the company asked local fishermen to bury any bodies they might find; company men would come to claim the following spring. Newspapers exhausted the different angles to covering the shipwreck. The story had been written.

Monarch

DECEMBER 7, 1906

~~~

Long before air travel around the Great Lakes, before freeways and highways created a network of passages for those seeking ways to more easily move from city to city in a once inhospitable terrain, before the era of the iron horse, when travelers rode the rails to reach destinations of business or pleasure, passenger boats ferried men, women, and children to busy ports open to the adventurous. It was a lucrative, competitive business, especially in the nineteenth and early twentieth centuries, before the building of highways and railroads.

The sailing wasn't necessarily easy or conventional. Passengers might be out on the water for days, only occasionally glimpsing land, facing the possibilities of uneasy rides, broken by storms that made the sailing rough, confined to a vessel that offered only marginal space in which to move freely.

The challenge, then, was for the transportation companies and individual boats to forge a memorable environment—and one that could be accomplished without disrupting the actual mechanics of sailing. For one, there was the aesthetic beauty of the boat. A vessel's appearance has limitations shaped by function, but that doesn't mean that design, or even a pleasing coat of paint, will not make it memorable to a ticket-bearing passenger. The side-paddlers, popular in the late nineteenth century, exemplify this. Or in the case of layered decks of passengers' quarters, the captain and crew quarters were often positioned nearby, giving those riding the boats an added sense of security. The white paint used on most of the vessels made them look clean and orderly: such small details mattered.

Much attention was paid, of course, to the passengers' rooms. If passengers were onboard for a night or two, comfort was no small demand. Every year seemed to foster new improvements, from wood-lined staterooms to luxurious dining facilities to spacious smoking rooms. Live entertainment became a regular feature.

Transportation firms specialized in running specific routes, and the lakes were spacious enough to accommodate all types, from relatively quick jaunts to long hauls, from business travelers to vacationers. As the nineteenth century drew to a close, passenger boats had become a vital part of Great Lakes commerce.

~~~

In 1890, John Dyble, a shipbuilder from Sarnia, Ontario, began work on a combined passenger and package vessel with a white oak hull reinforced by iron, in keeping with the mounting interest in iron-hulled boats. Dyble had experience in construction of passenger vessels. In 1882–83, while part of the Parry–Dyble firm, he had built the *United Empire,* a 252-foot passenger–package boat for the Northwest Transportation Company. By the time the new boat was launched in 1890,

Prior to her grounding near Isle Royale in a snowstorm in 1906, the 259-foot wooden steamer *Monarch* carried passengers and package goods.

Northwest Transportation was developing into the most successful transportation firm operating on the Great Lakes.

The *United Empire* was the way to sail in class and style. She served high-quality food, offered top-notch entertainment, and provided state rooms rivaling those of a fine hotel; she sliced through the water at a good clip and without apparent effort. Her captain, Edward Robertson, well respected at the *United Empire*'s ports of call, enjoyed fraternizing with his boat's passengers.

Dyble was hoping to duplicate the finer features of the *United Empire* on the new boat he was building for the Northwest Transportation Company. He succeeded. Appropriately named *Monarch,* the new vessel measured 259 feet, with a beam of just under 35 feet. She became the flagship of the Northwest Transportation fleet. Her scheduled Port Arthur–Duluth–Sarnia routes were the same as those of the *United Empire.*

The October 22, 1890, *Duluth Evening Herald,* in an article titled "A Beautiful Ship," gushed over the vessel its writer called "the finest running to Duluth":

> On her first trip, which was enjoyed by about 30 passengers, she made an average speed of 13 miles per hour. She was built, however, for a speed of 14 miles an hour and that rate can easily be attained. . . . This will make her the fastest passenger boat running into Duluth harbor.

The *Monarch,* at the beginning of her life on the lakes, was painted completely white, with the exception of a black smokestack. There was no passenger boat like her on the Great Lakes in appearance or performance.

The *Monarch*'s years of service were marred only by several minor scrapes—and one significant event. In 1892, she ran aground near Port Arthur, but she was freed after a portion of her cargo was removed. Six years later, while in harbor, she was struck by another boat entering the harbor; she suffered damage to her stern, but it was minor. Later in her life, she became icebound near the Soo and had to be rescued by salvagers.

The serious event occurred on Thanksgiving in 1896. The *Monarch,* with passengers and cargo, was bound from Port Arthur to Duluth. Stormy weather, with shifting wind, was predicted, but Captain Robertson decided that the *Monarch* was able to sail safely in the projected weather. He wound up facing much more than he bargained for. He took on gale-force winds that whipped up heavy following seas that crashed over the stern. Sleet was followed by blizzard snowfall that reduced visibility. Robertson and his crew maneuvered the boat through the night, avoiding troughs, shaking off boarding seas, holding a course that would take them to Duluth perhaps by midday or late afternoon.

The *Monarch* reached Two Harbors on the north shore at four o'clock in the afternoon. The sky was growing dark, but Captain Robertson felt confident in reaching Duluth rather than seeking shelter in Two Harbors. He had difficulty, however, in picking up Duluth's range lights, which he needed in order to line up with the narrow entrance to the Duluth harbor. He strayed close enough to shore to hear breakers. Finally, in what seemed to be the last possible minute, he saw the range lights and directed the *Monarch* in the proper direction.

But the ordeal was not over. Squeezing into the harbor entrance was going to be exceedingly difficult in such rough waters. Captain Robertson ordered full ahead when the *Monarch* approached the entrance. A massive wave lifted the boat and pushed her into the south pier. With the current directing the *Monarch* toward the north pier, the wheelsman took advantage of the full power and glided her through with no further damage. The *Monarch* arrived mostly intact, her hull slightly damaged, but safe from a nasty storm that could have been devastating.

The *Monarch*'s elevated status did not diminish in time. She earned handsome profits for her owners, who kept her up well. Her pilothouse was raised, and her Texas deck elongated; her appearance changed dramatically when her hull was painted black. Her overall luxury may have been surpassed when her owners launched the 321-foot *Huronic* in 1902. The need for her services might have diminished in the competition with the developing railroad service, forcing a reduced schedule in 1903, but the *Monarch* sailed on.

The 1906 shipping season was a good one, with bulk freighters hauling more cargo than the preceding year, and passenger vessels holding their own. Freight tonnage increased by 15 percent.

Disaster struck the *Monarch*'s last scheduled trip of the season, beginning in Port Arthur on December 6. The *Monarch* loaded a cargo of wheat, oats, flour, canned salmon, and other miscellaneous general merchandise and left Port Arthur at 5:25 p.m. Weather conditions were not favorable, but they were not prohibitive, either. Air temperatures were subzero, snow fell, and a fresh wind blew the boat across the water.

Captain Robertson was seasoned enough to be well acquainted with adverse sailing conditions late in the year. Of all the months in a year, November bothered boats the most. Cold, arctic air blew in from Canada, glazing Lake Superior with ice, and when meeting warmer air pushing up from the Gulf of Mexico, churning up the water, creating dense fog, setting off blinding snow, and making the sailing a miserable, occasionally dangerous experience. November shipwrecks outnumbered the losses of any other month.

Most vessels were in for the winter by December 1; they would be undergoing repairs, adding new equipment, or improving overall appearance while snow blanketed the upper Great Lakes region. Crews wanted to be home with their families by Thanksgiving. Still, as boats grew bigger and stronger over the years, shipping companies couldn't resist the profits brought in by one or two late runs.

For the *Monarch,* sailing conditions deteriorated quickly after she left Port Arthur. The wind shifted and was soon blowing a gale. The falling snow obliterated everything beyond 10 or 15 yards. The cold on the deck became unbearable. Still, the *Monarch* handled conditions well.

Captain Robertson grew concerned. In average sailing conditions, it took only about two hours and twenty minutes to move from Thunder Cape to Passage Island Lighthouse. Despite (or maybe because of) the storm pushing her, the *Monarch* moved rapidly. Earlier in the crossing, Robertson contacted the engine room and asked that they deploy the taffrail log, a torpedo-shaped mechanism that, trailing the boat, measured distance traveled. Sailing blind in what he figured to be in proximity of a narrow passage near Isle Royale, Robertson asked for a log reading. The machine had frozen and read that the boat had sailed only 10 miles. The *Monarch* had traveled much more than that.

Robertson reasoned that they should have already seen a signal from the Passage Island Light or at least heard the fog signal. He and his first mate braved the cold and, standing outside on the *Monarch*'s flying bridge, tried to locate the Passage Island Light. A deckhand, serving as a lookout, had been doing the same with no success. Robertson thought he saw the light but could not be certain. He should have been able to hear the fog signal as well, but all he could hear was the roaring of the storm. He returned to the pilothouse and ordered a slight course change—an alteration that would give more room in which to sail. He knew he couldn't depend on compass readings, which were notoriously unreliable around the island.

Suddenly, the *Monarch* bottomed out and ground to a halt. The boat, moving at full speed, grounded with tremendous force, leaving no guesswork about what happened. Captain Robertson returned to the deck to survey the damage. The boat was very near to shore, maybe no more than 10 yards or so. Robertson couldn't be certain. He

The Passage Island Lighthouse in 1882, watching over the waters between Passage Island and Isle Royale.

could make out the shape of a cliff towering over the beach. The waves were enormous. The *Monarch's* bow rose high in the air, much higher than the stern. Crew members and passengers rushed out to the deck, now tilting at a precarious angle.

There are conflicting reports about what happened immediately after the grounding. According to one source, Captain Robertson ordered his chief engineer, Samuel Beatty, to put the *Monarch* full speed astern; seeing the damage to the boat and fearing the consequences of backing her into the water, Beatty supposedly bucked the order and remained at full ahead. The other source claimed that Robertson had ordered the boat full ahead, claiming that he was very aware of the hazards of the *Monarch's* slipping into raging seas. The explanations ultimately didn't matter, nor were they confirmed or denied. The *Monarch* remained on the rock while Robertson tried to figure the best way to transfer personnel and passengers to shore.

To a casual observer, it might have seemed like a fairly simple chore. The *Monarch* came to rest about 25 feet from a large rock near shore. Several factors created a very different escape. First, there was the extreme danger posed by heavy seas. Robertson considered crossing in a lifeboat, but the attempt failed. The lifeboat was mangled in the attempt, and four sailors, who hoped to reach the rock and, using a long rope, create a lifeline, were fortunate to get back to the *Monarch* with their lives. Second, there was the extreme cold. The air temperatures dismissed any thought anyone might entertain of trying to swim to safety. Even if someone were successful in reaching shore, the saturated clothing would freeze.

But something had to be done soon. While the *Monarch's* bow, aided by its turning propeller, held fast to the rock she had grounded on, the stern was slipping below surface. There was imminent danger of its breaking away, causing greater flooding to the front of the vessel. The electricity, once one of the *Monarch's* fine features, had been extinguished by water flooding into the engine room This cast everyone on the boat into darkness, creating additional confusion in the pandemonium. Further, the *Monarch* was without heat.

Robertson, a veteran of thirty-five years on the lakes, puzzled through possible solutions to his vessel's predicament. It was possible, though highly unlikely, that the lighthouse keeper at nearby Passage Island had witnessed the accident and had alerted others about the *Monarch*. There was also a very minute chance that they would be spotted by another vessel in the area. Any boats venturing out into the storm would have stayed far removed from Isle Royale.

The solution came from a crew member. James "Jack" McCallum, brother of the *Monarch*'s second mate, a deckhand and last-minute replacement on the boat, suggested that a rope be tied around his waist and that he be lowered almost to the waterline. Other crewmen would then swing him back and forth like a pendulum until he reached the big rock. He could be passed a ladder to finish his crossing to shore and scaling of the cliff. Somehow, after a couple of failed attempts, he managed to make it to shore. He tied a line from the boat to a tree, and one by one, moving hand over hand, the *Monarch*'s twelve passengers and thirty of her crewmen passed over the tempestuous waters. One crewman fell into the lake and drowned. Once ashore, the new challenge was survival. By the captain's estimation, they were miles from any town, and everyone was too hungry and exhausted to attempt a trek through the arctic conditions. The stranded victims gathered fallen branches and driftwood to build fires, which Robertson figured would serve two purposes: as warmth and as a possible way to get the Passage Island Lighthouse keeper's—or a passing boat's—attention. The fires, along with a makeshift windbreaker fashioned from the collected wood, provided minimal shelter from the storm, which continued with no sign of relief.

Other provisions became an issue. There were no blankets (the one they had was given to stewardess Rachel McCormick), and food was nonexistent, at least in the beginning. The next morning, after spending a freezing night on the edge of Lake Superior, the group noticed that the storm had washed in some of the canned salmon from the ruptured *Monarch*. The individuals gobbled up the meager supply of food, which they recognized was only temporary nourishment.

Unbeknown to those huddled together on the island, the Passage Island Lighthouse keeper had seen the fires, but the heavy seas prohibited his launching a boat and investigating. He was imprisoned on his own island. He wouldn't get out the next day, either.

By Saturday, the castaways were growing desperate. They had manufactured a tent from one of the *Monarch*'s sails, but that was only marginally effective. The storm had eased, but just a small degree. Several men risked a visit to the *Monarch* for supplies. The stern had broken off and sunk; the bow was still hanging on a rise at a steep angle, and there was no estimating how much longer it would endure. The group split into three parties, each tending to a fire, each responsible for picking up wood necessary to keep them burning.

The night, the third since the *Monarch* ran aground, crawled past. When Sunday dawned, the group decided to take actions into their own hands. The storm was blowing itself out, but there had been no evidence that anyone knew that the *Monarch* was gone or that its survivors were trapped on the island.

Though far from ideal, Sunday wound up being a day of movement. The waves had diminished enough to permit a lighthouse assistant to row to the site of the fires he had seen. The rowing was an extremely strenuous 4-mile trip, and when he arrived at the site, he was unable to land his boat. Reginald Beaumont, the *Monarch*'s purser, gamely swam through the icy, wave-swollen water to the rowboat and appraised the astonished lighthouse assistant of the events of the past three days. He climbed into the boat, and the two headed back toward the lighthouse.

Meanwhile, four *Monarch* crewmen started out on foot in the direction of a known fishing camp on the other side of the island. They located several huts, but all occupants had packed up and abandoned them for the winter. Fortunately, the fishermen had left a small supply of provisions in the huts. The four men decided to spend the night in shelter before walking the provisions back.

Rescue operations progressed over the next twelve hours. Passage Island Lighthouse personnel saw a steamer, the *Edmonton,* downbound with a load of wheat, and flagged her down. The boat took Reginald Beaumont to Port Arthur, arriving at 2:00 a.m. Beaumont detailed the *Monarch* story to Northwest Transportation officials, and by 6:00 a.m. two tugs, the *James Whalen* and *Laura Grace,* expecting to encounter a group of hungry, exhausted, and half-frozen survivors, were on their way to Isle Royale. The tugs brought food, blankets, medical supplies, and two doctors.

Arriving midmorning, the tugs were not able to land near the encampment and, using their whistles, signaled that they would pick up the *Monarch* group on the other side of the island, in the lee of the diminishing storm. This meant a long hike across what resembled a frozen tundra. Those aboard the two tugs met a party of individuals suffering to varying degrees from exposure and frostbite. Miraculously, everyone had survived.

Northwest Transportation was not held financially accountable for all the possessions lost in the wreck. The company, although not required by law to do so, did pay the cost for the return home of everyone aboard. The estimated loss of boat and cargo came to $160,000.

This was Captain Robertson's final trip on the lakes. He retired but not before receiving a special commendation in Port Arthur on December 12. A little more than half a year later, on July 6, Jack McCallum was awarded a medal for his bravery in reaching shore and helping his fellow crew members and passengers. Chief engineer Samuel Beatty did not receive any commendation for his actions, but he may have walked away from the wreck with the most unusual distinction: only one year earlier, during the most savage storm in Lake Superior history, Beatty had been chief engineer on the *Monkshaven,* a 249-foot Canadian freighter that grounded near Pie Island and became the storm's first victim. Like those on the *Monarch,* the crew on the *Monkshaven* reached safety, only to contend with the forces of nature for an extended period of time.

〰〰

No one rushed to move the *Monarch*'s bow section. Northwest Transportation announced that it would accept bids for salvaging the wreck, but interest was nil. Instead, the bow wreckage clung to the rock, absorbing abuse from the wind and surf, bits and pieces of her stripped away and tossed on the shore. Shortly after the grounding, people visited the wreck site and removed artifacts from the vessel. The heavy machinery—the boilers and engine, which held some value—were on the stern, which had slipped backward into deeper water, perhaps as deep as 100 feet, presenting an intimidating challenge to all but the most well-equipped and experienced salvaging firms.

The *Monarch* grounded near shore, precipitating a heroic escape effort.

Nearly two years passed. Finally, Tom Reid, proprietor of the most highly regarded salvaging firm on the Great Lakes, purchased the salvage rights—a decision he would regret in short order.

Reid was familiar with the *Monarch*. He had come to the *Monarch's* aid when the vessel had become trapped in ice at the Sailors Encampment near the Soo Locks. The boat had been refitted earlier in the year, and the investment was threatened by a bitterly cold November freezing the lake. Reaching the *Monarch* amounted to more than Reid had bargained for: he took a small convoy of three vessels, but the sailing was very slow. Reid, though equipped to break through ice, devoted a week to plowing through subzero temperatures and thickening ice, "with the channel closing slowly behind them." Reid reached the *Monarch* and laboriously freed her.

The salvaging of the *Monarch* should not have been that difficult for Reid, who was accomplished at bringing up heavy machinery from the depths. The *Monarch's* stern, Reid's diver determined, had settled in just over 90 feet of water, and Reid had come prepared. He arrived with three tugs (*Salvor, George H. Parker,* and *Ottawa*), a barge (*Kelderhouse*), and a derrick-scow, fresh off a failed attempt to salvage the 300-foot freighter *Savona,* which had grounded the previous year. They managed to retrieve the vessel's engine and boilers, but the boat itself was beyond saving. They dynamited the boat and sold her remains for scrap.

With the conditions being the typically unpredictable November Great Lakes weather, Reid would have preferred to wait on the *Monarch* job until the following spring, but there were no guarantees that the bow would last another winter. Reid and his crew loaded the boilers and engine on the *Kelderhouse* and prepared to return to Reid's headquarters in Michigan.

The job hit a serious snag. A storm system blew in, and Reid decided to take shelter on Jackfish Bay on Lake Superior's northern shore. The man in charge of the derrick-scow, eager to get home, angrily complained about the stop. The convoy left the next morning, but the weather continued to present problems. Noting the dropping barometer, Reid again took shelter, this time in the lee of Michipicoten Island on Lake Superior's east side, not far from Canada. Once again, he heard bitter complaints from the commander of the derrick-scow, who insisted on sailing through the night. Reid went along with him.

The stranded *Monarch*.

Reid feared the huge waves whipped up by the storm and what they might do to his vessels, and those fears were realized when the derrick-scow was overwhelmed and capsized. Two men lost their lives, and Reid lost a vessel at an overall loss of $50,000.

"The *Savona* and the *Monarch*," wrote Mary Frances Doner in her biography of Tom Reid, "were two heartbreaking failures in the long list of Reid salvaging triumphs."

Chester A. Congdon

CANOE ROCKS, NOVEMBER 6, 1918

~~~

The freighter began its life as the *Salt Lake City*.

Constructed by the Chicago Ship Building Company for Cleveland's Holmes Steamship Company, the *Salt Lake City*, launched on Thursday, August 29, 1907, was a massive vessel for the times, measuring 532 feet in length and 56 feet in beam. She had thirty-two hatches covering a cargo hold divided into three sections. The owners held high expectations for the boat's earnings potential.

The *Salt Lake City*'s early years were uneventful but productive. She apparently suffered no significant bumps or bruises, and while she did not record any tonnage records (those belonged to the 600-footers built with greater frequency after the turn of the twentieth century), she held her own in the volatile shipping market. The Holmes Company sold the boat to the Acme Transit Company in 1911, and the company managed H. B. Hawgood Company, which ran her operation for a season. On February 2, 1912, the Continental Steamship Company of Duluth purchased the *Salt Lake City* and renamed her the *Chester A. Congdon* after one of Duluth's revered public figures.

Congdon, who grew up in upstate New York, graduated from Syracuse University in 1875; two years later, he received his law degree and began to practice in Syracuse. His ambitions eventually led to much more. He moved to St. Paul, Minnesota, in 1879, and, later, to Duluth. He taught, invested very successfully in iron and grain, and added to his résumé in politics. His name seemed to be connected to every significant group from banking to the Minnesota House of Representa-

The *Chester A. Congdon*, a 532-foot freighter originally called the *Salt Lake City* and renamed in 1913, experienced a minor run-in with another vessel on May 31, 1918. This would not be the case nearly six months later.

tives. It was appropriate that the *Salt Lake City* be renamed the *Chester A. Congdon* when a Duluth company purchased the vessel.

Two groundings, one in 1912 and another in 1915, blemished an otherwise spotless record. The first occurred in heavy fog, and both damaged plates, which were repaired without much difficulty.

The *Congdon*'s fatal accident was an entirely different matter, but it did not happen without due diligence on the part of captain and crew. At

Chester A. Congdon.

2:28 a.m. on November 6, 1918, the *Congdon* left Fort William, Ontario, in the Thunder Bay area, bound for Port McNicoll, Ontario, with 380,000 bushels of wheat. The boat had barely cleared Thunder Cape when she encountered a storm out of the southwest. Gale-force winds churned up the seas. Unwilling to proceed in adverse conditions, Captain Charles Autterson decided to drop anchor and wait for better sailing. The *Congdon* had been out for only about an hour and a half.

Six hours later, the wind did lighten up, and the *Congdon* was prepared to sail again. Autterson was still worried. While the wind wasn't nearly as heavy and the seas, while rough, were calmer, a heavy fog had settled over the lake. Autterson wisely cut the *Congdon's* speed and set a course for Passage Island. Autterson planned to sail for two and a half hours. If, by that time, the fog persisted, he intended "on stopping on account of the fog until we could locate something."

He met disaster before he needed to plan further. The *Congdon*, for reasons that were never explained, strayed south of its intended course and grounded not far from the Canoe Rocks. No one had heard the Passage Island Lighthouse fog signal, and the boat lacked communications equipment. The boat came to a hard, sudden halt.

The freighter did not appear to be in immediate peril. Her bow had come to rest in shallow water, and the *Congdon* was upright. She was, however, weighed down by her heavy cargo, so refloating the boat was out of the question until some of the wheat had been removed. Captain Autterson lowered two boats and dispatched them, one to Passage Island Lighthouse, 7 miles away, and one to Fort William.

The craft bound for Fort William, commanded by the *Congdon's* second mate and carrying two local fishermen, ran into trouble and didn't arrive at its destination until the next day. The second mate relayed the *Congdon* mishap story, and the Canadian Towing and Wrecking Company sent three vessels—the *Empire*, a wrecking barge; the *A. B. Commee*, a tug; and a short time later, the *Sarina*, another tug—to assist the *Congdon*, whose large crew was still on board. To those aboard the three new boats, the *Congdon* looked salvageable. The weather was reasonably calm, the grounded boat appeared stable, and the job of lightening her load seemed probable.

The group removed wheat from the *Congdon*, but their effort didn't last long. Inclement weather blew in and disrupted the work. Winds measuring 55 miles per hour buffeted the boats. The three vessels retreated to the shelter of a small bay on Isle Royale. They would wait out the storm and return.

Their plans were dashed when the storm subsided. Wind and strong waves had dismantled the grounded boat, split at the sixth hatch and broken completely, the stern portion eventually sinking

The *Congdon*, laden with wheat, grounded near Isle Royale, sustaining fatal damage when she split in two.

nearby. The bow, still on the rocks, was badly battered. When Captain Autterson and a shipping official visited the site, they took one look at the wreck, gathered some personal effects from the boat, and declared the *Congdon* a total loss.

Between the vessel and her cargo, the estimated loss was set at $1.5 million, making the *Congdon* the costliest loss in Great Lakes history and the first to exceed $1 million. Prior to the *Congdon*, the *Henry B. Smith*, a new freighter that had gone missing without a trace during the storm of 1913, had held the dubious Great Lakes record.

The timing of the accident was fortuitous in one respect: World War I was ending, and the crew of the *Congdon* celebrated Armistice Day in Fort William, parading in the street with the *Congdon*'s flag. The weather during fall 1918, nasty after a moderate summer, brutalized boats daring enough to challenge it. A successful shipping season bore the burden of rough sailing in October and November; twenty-one vessels were lost on the lakes during the 1918 season. Two French minesweepers disappeared on Lake Superior.

The fractured *Congdon*. The loss of vessel and cargo made the *Congdon* the first million-dollar loss on the Great Lakes.

On November 29, it was announced that investor James Playfair had paid $10,000 for what remained of the *Congdon*, but the investment turned out to be a poor one. The boat had disappeared: the two sections had sunk, the stern in shallow water, the bow in deep water, and neither proved to be worth the costs of raising them the following spring. The *Congdon's* only true value came much later, when sport divers sought to explore the wreckage of a boat easily accessible to anyone with the interest, time, and equipment to do so.

Kamloops

~~~

The *Kamloops*'s story began in England, where she was constructed by the Furness Shipbuilding Company for the Canada Steamship Lines in 1924. At 250 feet, the vessel was small by Great Lakes standards, which found new freighters measuring twice that length, but the *Kamloops* was built for purposes other than hauling iron ore and other bulk freight across the lakes. The *Kamloops*, a package, or tramp, freighter, was designed to move a diverse assortment of products between Canadian ports, her compact size allowing her to fit through locks too small for other bulk carriers. She completed her sea tests on July 5, 1924, and after a brief trip to pick up freight in Denmark, crossed the Atlantic Ocean with her first cargo load.

Canallers like the *Kamloops* were hard-working boats, beginning their shipping season as soon as the ice was melted or broken and continuing well into December. The *Kamloops* fell victim to this practice in 1926, when her season ended after she became icebound in the St. Marys River. The misadventure did not prohibit the Canadian Steamship Lines from assigning her work late the following season.

"The experience we had last year does not deter us," the company announced in a statement to the press, "because we realize that a thing like that may not happen again for another fifty years." The boats would sail as long as the weather held out.

A typical *Kamloops* trip found the boat visiting ports, usually in the Thunder Bay area, picking up or dropping off cargo, servicing cities not even considered by the larger freighters. On her return trip,

The unknown circumstances surrounding the loss of the *Kamloops* in December 1927 made the 250-foot, three-year-old package freighter one of the Great Lakes mysteries of its time.

she might haul grain or other bulk goods to posts such as Montreal, Toronto, or Quebec City. The result of all this activity was a busy but easygoing work environment, in which captain and crew grew to know the dockworkers and those at the many visited locks, with the crew working like a "big, harmonious family." At one stop, Bill Brian, the captain of the *Kamloops*, was presented a puppy that in no time became the boat's mascot.

The *Kamloops*'s cargo on her final trip of the 1927 season was typically diverse: coiled wire, salt, candy, shoes, building supplies, and parts for papermaking machinery. The boat was loaded but not overloaded. After these deliveries, cities would be forced to fend for themselves throughout the overbearingly cold winter. Most destinations had been stocking up on supplies and were prepared.

It would be a long journey with plenty of downtime—waiting at the locks, sitting around at the docks while the *Kamloops* loaded and unloaded—and Captain Brian disliked the time away from sailing. At this time of year, when storms could blow in with little warning, the weather made the waiting unnerving. Early forecasts now indicated an arctic cold front dropping down from northern Canada, and there was no telling what that meant.

On December 1, the *Kamloops* tied up at the Courtright, Ontario, docks to add bags of salt to her cargo hold. The next day, Friday, December 2, she spent the day en route, traveling up Lake Huron, sailing as fast as her triple expansion steam engine would take her. It was more of the same the next day. She locked through the Soo at noon on December 3. So far, the weather had cooperated, and the sailing had been slow but good.

That changed significantly as soon as the *Kamloops* wandered onto Lake Superior. A fresh, gasp-producing blast of cold air from the northwest shot in, raising collars and confining crew members to quarters. Choppy seas formed when friction from the wind met the water, rocked the boat, and threatened to shift cargo. Captain Brian, experienced in commanding package freighters through all types of weather, maintained his course. Sailing on a lake as vast as Superior offered options if the need should arise.

The wind velocity increased to gale force, batting around the *Kamloops* until Captain Brian reached a decision. He would seek shelter, drop anchor, and await better sailing conditions. Late fall storms had a history of blowing in and out in fairly short order. There was no sense in taking a beating. Brian dropped anchor near Whitefish Point, joining a small fleet of freighters taking shelter there.

The storm wasn't going away; if anything, it was intensifying. The *Kamloops* spent the better part of two days at anchor before Captain Brian decided to move ahead. He was already well behind schedule and could ill afford to fall further behind. For this leg of the journey, the *Kamloops* had a traveling partner, the 283-foot *Quedoc*, bound for Port Arthur. The *Kamloops* trailed the *Quedoc*, and though the *Kamloops* was not equipped with a radio and could not establish contact with the other vessel, the two boats were well aware of each other's presence and probably felt the reassurance of safety in numbers.

The storm worsened into one of the most intense on Lake Superior in years. Heavy snow fell; temperatures dropped to below zero. Those on the lake (and there were many) received unwanted souvenirs from their natural opponent: a thick white icing, developed from the freezing water and spray hitting the decks and deckhouses, enveloped the boats, wreaking havoc on hatch covers and adding considerable weight to the vessels. The *Kamloops* and *Quedoc* were two of the affected vessels.

Captain Roy Simpson of the *Quedoc* felt some sense of duty to the boat trailing him. Both vessels were bound in the same direction, using the same charts, but the off-again, on-again blizzard snowfall and heavy seas left both captains uncertain of their exact position. Simpson made estimates based on how he felt his course was being altered by the storm, and the *Kamloops* followed his lead. It was largely guesswork when the snowfall was so thick that Simpson couldn't see to the back of his boat. Taking soundings under these conditions was almost impossible.

The two boats soldiered on, each hour bringing them a little closer to their destination, each hour rubbing nerves raw in the respective wheelhouses. By late afternoon on December 7, the two boats, about a quarter mile apart, were in the vicinity of the northeasternmost point of Isle Royale. The lake floor topography in the area was unpredictable and treacherous. The lake bottom rose and fell suddenly, especially close to the island. Captain Simpson knew precisely the danger ahead when his lookout shouted. "Rocks . . . rocks . . . dead ahead!"

Simpson rushed to the wheel and turned hard to starboard. The wheel responded, and the *Quedoc* narrowly avoided the rocks. But the anxious moments were far from over. Simpson could see the *Kamloops*'s lights in the dusk, and the boat that been following him so precisely was now heading toward the same rocks he had just missed. He had to warn Captain Brian, but how? Neither boat had a radio, and there was no possibility of shouting through the storm. Simpson gave his whistle a series of warning blasts, a standard warning on the lakes, but the *Kamloops* kept coming. Barring a miracle, this was not going to end well.

What happened in the following minutes will never be known. The *Quedoc* had her own serious concerns, from staying out of troughs that might have flipped her over, to holding as steady a course as possible in the storm, to just making it to safety.

No one saw or heard from the *Kamloops* again.

~~~

The *Quedoc* reached port, battered and worn, but safe.

Other boats were not nearly as lucky. Between December 7 and December 9, when the storm swept across Lake Superior, five vessels, including the *Kamloops,* were destroyed. Of particular interest to Captain Roy Simpson was the plight of the 365-foot Canadian bulk carrier *Altodoc,* which ran afoul of the storm on December 7. Simpson's brother, Richard D. Simpson, was master of the boat, and by all reports the vessel had taken a thrashing before losing its rudder and, unable to steer, was blown to the rocks near Keweenaw Point. Fortunately for captain and crew, the *Altodoc* was equipped with a radio. An SOS was transmitted, and the Coast Guard rescued everyone aboard. The boat was declared a total loss.

At first there was little concern over the status of the *Kamloops.* The general opinion was that she had probably anchored somewhere near Isle Royale, waiting for the storm to blow out. Even Roy Simpson, the last to see the *Kamloops* on the water, expressed no worry. True enough, he had been preoccupied with news of his brother's boat, but curiously he had reported nothing about the *Kamloops* when he docked his boat. Newspapers, though interested in the *Kamloops*'s whereabouts, had nothing to report.

On December 12, five days after the *Quedoc* had last seen the *Kamloops,* a dedicated search commenced. The Canada Steamship Lines, owners of the *Kamloops,* dispatched two vessels, the *Midland Prince* and the *Islet Prince,* to search for the missing vessel. The Canadian government sent a tugboat to look around Whitefish Point, and another tug, the *James Wallace,* also joined the search. The Coast Guard eventually became involved, as did other boats scouring the area around Isle Royale.

Nothing turned up—no wreckage, no traces of survivors or victims, no crew possessions. Rumors, including talk of sightings, made the rounds, but nothing was substantiated. Captain Simpson was asked about what he had seen of the *Kamloops* near Isle Royale, but his account was hardly favorable. His attempts to warn the *Kamloops* of the rocks ahead had gone unnoticed.

"It was blowing such a gale of wind and snow that I couldn't hear it

myself," he said of his using his ship's whistle to get the *Kamloops*'s attention. "The *Kamloops* people obviously didn't hear it, either. But if the
lookout had been awake and tending to business, he would have seen
us turn, and the puff of steam would have told him we were trying to
signal him. There wasn't anybody else around to whistle at, was there?"

The *Midland Prince* and *Islet Prince* arrived in the vicinity of Isle
Royale, and these boats, along with fishing boats enlisted by the Coast
Guard, conducted an intensive search around the large island and
the water and small islands around it. The bitterly cold weather was
freezing the lake and making searching hazardous, and the search
was suspended by Christmas.

The *Kamloops*, authorities concluded, was lost with all hands.

〜〜〜

Winter passed with nothing new reported about the lost vessel. The
lake around Isle Royale froze over, as it usually did, and optimists gave
up hope of finding the *Kamloops* and crew. Shortly after the first of the
year, the Ontario Workman's Compensation Board ruled that all members of the crew could be presumed dead and their families eligible
for compensation. The *Kamloops* was now tagged with the sobriquet
"ghost ship," given to vessels that sailed away into oblivion without a
trace. Additional news about the boat was not expected.

Then, on May 26, after the ice on the lake had melted and spring
weather was settling on the northern portion of Lake Superior, a
fisherman named David Lind made a surprising discovery. Lind
was retrieving his nets when he came upon two bodies, both wearing *Kamloops* life preservers. The remains were located near Twelve
O'Clock Point on the northwest coast of Isle Royale.

The *Crawford*, a Coast Guard cutter involved in the *Altodoc* rescue,
hurried to where the two victims had been located, and, with help
from other small vessels, scanned the many nooks and crannies in
the area. They found wreckage freed by the melting ice, including life
rings, a battered portion of the pilothouse roof, hatch covers, a variety
of cargo, half a lifeboat, oars, and personal effects, including Captain
Brian's trunk. On June 4, fishermen found six more bodies, all badly
decomposed, on or near the island. These discoveries sent shock

waves through the shipping community. Answers—or at least partial answers—were allowing the piecing together of the *Kamloops*'s story.

Some crew members had apparently been able to leave the *Kamloops* prior to her sinking. A lifeboat found on the island in the proximity of the victims made that a certainty. All of the bodies, except the remains of First Mate Honore Genest, were wearing life belts. Some might have been washed off the lifeboat by the heavy surf, but at least some, including a woman found on the beach, reached land. Few would have lasted very long in their drenched clothing and subzero temperatures, but Genest was discovered near an attempted makeshift shelter.

How and where the *Kamloops* sank was a matter of conjecture. The recovered wreckage offered a strong indication of where the boat had slipped beneath the lake's surface. Most of those doing the guesswork agreed that the *Kamloops* had probably grounded on a shoal, remaining upright while Genest and the other crew members launched the lifeboat, eventually slipping into deep water and taking the lives of Captain Brian and those unable to escape the wreck.

Nearly sixty years would pass before divers found the *Kamloops* shipwreck. In the meantime, she retained her ghost ship status and remained one of Lake Superior's biggest mysteries.

～～～

In December 1928, Louis Coutu was trapping in a remote area near the Agawa River in Ontario, just north of Sault Ste. Marie, when he came upon a bottle with a handwritten note inside. He brought the bottled note to Sault Ste. Marie and stirred up a controversy when, rather than hand it over to officials, he proposed to sell it to the highest bidder. He walked back the idea after an ensuing outrage, saying, first, that he would turn it over to the *Sault Star*, and second, that he wanted to show it to the family of the letter's writer before he went public with it. The authenticity of the letter was doubted until, ironically, the handwriting was verified by the writer's family.

The letter's contents told a brief, heartbreaking tale: "I am the last one left alive, freezing and starving to death on Isle Royale in Lake Superior. I just want mom and dad to know my fate." The note was written by Alice Bettridge, the *Kamloops's* twenty-three-year-old assistant stewardess, who, indeed, had perished on the island. Her body had been recovered on the beach on June 4, 1928, and returned to Ontario for burial. She and Nettie Grafton had been the two women crew members onboard the *Kamloops* at the time of the sinking, and Bettridge was in such condition when she was discovered that the only way to positively identify her was by her teeth: Grafton had false teeth, and the woman found on the island had all her natural teeth.

~~~

There is an old saying that a shipwreck will remain undiscovered until she chooses to reveal herself. This seemed to apply to the *Kamloops,* which was not discovered until 1977. In the five decades that passed between her sinking and the finding of her wreckage, the *Kamloops* became a tantalizing mystery, spoken of and searched for with no tangible results. Much of failure to locate her can be attributed to the lack of the searching and diving technology available today; *underwater archaeology* had yet to become a popular term. Even now, there are hundreds—perhaps thousands—of wrecked vessels on the floors of the Great Lakes waiting to be found and explored.

Ken Merryman, a highly regarded shipwreck finder, took, by his estimation, one hundred exploratory dives before he and his team finally ran their hands along the *Kamloops's* stern railing. Their discovery on August 21, 1977, was the culmination of research and a process of trial and error that had taken them through the icy water in the area where the boat was believed to have disappeared. Merryman was twenty-seven years old when the group found the *Kamloops.* He had been diving for ten years, learning as he went along, experiencing the almost palpable excitement that divers feel when working their way along the remains of a once powerful, enterprising vessel.

"The wreck site of the *Kamloops* is more shrouded in mystery than any other wreck at Isle Royale," Daniel J. Lenihan wrote in his underwater archaeological study of the shipwrecks of Isle Royale. The *Kamloops* is located on a downslope, lying on its starboard side, in 180 to 260 feet of water, the stern at the shallowest point. It sank near Twelve O'Clock Point, where it was always presumed to be. The wheelhouse and forward housing are missing, but there is no clear indication of why and how she sank. The vessel's rudder and screw were relatively intact, leading some authorities to suggest that the Kamloops had lost her power at some point, was tossed around by the storm, and eventually pushed beneath the waves, drifting downward to where she rests today. This, of course, was purely speculation.

Discovery began when Roy Oberg, a local fisherman and helmsman of the *Voyager* ferry to Isle Royale, was using a side-scan sonar in a search of the area. The sonar indicated the presence of a large object near Twelve O'Clock Point, and he told Merryman and others about his discovery. Merryman, with fellow divers Randy Saulter and Ken Engelbrecht, without much specific planning, began diving in the area until they found clues—bundles of pipes, a ladder, and brass barrel— that they might be on to something. The search proceeded slowly, largely because before the mixing of gases, a diver had to be especially cautious about being endangered by diver's narcosis, a state of confusion brought on by deep diving. According to "Martini's Rule," an unofficial standard relating to diver's narcosis, every 30 feet of descent was similar to drinking one shot of alcohol. One had to show caution when diving the depths of a boat like the *Kamloops*. "You learn to operate while impaired," Merryman explained.

Merryman was on his boat when the other two divers came across the stern of the wreck. They could not positively identify the vessel in the dark, somewhat murky depths ("When you first see a shipwreck under water, you see a shadow"), but the three men were all but certain that they had located the *Kamloops*. They knew of no other sunken, unfound vessel in the area.

The team kept the exact location of the wreck to themselves—not to keep others from laying claim to the discovery but to keep salvagers and scavengers from picking the wreck clean of collectibles before they had the opportunity to examine the wrecked vessel. Sport divers could—and did—visit a sunken boat and strip it of anything that could be moved and placed in private collections. There was also the significant issue of victims: there was no telling how many of the *Kamloops* crew might still be trapped onboard, and making this determination before the boat was ransacked was crucial. Families needed closure.

In subsequent dives that fall and the following summer, the men made a positive identification of the *Kamloops* and were able to explore the wreck. The name *Kamloops,* partially obscured by rust and time, peeked out of the murky darkness. On board, the *Kamloops*'s cargo, including cases of Life Savers candy, scattered from the boat's collision with the lake bottom, looked as if it was awaiting unloading. Inside the engine room, one unfortunate victim, in a sitting position, pinned beneath wreckage, offered a ghostly presence. Given the amount of time that had passed between the boat's sinking and its discovery, the crewman was in remarkably good condition, with his chalky skin, caused by submersion in water, the only true sign that he had been there for any length of time. Divers, frightened by the apparition, claimed his spirit followed them throughout their exploration of the boat. Others found him benevolent, nicknaming him "Old Whitey."

How and why the *Kamloops* sank will never be definitively explained, nor, because of her depth, will she be heavily explored. Perhaps this is for the best: some questions should remain unanswered. The lake, it would seem, demands its secrets.

America

~~~

Back in the days when bulk freighters dominated the Great Lakes shipping commerce, diminutive workhorse vessels serviced small regional ports in any given area. They hauled smaller loads, brought much needed supplies, and acted as lifelines between towns and cities. These boats ran regularly scheduled routes. Their captains and crews were familiar and highly regarded figures. These were known as package freighters, and their connection to the posts they served became in many instances a part of a town's folklore or history.

Such was the case with the *America*, a boat that made regular rounds between Duluth, Isle Royale, and Thunder Bay from 1902 to 1928. The speedy little boat provided two additional valuable services: she carried passengers to and from Isle Royale and delivered mail to the island's sparse population and visitors.

Ellie Connelly, whose grandfather built a cabin on the island in 1914, recalled the congenial atmosphere created by the boat's arrival. "Boat day was huge because people were coming and going," she said. "There were regular visitors people looked forward to seeing ... and, of course, the mail and then the supplies. You'd go down there and meet everybody and say, 'OK, come over for cards on Wednesday.'"

When the *America*'s work came to a shockingly sudden and unexpected end, the *Fort William Daily Times Journal* published a warm summation that described her value to the community: "It was the *America* which did the local, routine work along the north shore, poking her nose into every little harbor on the coast line and keeping communication between the mainland and Isle Royale uninterrupted."

The *America* leaves Duluth Harbor.

~~~

The *America*, measuring just a few inches shy of 165 feet and weighing 681 tons, was constructed at the Detroit Dry Dock Company in 1898. Not intended to sail as a package freighter, the *America* was slotted to operate as a passenger vessel, shuttling people between Chicago and Michigan City, Indiana. An estimated crowd of four hundred watched her launching at the Wyandotte dock at three-thirty in the afternoon of April 2, 1898, and the boat was christened by the wife of one of the boat owners, beginning what became an eventful life.

The boat featured forty-nine well-appointed staterooms, and beside her regular jaunts, she would be used for special excursions or to back up other lines needing more passenger capacity. She carried about 1,200 passengers and became known as one of the fastest, smoothest rides on the lakes.

Ownership of the *America* changed hands in 1902, when the Booth Steamship Line purchased the boat and decided to redirect her use. The new owners wanted the *America* to work on Lake Superior, and rather than serve as a passenger shuttle, she was destined for the role

A lifeline between Isle Royale and the Minnesota mainland, the *America* carried passengers, supplies, and mail to the isolated island.

she would keep for the remainder of her time on the lakes. She would haul package goods as well as passengers, deliver the fresh catch of fish caught by commercial fishermen from different ports, and see that mail was delivered to Isle Royale. Before she began her duties in April 1902, the new owners added to the cabin capacity, giving the boat even more room for passengers.

One of these passengers spoke eloquently about the serenity he felt when riding on the *America*. He enjoyed the sights and the stops, including the visits for fresh-caught fish. "In each of these curving harbors," he wrote, "are the dwellings of fisher folk, their log homes being far enough back to escape the surf, while close to the jagged black shoreline are tiny shelters where fish are packed and salted. Alongside of these will be seen boats drawn up on pole skidways and reels for drying nets, while in front little docks jut out for making difficult landings."

The boat's busy schedule led to a checkered history of accidents. The *America* had been in operation for less than a month when she slammed into the south pier of the Duluth Ship Canal, resulting in heavy damage to the vessel's bow. Water flooded into the front of the boat, where hull plates were torn off. Port officials blamed the crew's unfamiliarity with the water's strong currents, along with the boat's sailing too fast for the canal, as culprits causing the accident. The *America* was dry-docked for repairs.

Two years later, five staterooms were damaged by another freighter's anchor, but the damage wasn't serious enough to shut down the *America*'s scheduled runs. This was not the case in July 1909, when the boat ran aground on the north shore and sustained damage to plates requiring repairs.

In writing about the *America*, Thomas Holden, an authority on Isle Royale, noted that "despite numerous lumps, bumps, near misses and unforeseen circumstances, *America* was nearly always on schedule."

In 1911, the freighter's hull was lengthened by 18 feet, and, perhaps as important, twelve new staterooms were added, allowing fifty more passengers. The enhanced 182.6-foot *America* was now able to haul nearly 100 tons more freight. The improvements were needed for economic reasons. A new highway constructed along the previously barren north shore cut into the need for boat delivery of package goods, causing the *America*'s owners to scramble to find ways to make up for the lost revenue.

The *America* rightfully attained the reputation of being the first boat out in the spring and the last to sail in the late fall. When Jacob Frederick Hector, the boat's long-standing captain, died in 1910, Edward "Indian" Smith, his first mate, took command. His knowledge of the lake, and particularly the waters on his vessel's route, was so extensive that it was said that he could "smell his way along the north shore."

That ability might have saved the *America* in September 1926, when his boat encountered the *Huronic,* a 321-foot Canadian passenger liner. Smith was at the wheel of the *America,* personally guiding his vessel through dense fog, when he saw the *Huronic* emerging from the pea soup on a collision course with his boat. His instantaneous reaction was to make a hard turn. He could not avoid a collision, but rather than absorb the worst of a full-force hit, the *America* received only a relatively harmless glancing blow.

Good fortune did not prevail in the predawn hours of Thursday, June 7, 1928. The *America* was taking her customary route, checking in to Grand Marais before sailing to Isle Royale. Captain Smith had just turned over the pilothouse command to First Mate John Wick and had gone down to his cabin to rest. The boat had dropped off two passengers at Washington Harbor on the island's northeast tip and was leaving the harbor.

Wick was an able officer, but he did not know the *America* or the area around the island very well. He had recently transferred to the *America* after a stint as first mate on the *Jack*, a similar freighter of the Minnesota Atlantic Transit Company. Wick had left what was known as the "Poker Fleet" because the *Jack*'s commander, Gus Ege, refused to recommend him for command of another boat in the fleet.

Five minutes after Captain Smith turned over the pilothouse to his first mate, the *America* ran aground, hitting bottom on a reef four times and tearing a hole in the boat's single steel bottom. Hearing the collision with the reef and Wick's frantic ringing of the bell to warn all on board of impending doom, Smith rushed to the wheelhouse for an appraisal of what had happened and to survey the damage to the vessel. The pumps were working, but they could not handle the water gushing into the boat.

"Beach her, beach her," Smith ordered wheelsman Fred Nelson. Smith aimed to beach the *America* on a small gravel beach nearby, saving his vessel from sinking, but there was too much working against him. Water continued to flood the stern of the boat, making her prey for the rising topography of the lake bottom. The *America* hit bottom again about 30 yards from the beach, and the small freighter ground to a halt on a sloping shelf of submerged land. The boat's sinking was evident, but there was no panic among passengers and crew. "The boat started sinking slowly," Nelson told the *Duluth News Tribune*. "All five of the ship's life boats were launched. Members of the crew were assigned to take charge of these boats, and everyone was taken off. . . . There was no confusion while the life boats were being lowered. Everyone behaved wonderfully."

Ten passengers and thirty-one crew members boarded the lifeboats, and aside from a pet dog tied to the stern, there were no casualties. One passenger, H. S. Cottier, corroborated Nelson's account in an interview with the *Fort William Daily Times Journal*. "The ship began to settle and all we had to do was get into the boats," he said. "There was no panic whatever, and it was not until an hour later, when it was just breaking day, that the good ship sank almost out of sight."

Captain Smith was the last to leave. The *America* slid slowly down the underwater shelf until only a small portion of the bow jutted out of the lake. Smith stayed with his vessel, looking mournfully at what had been his long-standing and sole command, supervising the safe removal of everyone onboard, until it became clear that he had to abandon ship or face the consequences of being onboard when the boat eventually sank. He stepped into a lifeboat, then headed for the gravelly beach he had hoped to reach on the *America*.

The boat refused to slip underwater—at least not right away. The forward house and decking remained above the surface, the subject of many photographs and news stories. The *America* had been like an old, visiting friend, and talk about salvaging, repairing, and refloating her began almost immediately. She seemed so accessible. A lengthy history of attempting to salvage the *America* was about to commence.

The early morning grounding of the *America* on June 7, 1928, was the last of a number of accidents suffered by the 183-foot steamer, one of the most popular visitors to Isle Royale.

Fortunately, all passengers and crew aboard the *America* escaped the sinking vessel. Attempts to raise or salvage her were unsuccessful.

The U.S. Steamboat Inspection Service and the *America*'s owners investigated the accident and concluded that First Mate Wick was solely responsible by choosing a course too close to a known and charted reef. He was reprimanded for careless navigation, the insurance underwriters settled with Booth Fisheries, a buoy marker was placed near the wreckage as a warning of the submerged vessel in shallow water, and the immediate aftermath of the sinking ended.

But the package freighter's story was far from over. The predominant question was not whether the *America* could be salvaged, but who would do it. Booth announced that it was finished operating in the area and that insurance firms were entertaining bids on the hull, setting off unsubstantiated rumors that the vessel might have been scuttled for the insurance money.

Salvaging the wreck seemed possible, if not probable. Soon after the *America* struck the reef, when it appeared likely that she would sink in shallow water, chief engineer Frank McMillin had ordered boiler pressure to be relieved and all surfaces greased to help keep the engine room functional for the recovery of the boat after she was salvaged. Bringing the *America* to the surface didn't seem to be a problem. As time illustrated, having the funds to do so was the problem.

Captain Cornelius O. Flynn was the first to determine this. A vessel owner and captain, salvager, and diver, Flynn bought the *America*, declaring that he intended to place the boat back in service. He had surveyed the wreck and felt that his plan was feasible. His timing, it turned out, was not. The country was entering the Depression, and the Duluth resident could not find a way to obtain the funding necessary for his project. Further, harsh winters in 1928 and 1929 badly damaged the portion of the bow still exposed to the elements, and when the ice around the vessel melted in 1930, the bow finally slid out of sight.

Flynn hung on to his dream, but he finally quit pursuing it when he conceded to financial realities. He did not, however, forsake ownership of the *America*. His son, Paul Flynn, eventually inherited the *America*, and the younger Flynn considered picking up his father's pursuit of salvaging the vessel. He, too, buckled under the heavy costs involved. The reality was difficult to accept. When the Flynns were hoping to raise her, the *America* looked to be in good shape, excepting the hole in her hull from the grounding and the damage to her bow. The job required creativity. The salvage business, greatly advanced over the past half century, was known for its innovative approaches to difficult problems.

The *America* did not fade from memory. Maybe her proximity to the surface (the bow, though totally submerged, was only 4 feet from the surface) enticed interest, or maybe all the stories about her past kept the *America* on the minds of so many. Whatever the reason, the fascination stuck—perhaps in refloating her and using her as a museum ship.

James R. Marshall took a turn at trying to rejuvenate the boat in 1965. Marshall, a Lake Superior historian, author, and editor, encountered numerous problems in his endeavor, from bad weather conditions to a boat that continued to deteriorate to a battle with opponents who wanted the *America* to remain where she was. Marshall's interest

The *America* sank in shallow water, making the wreckage one of the most visited diving sites on the Great Lakes.

in salvaging the boat rose from a deep love of Great Lakes history. He had nothing to gain from the adventure. Sport divers had stripped the *America* of anything valuable or collectable, and he was aware of the expense of the project. Still, he thoroughly researched the job and talked extensively with the now-aging Paul Flynn.

"Our plan was reasonably simple," Marshall explained. "Flynn had been right about sealing the forward and aft sections. About 60 percent of the hull was not a problem, once the forward main deck had been cleared of collapsed superstructure. Once she was afloat, we planned to bring her back to Duluth for a complete refurbishing. We would then turn her over to the St. Louis Historical Society for all to come and see."

The reasonably simple plan turned out to be impossible to execute. Marshall had assembled a dream team of experts to assist him, but they ran into all kinds of issues. The weather during late 1965 was stormy and cold, forcing workers to halt their efforts until the following spring. Dynamite used in the process blew a large Y-shaped hole in the hull near the vessel's keel. Repair bills piled up, and Marshall decided over the passing months that it was "pump the *America* soon or else."

The end came from an unexpected source: the U.S. District Attorney in Grand Rapids, Michigan, who opposed the use of explosives in the salvaging. Rumors were making the rounds that Marshall's opponents were thinking about bombing the *America*, and to top it off there was some question about who owned the boat.

Marshall was finished. When organizing his project, he had not factored in any opposition to his plan. He had obtained the backing of Minnesota Congressman John Blatnik, and he had kept the politician up to date on his progress. He had not considered that other well-meaning groups might not want to see the *America* moved.

The *America* became one of the most popular diving sites on the Great Lakes, and the most visited wreck near Isle Royale. The Great Lakes Shipwreck Preservation Society devoted hundreds of volunteer hours to strengthening the weakening walls and decks of the vessel, hoping to hold it together for future divers. They knew as well as anyone that their efforts were only temporary. Nature always won.

George M. Cox

~~~

The loss of the passenger boat *George M. Cox,* like the loss of other vessels after grounding, stands as a prime example of an accident that never should have happened. It occurred in dense fog near Isle Royale, in calm waters, as a result of human error. After a thorough investigation, the captain and first mate lost their licenses, and neither would sail again. The *Cox* was a total loss, though decades later it would become one of the more popular dive sites on Lake Superior.

Luckily, all passengers and crewmen survived, and only a handful had injuries of any significance. Unluckily, the vessel had just been reconditioned and renamed and was on her first trip after a two-year layoff.

The *George M. Cox* began her eventful life in 1901, when, sailing under the name *Puritan,* she operated as a luxurious passenger vessel. At 233 feet in length and 40.5 feet in width, she had two decks and offered the strength and speed to move passengers smoothly and safely. The Holland and Chicago Transportation Company ordered her construction, but before the hull was even completed, the company was purchased by Graham and Morton Transportation Company. John H. Graham and J. Stanley Morton ran a service of high-end passenger vessels connecting Chicago, St. Joseph, and Benton Harbor on Lake Michigan, with occasional forays to Milwaukee and Mackinac Island. During the production season, she also handled cargoes of fruit.

The accommodations offered some of the finest amenities of the day, from electricity to the elegant mahogany of her forty-two staterooms, from a grand staircase to a dining room forward and a large smoking room aft. The boat's equipment, including four specially designed boiler units and triple expansion engine, all but guaranteed an easy ride for the vessel's first- and second-class passengers.

The *Puritan* was launched in 1901, and her early years of service lacked serious incident—at least on the water. Change seemed to characterize her existence, and even that was of major consequence. She received new boilers in 1905 and was lengthened by 26 feet in 1908. During World War I, she was camouflaged and modified for ocean sailing for the U.S. Navy. Her main duties involved transporting troops. After the war, the *Puritan* was sold yet again, overhauled, and placed back in the passenger business. The boat was chartered by Chicago's Michigan Transit Service, which purchased the vessel in 1924. The company, like those before it, moved passengers back and forth between Chicago and northern Michigan.

The Depression put the *Puritan's* years of service in limbo. People were not taking expensive vacations as incomes dried up or disappeared. The *Puritan* had escaped noteworthy damage while tied up

The *Puritan,* one of the most luxurious passenger vessels on the Great Lakes at the beginning of the twentieth century.

at a dock in 1927, when she broke loose from her mooring and was pushed around the harbor in the same storm that claimed the *Kamloops*. She could not dodge the financial crisis two years later.

The *Puritan* lay idle, docked in Manistee, Michigan, while the country endured the Depression. Not surprisingly, the boat's owners were none too pleased with the lost earnings and the costs of maintaining a nonworking vessel. The boat was eventually sold to the Isle Royale Transportation Company, a firm run by George M. Cox, a wealthy New Orleans shipbuilder and brewer. Cox, a stockholder in the Duke Transportation Company, had grand plans for his latest purchase. He would refurbish her, rename her, and use her, along with another transportation acquisition, the larger, 310-foot *Isle Royale*, to usher passengers to northern Lake Superior and the island. According to the plan, the *Cox* would shuttle between Chicago and southern Canada, with weekend excursions to Mackinac Island, while the *Isle Royale* handled traffic around her namesake.

"The boats are elegantly equipped, and everything that can possibly be done will be offered for a passenger's pleasure," Cox told the *Manistee News Advocate*, adding that this did not mean that there would be any tolerance for gambling or disorderly behavior. "Our purpose is to supply two ships, and perhaps more, where every family will be offered clean and wholesome amusement and plenty of good times."

Cox had a specific pleasure cruise in mind for the first trip of the vessel bearing his name. The Century of Progress Exposition was opening in Chicago, and Cox deemed it an ideal occasion to move passengers from Port Arthur to the Windy City. He was so excited by the gala occasion that he decided to take the *Cox*, along with a group of friends, on the trip.

~~~

The *Cox*, resplendent in a fresh coat of white paint, offset by a newly painted jet-black smokestack, left Chicago on May 25, 1933. This was going to be an affair that allowed George Cox the opportunity to show off his new boat. Two days prior to the boat's Chicago departure, while the craft was still in the shipyard in Manistee, hundreds of people, along with the press, inspected the *Cox* and voiced their approval. There was entertainment onboard, and it was clear that Cox meant every word he spoke about the boat's pleasing her passengers. At the helm was Captain George Johnson, a Great Lakes veteran from Traverse City, Michigan.

The trip was designed for relaxation, with a couple of stops before reaching Port Arthur. Crew members greatly outnumbered the tiny passenger list, which stood at eighteen, with a capacity group waiting to board in Port Arthur. Celebratory crowds greeted the *Cox* at her planned stops. She left Houghton, Michigan, on the afternoon of May 27, with a short jaunt to Isle Royale ahead.

What happened when the boat approached the island became the subject of debate and speculation. Captain Johnson turned the pilothouse command over to First Mate Arthur Kronk with specific instruction concerning making a course change before the *Cox* reached the treacherous waters near the Rock of Ages Lighthouse. The underwater topography in the area was especially dangerous, with lake bottoms rising from deep to very shallow in short order. The Rock of Ages Lighthouse, a 117-foot tower built on a rock outcropping and initially lit in 1910, was constructed as a means of warning vessels of the hazards in the area.

From his vantage point in the lighthouse, keeper John Soldenski peered through a thick, low-hanging fog, amazed by what he saw. Although he could not make out the vessel, he could see its two masts poking through the fog, the boat traveling too fast for conditions, headed directly toward the reef the lighthouse was equipped to caution boats about. Soldenski rushed to his fog whistle, but the boat kept coming toward the lighthouse. The reef lay between the unidentifiable steamer and the light.

The *Cox*'s first mate, it so happened, had not followed his captain's instructions to alter the boat's course. He would later explain that a deviation of the boat's compass reading had led to some confusion. This was not an uncommon phenomenon near Isle Royale. But Captain Johnson stated that the *Cox* had heard the Rock of Ages alert at least an hour before his boat hit the reef, and he had thought little of it. There was plenty of time to alter course and avoid danger.

Rock of Ages Lighthouse during construction.

Soldenski's frantic attempts to warn the boat of danger ahead were probably futile. Fog whistles had a strange way of echoing in the low visibility, and even if this had not been the case in the late afternoon of May 27, the *Cox* was moving too fast to react in time to avoid disaster. It was roughly six o'clock, with dinner being served in the dining room, when the *Cox* ran aground. The collision with the reef was violent, largely due to the boat's speed at the moment of impact. The grounding was so forceful that it ripped the engine and boilers from their moorings. A hole in the boat's hull opened the stern to inrushing water. The *Cox* immediately began listing to her port side.

In the dining room, passengers, wait staff, and other personnel were thrown to the floor. Food, plates, and utensils went flying. Furniture slid across the floor and crashed. Even George Cox suffered from the effects of the sudden grounding, receiving minor injuries from the experience.

Adeline Keeling, a twenty-three-year-old staff nurse on the *Cox*, described the accident and its immediate aftermath in an interview published in the *New York Times*. "There was a heavy thud, followed by a series of crashes," she said. "The passengers were at dinner at the time. I saw a heavy buffet slide across the floor and crash into tables and a partition. I was in my stateroom and was thrown against a door and stunned. The stewardess, Beatrice Cote, helped me to my feet, and was herself knocked down in the second crash." Cote injured her back in the fall and, after rescue, was transported to a Fort William hospital. The severity of other injuries ranged from light to serious. John Ganzara, a deckhand, hurt his hand, legs, and shoulder. Alex Mack broke a leg. George Williams suffered from a scalp cut.

While those injured were attended to, activities on the boat moved with great urgency. The *Cox* had transmitted an SOS following the grounding. Lightkeeper Soldenski launched a gas-powered lifeboat and sped to the scene. The *Cox*'s five port lifeboats were calmly lowered (the starboard boats were rendered useless, due to a severe list of the *Cox*), and Soldenski towed them to the Rock of Ages Lighthouse. The Portage Coast Guard, alerted to the *Cox*'s plight, left for the wreck site, but all onboard were gone by the time they arrived. It had taken only forty minutes to completely abandon ship.

The Rock of Ages Lighthouse.

The passengers and crew safely reached the lighthouse, but it lacked the room to accommodate everyone. Those rescued took turns resting inside the lighthouse and braving the cold outside. Soldenski's wife served the unexpected guests hot coffee. Some of those rescued tried to sleep on the lighthouse staircase, but for most, a long night awaited.

The morning hours of May 28 were busy at the lighthouse. The Portage Coast Guard boat arrived and carried forty-three passengers and crewmen to the Washington Island hotel dock on Isle Royale. When the boat returned to the lighthouse, Captain Johnson requested that the crew recover as many bags of luggage as possible from the wreckage. Seventy-one pieces were brought back.

The Coast Guard cutter *Crawford* arrived and assisted with the removal of those still at Rock of Ages. Passengers and crew were transferred from there and from Washington Island to Houghton, closing a rescue operation that involved more people than any other in Lake Superior history.

~~~

The *Cox* story dominated the news over the following days. She would remain afloat, her stern completely submerged and her bow rising more than 100 feet in the air, until summer. Further visits to the wreck yielded more possessions and furnishings. The bow eventually broke off, and the *Cox* sank in early July, her wreckage strewn in 10 to 100 feet of water. The boat had been declared a total loss well before she sank.

In the months between the accident and the boat's sinking, efforts to salvage the *Cox* and her contents resulted in mixed success. The boat, with a huge hole torn in her hull and the engine room works ripped away during the grounding, was hopeless. Salvagers recovered a strong box with money, jewelry, and stocks and bonds inside. The vessel's safe was also brought up.

A formal inquiry was called to look into the causes of the accident, with the captain and first mate in focus. The inquiry convened on May 30, 1933, in Houghton, under the direction of Captain John Hanson and Alfred Knight of the U.S. Bureau of Navigation. Captain George Johnson, highly praised by newspapers for his actions in safely removing everyone onboard the *Cox*, was the first witness called to testify. Johnson did not back away from pinning First Mate Art Kronk with the responsibility for the *Cox*'s being in the hazardous area near Isle Royale. Johnson testified—and his testimony was later corroborated by others—that he had set a specific course for Fort William before retiring to his quarters and leaving Kronk in charge. Rather than follow his directives, Kronk had set a different course—one that led to catastrophic results.

Johnson said he was in the wheelhouse when the *Cox* encountered the heavy fog. "The sounding of the Rock of Ages fog siren was well determined at 5:20 p.m., exactly one hour before [the *Cox*] piled up on the reef," Johnson testified. "The vessel proceeded at a moderate speed until 6:10 p.m., when the fog sirens on Rock of Ages became more distinct."

The speed at which the *Cox* was traveling at the time of impact with the reef was, under the conditions, of great interest to the inquiry. Vessels are supposed to cut speed in foggy conditions, but there was no accurate way to determine the *Cox*'s speed. Johnson confessed to

The 259-foot passenger liner *George M. Cox* grounded in heavy fog on the Rock of Ages reef on May 27, 1933, as owner George M. Cox entertained passengers on the vessel's maiden voyage. Herculean efforts rescued those aboard the grounded *Cox*.

the board of inquiry that the boat was moving faster than he would have liked, but he could not offer the actual speed. Even his accounts in newspaper interviews varied. In a May 29 interview with the *Superior Evening Telegram,* he told a reporter that the *Cox* was doing 17 knots when she hit the reef; one day later, he was quoted by the *Daily Mining Gazette* as saying the boat's speed was 10 knots. In view of the force of the grounding and the damage to the *Cox,* the latter seemed like a low estimate.

Art Kronk followed Johnson. His appearance began late on the opening day and continued the next morning. Kronk found himself on the defensive, vehemently denying Johnson's assertions about his role in the accident, as well as other testimony by Johnson that portrayed him in a less than favorable light. Johnson claimed that Kronk had been the first officer to leave the *Cox,* that he had been on a lifeboat with only a single passenger, a woman, and that he, Johnson, ordered Kronk to return to the *Cox* for more passengers. Kronk denied the allegations (though Johnson's remarks were later backed up by other testimony), stating that he had stayed with the *Cox* until the bitter end.

Kronk's abilities as an officer were already in question. As first mate on the *Kiowa,* he had been onboard another sinking boat. The *Kiowa,* fighting a blizzard in 1929, had grounded off Sable Point. The captain had drowned, but Kronk had had his license suspended for thirty days for negligence. Now, less than four years later, he was facing more disciplinary action for his role in another lost vessel.

His role in the inquiry was contentious, at the very least. He angrily answered some of the more pointed queries. On one occasion, he broke down in tears, pounding the table and saying he was being "framed by a dirty bunch of crooks." Then, the same evening, he got into a physical altercation with M. L. Gilbert, the Isle Royale Transit Company's vice president and marine superintendent, in the hotel lobby.

The board of inquiry testimony was compelling. When the hearings concluded, the board found Johnson and Kronk guilty of "reckless navigation in a fog and inattention to duty." The U.S. Steamboat Inspection Service suspended both men's licenses, and neither man sailed again.

Emperor

~~~

Fatigue.

When the word is used in discussions about shipwrecks, it is usually applied to the construction of freighters, as in metal fatigue. From the beginning of the use of steel in bulk carrier construction and the loss of vessels from hull failure, heated arguments have focused on whether steel was strong enough to stand up to the beating it took in stormy weather, to the damages inflicted during the loading and unloading processes, to standard day-to-day operations, and to time and how years of service might affect the strength of steel. These and other factors were batted about in the early days of steel use (the late nineteenth and early twentieth centuries), when the sample size was too small to draw conclusions, to later days, when boats such as the *Carl D. Bradley* and the *Daniel J. Morrell,* which had both been constructed near the beginning of the use of steel in naval architecture but had served long and well on the lakes, sank after hull failure in storms. Was metal fatigue responsible for the sinkings?

Science and technology vastly improved the steel used in boat construction, but another type of fatigue has probably contributed to a large number of disasters. *Human* fatigue.

For the sake of safety and efficiency, the pilothouse and engine room crews must be alert and operating at full capacity at all times on duty. This might seem obvious, but it is not always the case. Circumstance, be it a storm or personnel shortage or other factors, can lead to fatigue that endangers vessel and crew.

Such was the case when the *Emperor,* a 525-foot freighter loaded with iron ore, sank on June 4, 1947. Twelve men lost their lives.

~~~

When the Collingwood Shipbuilding Company laid her keel in 1910, the *Emperor* was destined to become the largest freighter constructed in Canada to that point. Collingwood, Ontario, on Lake Huron, as a seafaring city, could compete with the best that Canada had to offer. The city's shipbuilding efforts began shortly after William Watts arrived in 1850, with his construction of skiffs used by area fishermen. The railroad arrived a few years later, on January 1, 1855, and lake commerce was quickly established. Collingwood not only became a center for the arrival of immigrants and the shipping of grain and package goods; it eventually became a focal point for the construction of freighters. The Collingwood Shipbuilding Company was founded in 1899.

The *Emperor* followed the early-twentieth-century trend of constructing longer boats with ample power and bigger cargo holds. Two Scotch boilers fed steam to a triple expansion engine capable of producing 1,500 horsepower that moved the fully loaded vessel at a crisp 11 knots.

The *Emperor,* a 525-foot freighter operated by the Canadian Steamship Lines, was loaded with iron ore when she grounded near the northeastern tip of Isle Royale, breaking in two and costing twelve men, including the captain, their lives.

Inland Lines of Ontario, owner of the *Emperor,* launched the boat on December 17, 1910, but had to wait until the following spring to put her into service. Her maiden voyage might have predicted tough times ahead. The vessel had not sailed far when she broke her main shaft in Thunder Bay, necessitating a tow to De Tour, Michigan. She was repaired and set to work. This was only the beginning of the *Emperor's* early misfortunes. Later that same year, on the Canadian side near the Soo Locks, the *Emperor* ran over an anchor, tearing a hole in her bow. She sank in shallow water and blocked the channel. She was repaired, but it had been an expensive year for Inland Lines.

The boat was sold to Canada Steamship Lines in May 1916, and she performed over the next three decades—not without incident but well enough to be a strong, profitable freighter.

~~~

What precisely happened to the *Emperor* on June 3–4, 1947, will never be known for certain. The Coast Guard conducted a thorough investigation that pieced together the boat's final voyage, but there were too many unknown factors to draw a conclusion. Still, there was no disputing the conclusion that the *Emperor* had gone down as a result of avoidable human error.

July 3 had been an eventful day. The *Emperor* dropped off a load of coal in Fort William before moving on to Port Arthur for a load of iron ore destined for Ashtabula, Ohio. As per custom, the first mate, James Morrey, supervised the loading. It took between six and seven hours to drop 10,429 tons of iron ore into the *Emperor's* cargo holds, time the first mate otherwise would have been off duty and resting. By the time the boat was ready to go and was headed out to the lake at 10:33 p.m., Morrey was facing his usual turn in the pilothouse.

The *Emperor* lacked a third mate on this particular run, so Morrey's assigned 12:00 to 6:00 a.m. watch was grueling, especially following a long loading process. Captain Eldon Walkinshaw retired to his quarters. Morrey took a seat in the pilothouse, ready to start his shift.

According to a surviving wheelsman, the freighter's course had been set by the first mate. This would have been the course plotted for good sailing conditions, which they were on that night. It was clear with very little wind. Visibility was excellent. The *Emperor* had taken this course in the past, and those in the pilothouse would have been aware of the hazards they faced as they drew near Isle Royale. So what happened?

The Coast Guard figured that Morrey, exhausted from his work without benefit of the customary break, dozed in his pilothouse chair. There was even speculation that the wheelsman might have nodded off here and there. There was no plausible explanation for how the two men would have missed the clearly visible navigation lights along the way—markers that would have warned them that they were straying from a safe course and heading into danger. When a course change was eventually ordered, it came too late to evade the narrow passageway between Isle Royale and Passage Island.

The Canoe Rocks reef, off Isle Royale's northeastern tip, was known as very hazardous, as the *Chester A. Congdon,* a boat slightly longer than the *Emperor,* discovered in 1918. A warning light had been installed on nearby Blake Point, but it apparently was not seen by the pilothouse crew on the *Emperor.*

Would radar have helped? The *Emperor* was not equipped with it, but that was not unusual at the time. In 1945, the *Mackinaw,* a Coast Guard icebreaker, became the first vessel of any kind to install radar, and a year later, a half-dozen freighters became equipped with it. Radar was expensive and unproven on the Great Lakes. It effectively spotted other vessels and land, but the reef was submerged, and in any case, the warning lights in the area should have alerted the pilothouse of the dangers ahead.

The *Emperor* struck the reef with a force that immediately split the boat. Chief engineer Merritt Dedman, asleep in his bunk at the time of impact, rushed to the engine room and instantly saw that the boat had lost her rudder and was in the process of sinking. Captain Walkinshaw, also awakened by the noise from the collision, surveyed the damage, sent out an SOS, and issued an abandon ship order, all within ten minutes of impact.

The port and starboard lifeboats were launched in an orderly fashion, but those in the boats ran into problems. The starboard boat carrying ten sailors was filling with water from the onset, most likely

from a lost bilge plug. Those in the port lifeboat were contending
with something more serious when the badly listing *Emperor* slipped
below the surface. "She was capsized by the suction of the sinking
ship," Second Mate Peter Craven told the *Port Arthur News Chronicle*,
speaking of the troubles faced by those on the port lifeboat, "Most of
the missing were in or about this second boat. Down we went. When
I came up, I reached the surface the moment the boat came up over-
turned."

Fortunately for those on both boats, help was on the way. The *Kim-
ball*, a 125-foot Coast Guard cutter putting up channel markers in the
vicinity, heard the SOS and rushed to the site of the sinking, arriving
in twenty-five minutes. They recovered survivors in both lifeboats and
seven who managed to swim to Canoe Rocks. They also retrieved the
body of the *Emperor*'s main cook. Twenty-one were saved, and unfortunately twelve perished, including three (Walkinshaw, Morrey, and
wheelsman John Prokup) who might have been able to provide details
about what led to the sinking.

After conducting its investigation of the accident, the Coast Guard
placed the blame on the first mate, marking the wreck as the result
of human error. It noted the mate's exhaustion and did not speculate
as to whether he had fallen asleep or was simply too tired to make
the needed changes in direction. All that mattered was the *Emperor*,
a seaworthy vessel, was gone.

~~~

In his 1997 book *Haunted Lakes*, Great Lakes historian Frederick Stonehouse examined unusual phenomena associated with the Great Lakes
shipping industry. He looked at superstitions, such as hunches, the
dislike of starting trips on Fridays, bad luck vessels, or tossing coins
over one's shoulder at the beginning of a trip. He wrote of lighthouses'
strange phenomena, and how some were said to be haunted by their
former keepers. He gave accounts of vessels supposedly haunted by
crew members lost in their sinking.

He offered convincing evidence of possible truth in even the more
outrageous of the claims, but he was also quick to note that while they
might make entertaining stories, the tales might be lacking overall

veracity. "I neither believe nor disbelieve in ghosts, and have no special sensitivity to the spirit world," Stonehouse declared in the book's preface. The stories, he averred, are of interest because they add texture to history; they speak of traces and beliefs of the past.

The *Emperor* figured in the book. A diver exploring the wreck had what Stonehouse called "an eerie experience":

> Swimming into one of the deckhand's cabins, he was startled to see the apparition of a crewman laying peacefully in his bunk. The ghost looked blankly at the diver, who quickly determined that he had seen enough and left for the surface.

Was this account an example of a diver's vivid imagination, poked into motion by the murky black depths of Lake Superior, the remains of a gigantic boat now frozen in time on a lake bottom, the silence of a scene, and a belief in ghosts, spurred on by faith in eternal afterlife, coupled with all the stories about hauntings that one hears from early childhood, in books, movies, and even oral history? Whatever the case, the diver's tale adds to the story of a vessel and keeps alive a history that might have been forgotten.

PART III
Three Killer Storms

Lake Superior's
Toughest Storm, 1905

~~~

The eleventh month of the year has been a scourge to the shipping industry since the beginning of moving cargo on the Great Lakes. Meteorologists refer to November as a transition month, and for great reason. The weather can be mild and warm, cold and dangerously stormy, or, most likely, a combination of both. A master can guide his vessel, laden with a full load of cargo, onto calm waters, only to encounter deadly sailing conditions in the span of a few hours. Worse yet, for captains and crews of large freighters, overconfidence clouds judgment and leads shipping officials and "heavy weather" captains to believe that the vessels are up to the task of taking on anything Mother Nature throws at them.

The three largest vessels lost on the Great Lakes (the *Edmund Fitzgerald*, 1975; the *Carl D. Bradley*, 1958; and the *Daniel J. Morrell*, 1966) were wrecked and lost all but three men among them on Lakes Superior, Michigan, and Huron, respectively, in November storms. Countless others were lost or destroyed as well. Factors contributing to the losses include inadequate weather forecasting in the days prior to radar, satellite tracking and communications, GPS, a good understanding of upper air patterns, an adequate number of reporting stations, and a general distrust within the shipping industry of weather forecasts. And, of course, greed. In November, with the shipping season reaching its end, shipping companies tried to squeeze in a final trip or two. Boats would be serviced in the layup months ahead, and if they were seaworthy, they operated.

The Duluth harbor canal in stormy weather, circa 1906.

Success courted disaster. The Minnesota iron ranges supplied as much ore as the freighters could haul. U.S. Steel owned its own fleet of boats, the Pittsburgh Steamship Company, capable of supplying the corporate giant with the iron ore needed for an ever-increasing demand. By early 1905, the fleet consisted of 112 vessels. The company needed them. The 1903 and 1904 seasons had seen a downturn in shipping tonnage, but there had been a substantial rebound in 1905: 40 percent greater tonnage than the previous year, in weather less than cooperative. Minnesota's eastern coast had been raked by a greater than average number of storms, yet the boats continued to sail.

Herbert Richardson, the thirty-eight-year-old U.S. Weather Bureau forecaster in Duluth, took his job very seriously. The Duluth harbor was second only to New York's in annual traffic, and while sailors and their bosses might have been dismissive of the weather predictions and warnings, Richardson knew that he would be blamed if an improper forecast cost a company a boat. Captains might choose to look beyond his warnings, but if anything went wrong, Richardson stood to be excoriated for not warning strongly enough. That was doubly true if the Witch of November decided to pay the area a visit.

The third week of November 1905, a nasty storm stirred up the waters of Lake Superior with heavy snow and winds at 60 miles per hour. Richardson, who could see the water from his brick home built high on a hill, held his breath and gazed at the lake, hoping that the boats' skippers would take his forecasts seriously and stay in. Fortunately, they did. Unfortunately, there was a saying in shipping lore that declared that smooth sailing would follow a storm for at least a week, and that old saw, plus the fact that companies had lost precious time at the end of the season, only days away from Thanksgiving, probably meant that companies would disregard any cautions about impending bad weather.

On Monday, November 27, the reports Richardson was receiving from Weather Bureau headquarters in Washington, D.C., were ominous: two strong weather systems, a cold Canadian air mass and a warm, moist system from the Gulf of Mexico, were on a collision course, and that always meant stormy, violent weather. Richardson issued his cautions and ordered the large storm flags hung near the docks. Then he did all that remained to be done: he waited.

~~~

He didn't have to wait long. A day earlier, on Sunday, a number of freighters stalled at the Soo Locks during the previous storm had been released and were making their way to destinations along the Great Lakes. Three vessels—the *Crescent City,* the *William Edenborn,* and the *Madeira* (a three-masted barge towed by the *Edenborn*)—were bound for ports in Minnesota. It had been sunny and calm at Sault Ste. Marie when they departed; it would be much different as they approached their destined ports.

At 406 feet, the *Crescent City* was dwarfed by the 500-footers under construction since the turn of the twentieth century, but she was a steady worker for the Pittsburgh Steamship Company. Built by the Chicago Shipbuilding Company in 1897, the *Crescent City* had served the Zenith Transit Company prior to her sale to Pittsburgh Steamship in 1901. On her trip to Minnesota on November 27, 1905, she was traveling light, with a crew of twenty-five, bound for a load of iron ore in Two Harbors, a port roughly twenty-five miles north of Duluth. From there, she would move on to Ashtabula, Ohio. She would drop off the iron ore and call it quits for the season.

The early portion was uneventful, which sat well with Captain Frank Rice and his crew, especially at this time of year. The weather began to deteriorate as the *Crescent City* reached western Lake Superior. A blast of frigid Canadian air sent temperatures plunging. Shrieking winds created the all too familiar "Christmas tree waves" and the chop that sailors dreaded. The *Crescent City* sailed straight into the storm, fighting to avoid becoming trapped in the kind of troughs that had overwhelmed boats throughout the history of commercial shipping on the lakes. Captain Rice fought a losing battle in holding his vessel's course.

Wheelsman Charlie Abrams recognized the warning signs and knew the freighter was in peril. The barometer was dropping, temperatures hovered around zero, and soundings indicated the *Crescent City* was in 100 feet or less of water. "I have sailed the Great Lakes for the last ten years," he would say, "but never have I seen so desperate a position or seen so terrible a storm."

At some point in the wee hours of the morning of November 28, Rice reached a decision. He would not attempt to dock in Two Harbors. It was simply too risky. Instead, he would head south to Duluth. There was a chance, however slim, that the storm would abate by the time the *Crescent City* reached the two narrow stone piers leading to Duluth's harbor.

"It was blowing at that time, I should judge, from sixty to seventy miles per hour from the northeast, accompanied by heavy snow,

The 406-foot *Crescent City*.

Unable to battle fierce winds and seas in the 1905 storm, the *Crescent City* was tossed into shallow water, where she grounded just offshore. The captain and crew escaped to land, only to face a challenge to survive the ordeal in frigid temperatures.

almost impossible to see one end of the boat from the other," Rice told company officials afterward. "Orders were sent the engineer to work the engines and boilers at their full capacity to try to get the boat to head to the wind and sea, and headed down the lake. We tried to get the boat around six times in succession, but she would come in the trough of the sea and no further; [we] found it an impossibility to get her headed to the wind and sea. I then headed her for Duluth."

That, too, turned out to be a futile undertaking. The waves near the canal were too mountainous to entertain the notion of entering the harbor, so Captain Rice decided to sail on and hope for the best. The wind and water continued to batter the *Crescent City* and push her closer to shore.

"My mate reported fifteen fathoms of water," Rice reported. "I then stopped the engines and let go my starboard anchor. The vessel swung to her anchor and held there. As a matter of protection though, we let go the port anchor and gave her all chain on each. We rode to the said anchors with the engines working ahead on to the anchors until three o'clock A.M., when the storm reached hurricane velocity, striking us on the starboard bow and swinging up head north. We then worked the engines wide open, working our helm hard port, endeavoring to bring the ship's head to her anchors in wind again. At this time, the snow storm was thicker than it had been any time and we knew nothing until we saw the cliffs of the North Shore. The engines were checked. I saw that we were going on a pointed bluff, where I knew if we stopped it would be a total loss to the ship, and the crew also. I backed the engine, giving the signal to the engineer to back strong."

None of these measures were effective. The storm pushed the *Crescent City* on land with great force, so much so that the boat was almost entirely out of water when it came to a stop. The crew was safe, but the vessel was a total loss.

~~~~

Duluth boasted of one of the busiest and most beautiful ports in the United States. It could also be one of the most challenging, due greatly to a long canal leading to the docks. The canal's construction began in 1871, after much legal squabbling between Duluth and Superior, Wisconsin, a nearby city competing for lake traffic after the construction of the first of the Soo Locks in 1855. The fighting between the two cities led to the creation of a legend, in which every man, woman, and child supposedly banded together to hand-dig the canal before a court injunction prohibited it. In fact, citizens did help with the working on the canal, digging out the final connection between the canal and Superior Bay, but it was nowhere near as dramatic as the legend, developed over the years. Given Duluth's natural beauty, with an eye-widening shoreline offset by homes built on the hillsides surrounding the city, the canal was the perfect fit.

Duluth was expanding enormously when the canal opened. The population of about three thousand ballooned to thirty-three thousand in the ten-year stretch from 1880 to 1890. Scandinavian immigrations poured in. The Lake Superior and Mississippi Railroad, servicing the newly discovered but very profitable iron ore range, was built. This small town, built on the banks of a massive lake carved out by a glacier, was soon the hub of the Great Lakes shipping industry.

To build the Duluth harbor, the lake bottom needed to be dredged and a canal built. The resulting harbor became one of the most attractive on the Great Lakes.

Weather played a notable role in the canal's history. Severe winters and lake storms, with their ice and heavy waves, weighed heavily in the weakening of the wood framing the canal's 1,700-plus feet. At the turn of the century, the two long piers had their wood replaced by concrete, the south pier opening in 1901, the north pier in 1902.

A crowning touch was added early in 1905, with the opening of the Duluth Transfer Bridge, a large structure rising over the canal and connecting people between Duluth and Park Point. Cars and cargo also crossed the platform, making the bridge as functional as it was attractive. Tourists rushed to see it.

But for all its exquisite design and usefulness, the canal could be treacherous when the weather turned bad. At 300 feet in width, the canal posed little problem when the seas were calm; the bigger vessels simply made wide turns into the canal. On rough days, waves and a strong undertow at the canal's entrance could present difficulties for even seasoned mariners.

This was illustrated in the early morning hours of November 28. The weather was snowy and cold, and the sea conditions were deteriorating, but nothing like the waves building over the hours ahead. The *Arizona,* a small 189-foot wooden lumber hooker, was fighting a losing battle with the elements as it approached Duluth. Built in 1868, shortly

A freighter leaves Duluth Harbor during construction of the Aerial Lift Bridge.

The beautiful aerial bridge near the entrance of Duluth Harbor.

after the Civil War, the *Arizona* had caught fire near Marquette, Michigan, in 1887 and barely survived. After extensive repairs, she was back on the water, picking up and delivering lumber around the lakes.

Captain Walter Neal applied his hearing as he grew closer to Duluth. He listened for the sound of fog whistles. It was almost 1:00 a.m. when the *Arizona* approached its port of destination, but the waves and the undertow almost took her down. Out of control, the *Arizona* spun completely around on three occasions during the last quarter mile of her trip, yet somehow, after the third turnaround, the *Arizona,* her rudder badly damaged, found herself aimed straight into the canal. Captain Neal commented later that only blind luck had been with him. He directed his vessel through the canal without further incident, marking the *Arizona* as the first boat—and one of the only vessels—to navigate the canal during the storm.

~~~~

Elsewhere on Lake Superior, the *William Edenborn* and the *Madeira,* the schooner barge she towed, were fighting for their lives. The two vessels had sailed under similar circumstances as the *Crescent City,* experiencing an uncomplicated passage after leaving the Soo Locks and proceeding across Lake Superior, only to face increasingly hostile weather as they neared the northern shores of Minnesota. Air temperatures were bone-numbing cold, and the wind blew steadily at 60 to 70 miles per hour. Both boats were of ample size to operate under usual sailing conditions, or in fresh, somewhat strong weather, but they had not been constructed for efficiency in conditions like this.

The 478-foot *Edenborn,* sailing under ballast, did not have the capacity for towing a large barge such as the *Madeira* in heavy weather. The *Madeira,* constructed in 1900 by the Chicago Shipbuilding Company, was, at 436 feet, not only very large: she also had the distinction of being built to operate solely as a barge, a rarity at the turn of the century, when lakers were being elongated to hold increased tonnage and fewer vessels were employed as the less cost-efficient barges. The *Madeira* lacked an engine other than a small one for raising and lowering her anchors, so hauling her taxed the *Edenborn.* The *Madeira* carried a crew of nine, including the captain, John Dissette.

The 478-foot *William Edenborn*.

The 436-foot *Madeira* was in tow of the *William Edenborn* when she broke loose and grounded near the northern shore. An amazing rescue, led by a seaman who scaled the face of an imposing bluff, saved most of the vessel's crew.

The two vessels went through the Soo Locks on November 26. The weather was good, and no weather warnings had been posted. Both vessels were sailing light, using water as ballast. "Everything proceeded as usual on the trip until about six or seven o'clock of the 27th of November, when the wind began to blow from the northeast, accompanied with blinding snow," Captain A. J. Talbot remembered. "From that time on the wind developed into a hurricane, constantly increasing in force."

The two vessels labored in the worsening weather. Blinding snow reduced visibility until those in the forward section of the *Edenborn* could barely see the aft section of the boat. Waves broke over the spar decks. Gale-force wind out of the northeast pushed the two vessels, lifting the *Edenborn*'s stern out of the water and forcing Chief Engineer Silas H. Hunter to throttle down to avoid damage to the boat when her overspinning propeller slammed back down into the lake. "The stern would fly out of the water and the engine would race and we would throttle the engine whenever the wheel would fly out of the water," said First Assistant Engineer Lester Hineline. Added Hunter: "I was in the engine room all night and my first assistant was at the throttle from twelve o'clock on. I have sailed thirty five years and have sailed twenty nine years as a licensed engineer. During all of the night of the 27th and 28th the wind and sea were the most violent I have ever experienced."

Then, at the height of the struggle, the towline connecting the two boats snapped. The *Edenborn* continued to sail on in the darkness, leaving the *Madeira* to fend for herself. "I saw nothing more of our steamer from that time on, although I kept sounding the Company's signal from that time on," Captain John Dissette of the *Madeira* stated later. "When I ascertained that our tow line was gone I at once took measures to use our anchors as promptly as possible. Realizing that one length of the cable would be insufficient, I hove up with the windlass the entire length of the cable, 180 fathoms. This was done immediately after the line parted."

The *Madeira*'s fate had been sealed. With no power to drive it, the barge and the crew were at the mercy of a pitiless sea. The schooner would be tossed around until she sank or ran aground. The rocky shore, guarded by towering bluffs, lay ahead.

The end came for both vessels within about an hour of one another. The *Edenborn* struck land first, crashing, bow first, onto the shore near Split Rock. Hatch covers blew away. A split tore into the deck near the number nine hatch. James Johnson, the *Edenborn*'s third engineer, fell through a hatch and was killed. "He had a habit of walking on the hatches," Captain Talbot said of Johnson. "I had on previous occasions cautioned him about taking the middle of the ship and called his attention to the danger of walking on hatch covers. While I did not see him fall in, I presume he did on this occasion as on previous ones walk in the middle of the ship, and fell into the hold." Three others, accompanying Johnson in an effort to launch the stern lifeboat and life raft, also fell through hatch openings, but they survived with only minor injuries.

While those aboard the *Edenborn* scrambled to get off a boat being pounded relentlessly by stormy waters, those on the *Madeira* watched helplessly while the shoreline indicated an inevitable collision. Rocks, boulders, and a stretch of 70-foot cliffs lined the shore. The *Madeira*'s bow slammed into land with tremendous force. The barge started to split on impact, helped along by the ebb and flow of the violent seas. The nine men aboard the *Madeira* knew that the odds were greater than even that they would be pulled back into the lake, into deeper water, where they would have no chance of survival. They needed to get off the boat.

This looked improbable. The *Madeira* had beached on Gold Rock, an isolated area near Split Rock, and the nonexistent shoreline consisted of boulders and rocks. Even if they were able to lower themselves, they would not last long in the frigid weather. The only realistic chance lay 70 feet above them at the top of the cliff, and reaching that would entail a climb up a sheer, icy surface.

First Mate James Morrow had an idea. Waves pushed the *Madeira* in a regular, rhythmic pattern. Was it possible to scale a mast to a point where, after carefully timing the *Madeira*'s forward thrust, he might be able to jump onto land at the top of the cliff? He climbed the mizzen mast but quickly determined that his plan to leap to land was out of the question. During his trip back down, the barge shook violently, and he was thrown into the water. He was never seen alive again.

Fred Benson, a powerfully built Swedish crewman, was next to make an attempt. He seized a coiled rope and leaped onto a ledge near the base of the cliff. He managed to gain a foothold, and from there he pulled himself up the face of the cliff. He eventually reached the top. He secured the rope to tree, weighed the other end of the rope with rocks, and lowered it to the bow section of the *Madeira*. One by one, three men pulled themselves, with Benson's help, to the top of the cliff. One carried a longer, stronger rope. They lowered it to the stern of the *Madeira*, and four sailors, including Captain Dissette, joined them. In the end, all but one of the nine escaped what looked to be certain death. The last of the crewmen had barely reached safety when the broken barge was dragged back into the lake.

The eight had no time to savor their good fortune. They were out in the middle of nowhere, wet and freezing, with no food or shelter, with no faith that anyone would come to their aid in the hours ahead. They gathered wood and built a fire.

~~~

The *Edenborn* and *Madeira* were not the only boat and barge to cross Lake Superior that day. A 454-foot freighter, the *Lafayette*, left the Soo Locks, towing a barge, the *Manila*. They were bound for a load of iron ore in Two Harbors. It was to be the last haul of the season for both vessels.

Built five years earlier by the American Shipbuilding Company in Lorain, Ohio, the *Lafayette* was part of the Pittsburgh Steamship Company's "College Line," five identical freighters named after universities. At 436 feet, the *Manila* was nearly as long and heavy as the *Lafayette*, a size that would come into play at the end of the two boats' eventful crossing of the lake.

The weather at the Soo Locks had been so calm that Captain Dell P. Wright had not bothered to order ballast water pumped into his empty freighter or her accompanying barge. The added weight might not have been needed at the beginning, but as the weather worsened and the two vessels found themselves caught in the maw of a vicious nor'easter lashing the western region of the lake, weight might have helped to hold course. Wright finally added water but to little use. In the ever-building waves and blizzard snow, he lost his way. He ordered his engineer to cut power and tried to maintain a course that he estimated would take the two vessels closer to Wisconsin, where they might find relief in the lee of the state's shoreline.

The storm stirred up havoc everywhere. The wind was deafening. The blowing snow blinded anyone attempting to see through it. No one dared step outside without risking being swept overboard by waves boarding the boat. When he could see the *Manila*'s lights behind the *Lafayette*, Wright saw chaos. The *Manila*, rather than following directly behind the *Lafayette*, zigzagged in whatever direction the waves took it. Wright considered whether to continue to tow the barge or cut the towline and hope the *Manila* could drop anchor and ride out the storm.

"By this time the seas had become so immense that when riding them the ship would pivot around and was almost unmanageable, the engineer having to throttle her on every sea at half speed," Captain Wright explained. "At times I would see the barge's light abreast of me to the northward and in a very few minutes abreast of me to the southward, it being impossible to keep the ship on her course."

The 454-foot *Lafayette* was towing the 436-foot *Manila* when the storm pushed the two vessels ashore. The grounding broke the *Lafayette* in two.

George Balfour, trailing the *Lafayette* in the *Manila,* helplessly watched the events unfold around him. Without an engine, his barge could be of no assistance in the storm, and he had no control over where the lake waters took him. "The captain of the steamer towing us attempted to come about and head into the sea and to ride out the gale in that manner," he recalled, "but he was unable to keep his ship's head to the wind, and after several unsuccessful attempts we proceeded a ways. At about three o'clock in the morning the *Lafayette* signaled me to stand by my line, but at the same time I observed that the *Lafayette* made attempts to swing off toward the South Shore, and I could see his maneuver was to get as close to the South Shore as possible so that we could come to anchor, but his efforts in that direction were unsuccessful, the sea picking the steamer up and swinging it away."

Captain Wright was stunned to hear waves crashing on the shore off the starboard bow of his boat. The *Lafayette* and *Manila* had been blown across the lake and were about to be driven aground some-where on the Minnesota coast. He would learn that they were about 6 miles north of Two Harbors, at the base of tall bluffs, which, while not as imposing as those towering over Split Rock or Gold Rock to the north, were more than enough to any wet, freezing sailor attempting to scale them. The *Lafayette* crashed into the shore, her bow almost perpendicular to the rocks, with the *Manila* close behind. The *Lafay-ette*'s crumpled bow was completely broken when the *Manila* collided with her, and the freighter began to break apart. The two vessels were so close when they came to rest that four of the *Lafayette*'s crewmen were able to escape by jumping onto the *Manila*'s deck. This proved to be only a temporary solution. The raging surf pulled the two boats farther apart, making a leap too dangerous to attempt.

Fortunately for those on the *Manila,* the barge was positioned close enough—and parallel—to the shore to make escape an easier task than getting off the *Lafayette.* The men on the *Manila* escaped by climbing on the branches of trees overhanging the barge, or by lowering themselves on a ladder. Once ashore, they rushed to assist the men trapped on the *Lafayette.* The men on the bow, now rapidly breaking apart, were able to jump down. Those on the stern tossed a weighted line to the shore, and when it was secured to a tree, they pulled themselves, hand over hand, to safety. Fireman Patrick Wade slipped from the line and became the day's sole casualty when he was crushed between the two stricken vessels.

When everyone was on shore, the men began the chore of climbing the bluff. What lay ahead was anyone's guess.

~~~

For those stranded when their boats grounded on the shores of western Lake Superior, the nightmare of the horrible storm was just beginning. Their wet clothing clung to their bodies and froze in the subzero temperatures. They had nothing to shelter them from hurricane-force winds. They tried to ignore gnawing hunger. They couldn't guess where they were. But they had to do *something*. Frostbite and hypothermia sniffed at their little remaining energy.

The *Crescent City* crew, perhaps most fortunate of all those stranded, took action almost as soon as they climbed down their ladder to safety. Captain Frank Rice and the *Crescent City*'s first mate volunteered to watch over the grounded freighter until daybreak. The others were to fan out, walk until they located a phone, call the Pittsburgh Steamship office in Duluth, report the *Crescent City*'s predicament and position, and return and await rescue. With any luck, they would accomplish all this in little time—and, with equal fortune, they might find a cup of coffee and breakfast along the way. God willing, dry and warm clothes might be involved.

After all they had been through, they were a ragtag group, no doubt imposing to the eye. Many sailors were rough in appearance on a normal day, but this group, icy and covered with dirt, some bloody, and exhausted from the day's events, probably looked more like escapees from a chain gang than proper churchgoing citizens. That they had no cars and were walking in the driving snow didn't help, either.

Watchman Arthur Daggett was a study unto himself. Short, built like a fireplug, quick tempered and easily provoked, Daggett was an able sailor designed for a lifetime on the lakes and visiting all the dusty port taverns to trade stories about his exploits—and he had stories to tell. He was only twenty-eight years old, but his star-crossed career had placed him in three separate accidents on three separate boats. The first, in 1897, found him treading water after his boat, a wooden schooner, sank; he managed to stay afloat until he was picked up by another vessel in the area. Second, he had been on the *Thomas Wilson* when she was rammed by the *George G. Hadley* in 1902. He and a fellow crewman jumped off the whaleback as she was sinking. Daggett survived; his crewmate did not. Daggett tread water for an hour before he was picked up. Now . . . the *Crescent City*. The debate was whether he was the luckiest or unluckiest man alive.

Crescent City's second mate, H. J. Stephens, and engineer A. E. Buddameyer were first to accomplish their mission of finding a phone. They knocked on the doors of several rural homes, but no one allowed them to enter. They eventually found an elderly couple willing to accommodate them, but they had no phone. The couple offered them much appreciated coffee and bread and gave them directions to an office with a phone. Stephens and Buddameyer's conversation with the Pittsburgh Steamship official broke up in the storm, and the two decided to head to Duluth and visit him in person. This required another long walk and a trolley ride, but they finally made it. They told company official H. W. Brown what had happened and gave him the *Crescent City*'s approximate location. Brown gathered the information, took the two men to a hotel, and provided them with enough money to purchase new clothes. The rest of the crew, Brown assured them, would be taken care of as soon as possible.

The crews of the *Edenborn* and *Madeira* would have their own stories about finding help. Those on the *Edenborn* whiled away the hours following the boat's grounding on the vessel's forward section, which was in no danger of sinking. At daybreak, one of the sailors used a life raft to reach shore. He tied a line from a tree to the *Edenborn*'s bow, a makeshift breeches buoy was constructed by hanging a chair to the line, and First Mate William F. Hornig worked his way to shore. Hornig set out to find a phone, fighting his way through snow. He located a logging camp nearby, but there was no phone there. The nearest phone, they estimated, was 10 miles away. After two failed attempts to fight through deep snow to the site, Hornig hired a local fisherman, Octave Iverson, to use his snowshoes to walk to Two Rivers and hand-deliver a note to a Pittsburgh Steamship representative. It took twelve hours for Iverson to reach his destination, but the letter was delivered, and the official set out to find a boat to pick up the crew. No one knew the *Madeira*'s fate, though there was hope that the crew and barge might be discovered somewhere near the *Edenborn*'s location.

The sunken *Madeira*, of course, would not be located. The eight surviving sailors began their search for help after spending a night and all the next day by a fire they had built near the top of the cliff. They didn't have to look for long. They found a tiny shanty in the woods, whose owner, a man from Superior named Rick Hansen, took them in and fed them his meager supply of food. He then led the crew to another cabin, this one larger but no better prepared to provide for guests. The crew was badly frostbitten and suffering from exposure, and Captain Dissette had hurt his back in the wreck. They needed rest. When the men had warmed enough to go, they were taken to the same lumber company that had assisted those from the *Edenborn*.

Heavy wind and waves buffeted the *William Edenborn* until she was hopelessly lost along the dangerous north shore. She grounded, leaving her crew to a desperate battle to survive for days in the wild.

"Owing to the fact that my feet were frozen and my back injured I was unable to accompany the men that afternoon," Dissette told Pittsburgh Steamship afterward, "but on the following day Hansen took me to the same lumber camp."

Help, the men learned, was on the way.

~~~

The large red storm flag had been posted by the time Captain Richard Humble guided his boat, the *Mataafa,* out of the Duluth harbor and onto the lake. The waves had kicked up a bit, but they weren't anything Humble had not seen during his six years as skipper of the *Mataafa.* He could never have imagined that he was about to sail into a historic storm that would make his boat famous—and give him notoriety he would have given anything to avoid.

At thirty-two, Humble was younger than most holding his position, but he was a first-rate mariner. Boyish and handsome,

Captain Richard Humble of the *Mataafa.* His efforts to save his crew from its ordeal were nothing less than heroic.

with a fondness for cigars, Humble looked more like a deckhand than one in command of a vessel like the *Mataafa.* He had moved quickly through the ranks, proving his ability at every level. Humble grew up in Lexington, Michigan, and met his wife, Jesse, there. They married in 1902 and shortly afterward moved to Conneaut, Ohio, a town not far from Cleveland. He would not be with Jesse and their baby daughter for Thanksgiving, but the winter layup was just around the corner.

The *Mataafa,* constructed by the Cleveland Shipbuilding Company and launched in 1899, was 430 feet in length and carried a crew of twenty-four. The freighter's history, in and out of the water, had been colorful prior to November 27, 1905. She had first sailed as the SS *Pennsylvania*, but after a few months was purchased by the Minnesota Steamship Company and renamed *Mataafa*. In her first year of service, she sustained minor damage when she struck a rock in the Straits of Mackinac, was repaired in Chicago, and was damaged again when she grounded near the Soo Locks. A change in ownership occurred in 1901 when the newly formed Pittsburgh Steamship Company bought the Minnesota Steamship Company.

A number of factors conspired against the *Mataafa* at the time of her departure on November 27. She had been well constructed, but at 1,800 horsepower she was underpowered for a battle against a violent late-season storm, especially when she was loaded with iron ore and towing a barge as large as the *James Nasmyth,* a 366-foot, 3,822-ton barge loaded with coal. One construction feature weighed heavily in the journey: the *Mataafa* had been designed without the standard aft deckhouse, which held crew quarters and the galley. Instead, the men bunked and ate below deck level. In addition, the *Mataafa* lacked the long, below-decks corridors connecting the forward and aft sections of the vessel, allowing sailors to walk the length of the boat without stepping outside in stormy weather; these lengthy passageways were becoming standard in shipbuilding of the day.

The *Mataafa.*

The *Mataafa*'s crew on deck.

These factors, along with the weather and Captain Humble's decisions, contributed to the *Mataafa*'s fate. A storm had been forecast, but when the *Mataafa* left Duluth Harbor at three thirty in the afternoon, sailing conditions were all right. The barometer was falling, and the seas were getting rougher, but the *Mataafa* was a big, capable boat. Like other ship commanders, Humble had remained dockside during the previous storm on November 23. He was now eager to sail and complete this last trip of the season. By his estimation, the likelihood of back-to-back gaggers in so little time was slim.

"The weather conditions," Humble would say, noting that he was aware of the storm warnings, "were such that I did not deem it advisable to remain in port and accordingly started down the lake." He was not alone in his thinking. No one on the *Mataafa* crew voiced any concerns about sailing, and by all indications, it was business as usual on Lake Superior that day, with dozens of boats and barges on the water, oblivious to weather projections.

One other freighter-and-barge combination ran into the storm's fury on Minnesota's northern shore. The *George Spencer*, a wooden bulk carrier, and the *Amboy*, a three-masted wooden schooner in tow, were sailing from Buffalo to Duluth when their path intersected with nature's halfway between the Canadian border and Duluth. Both vessels were loaded with coal.

The two vessels were becoming antiquated in the age of the elongated steel freighters capable of hauling more tonnage than the *Spencer* and *Amboy* combined. The 246-foot *Spencer*, built in 1884 by the Thomas Quayle and Sons Shipyard in Cleveland, had the distinction of being one of the first boats to load iron ore at Two Harbors, which had opened just before the *Spencer* was launched. The *Amboy*, constructed ten years earlier, specifically for the iron ore business, was, at 209 feet, capable of hauling 1,500 tons of cargo per trip. Her productive years of service on the Great Lakes were offset by a series of mishaps that included groundings and on one occasion a near foundering during a storm.

The two vessels were sailing blindly on November 28, 1905, after encountering heavy snow and gale-force winds in northern Minnesota. With compasses spinning and visibility nearly zero, Captain Frank Conlin ordered the *Amboy* cut loose. The fifteen men on the *Spencer* and the nine on the *Amboy* were on their own. The sea tossed them around without mercy.

Both boats hit bottom about 200 yards from shore. They would later learn that they grounded near Thomasville, a town northeast of Split Rock. Without heat and with the storm intensifying by the hour, the crews of both vessels knew that it was only a matter of time before their boats were battered into splinters. They had to find a way to reach land.

Fate cut them a break. A handful of fishermen heard their distress whistles and worked heroically to help them. The stranded sailors tied lines to pieces of wood and life buoys, threw them overboard, and let the waves carry them toward shore. The fishermen waded chest deep into the icy water and retrieved them. They affixed the lines to trees. *Amboy* watchman James Gibson, moving deliberately, hand over hand in the wind, made it to shore. He and the fishermen rigged a breeches buoy, and all those aboard the two grounded vessels were brought safely to shore. Their thirteen-hour ordeal had ended.

~~~

Captain Richard Humble was concerned. The beginning of the trip of the *Mataafa* and *Nasmyth* had been uneventful. The two vessels made good time as they sailed north toward Two Harbors. They were to turn east toward the Apostle Islands before crossing the lake, dipping down to Whitefish Point, and heading to the Soo Locks. The final destination was Lake Erie and its steel mills—a long trip, but one Humble had taken many times over his sixteen years on the lakes.

The predicted storm, with wind out of the northeast, was brewing. It hit Duluth at 6:00 p.m., with heavy snow and winds exceeding 40 miles per hour. Humble ordered his engineer to face the storm with full power, but the two boats struggled for any progress. They were up against roaring winds as they began their turn east to the Apostles, and Humble, not unlike every master directing a vessel in a mighty storm, feared what might happen if the *Mataafa* and *Nasmyth* became caught up in a trough. "The sea had gotten to be so large that it was running over our decks from both sides and was loosening some of the hatch fastenings on the hatches," he noted.

He surrendered to the storm at 4:00 a.m., after more than twelve hours of punishment from the forces of nature. As Humble saw it, he had three options. He could lower his anchors and try to ride out the storm, a proposition with little appeal, since the *Mataafa* and *Nasmyth* were already taking a steady pounding from the storm, and there was no prediction exactly how much longer it would go on. He could try to dock at Two Harbors, which was nearby but would require some tricky maneuvering to locate and enter. Or he might return to Duluth. Humble considered all three options and chose Duluth. "A great many of our hatch bars had become loosened with the heavy seas," he explained, "and I was afraid we were going to lose our hatches, and I knew I would soon have to seek shelter some place. The snow finally cleared up and I could see the shore, and also see Duluth."

The fight to return continued for hours. Humble reasoned that full power from the engine room, accompanied by a strong push from following seas, would hasten the trip to Duluth, but it didn't work that way. Just holding course turned out to be a burden. The largest seas Humble had ever seen lifted the stern out of the lake, and the engineer had to power down to avoid the tremendous shudder that rocked the boat when the overspinning propeller slammed back down into the resistance of the waters. The men shoveled coal as fast as possible to keep power at a maximum. In the front of the boat, the wheelsman was fortunate to break even in his attempts to steer the *Mataafa* and *Nasmyth* away from the shore.

The plodding pace actually worked to the benefit of the two boats. The Duluth harbor, it turned out, experienced problems that might have been exacerbated had the *Mataafa* arrived earlier in the day. Shortly after noon on that November 28, the *R. W. England,* a 368-foot steamer under the command of Richard England, was prepared to enter the long, narrow canal leading to the Duluth harbor. The boat had begun its turn into the canal when England judged that his craft would not make it, and he ordered his wheelsman to turn hard and

The *R. W. England* (seen here at her launching) grounded after missing the Duluth harbor in hurricane-force weather.

back into the lake. The boat successfully completed the maneuver, but the towering waves, whipped up by winds gusting to 80 miles per hour, pushed the *England* toward the shore. She was driven aground 2½ miles south of the canal, her stern coming to rest on a sandy beach, well out of the water and free of any danger.

Approximately a half hour later, the *Isaac L. Ellwood,* her cargo hold loaded with iron ore, attempted to enter the canal. The *Ellwood* had taken a similar approach as the *Mataafa,* leaving the previous day, when sailing conditions seemed manageable. She was scheduled to stop at Two Harbors, but by the time they were approaching the port, snow was falling heavily, and the seas were rough enough that Captain C. H. Cummings judged it too risky to attempt to enter the harbor. Instead, he decided to stay in the area and enter the harbor when conditions improved.

"We remained outside, part of the time heading into the wind and part of the time going with the wind and sea, for the purpose of remaining in the vicinity of Two Harbors, hoping the gale would subside," recalled Chief Engineer Thomas Treleaven. "We continued these tactics until 9:15 o'clock a.m. of November 28, when the wind and sea became so violent that it was deemed inadvisable to longer remain outside."

The 478-foot *Isaac L. Ellwood* glanced off Duluth Harbor's north pier but was successfully towed to safety shortly before the *Mataafa* arrived at the site in the same storm.

The storm had become so fierce that it had loosened some of the vessel's hatch covers, creating a clear and present danger to vessel and crew. "Two sections of No. 12 Hatch came off and we succeeded with difficulty in again battening it down," Alex Brown, the *Ellwood*'s first mate, said later. "All the other hatches began to show indications of loosening because of the heavy seas that were sweeping our deck. We then deemed it inadvisable to proceed further down and turned about seeking a port of refuge, heading for Duluth."

As the five-year-old, 478-footer attempted to enter the canal, a gigantic wave lifted her, causing her stern and then her bow to hit lake bottom. "When we were probably within a length of the piers, I felt her touch bottom," Captain Cummings said. "I distinctly felt her strike bottom three times. Then we came in and hit the north pier with our starboard bow. After striking the north pier with the bluff of her starboard bow, she sheered toward the south pier, her stern swinging to the northward, which caused the vessel to collide about amidships with the outer end of the north pier, breaking a hole in the vessel's side, at a point about amidships."

People gathered nearby were horrified by the sight of the *Ellwood*'s bouncing off the north pier and then smashing into the south pier. Water flooded through the tears on both sides of the boat. Cummings guided the *Ellwood* down the length of the canal and into the inner harbor, where he was met by tugboats that ushered her into shallower water. She immediately sank to the bottom in just over 20 feet of water. No one was seriously injured.

The *Mataafa* turned up an hour later. Captain Humble had another decision to make as the freighter and her escort approached Duluth. The two vessels had taken such a beating by the storm that Humble figured that there was no way both would be able to negotiate the canal together. It would have been tough enough for a single boat to pass through the narrow passageway in seas tossing vessels around like toys; two boats would only get in each other's way. Humble calculated that the *Nasmyth*, if cut loose, could drop anchor, ride out the storm, and be pulled to safety when the waters settled down. He contacted Captain Donald Graham, the *Nasmyth*'s skipper, and relayed his plans. In hindsight, it was the correct decision: the *Nasmyth* survived the storm and was retrieved without serious damage.

A large crowd had gathered dockside in Duluth. That was common in the port town. People would assemble, even in nasty weather, to watch the boats come and go. Captains would acknowledge them with blasts from their boats' whistles, and those gathered would respond enthusiastically. There had been roars of approval when the *Ellwood,* after careening off the stone walls of the canal, sailed into the inner harbor. Now, with the *Mataafa* making its wide turn at the entrance of the canal, the onlookers held their collective breath.

The strong currents near the opening of the canal could present problems for the big bulk carriers sailing through them. And the currents, combined with the incredible push from the waves, were treacherous as the *Mataafa* aimed its bow at the center of the canal. Humble called for full speed, hoping to power the *Mataafa* through the roiling waters. Nothing helped. An enormous wave rolled under the boat and raised her stern high out of the water. The *Mataafa*'s bow submarined until it hit bottom. The stern came down and sent a tremendous shudder throughout the boat, the *Mataafa* surging forward and into the north pier. "It sheered to the starboard end of the north pier," Humble explained, "and I ordered my wheel hard to the starboard in the hopes of clearing the north pier, but we could not swing quick enough and hit it a hard blow on the bluff of the starboard bow, doing considerable damage to the bow."

Mataafa impaled on the north pier. Huge crowds gathered in support of the stricken *Mataafa,* in clear view of people onshore. It seemed impossible to believe that a powerful vessel was incapable of being saved or assisted so close to safety.

But the lake was nowhere near finished with a freighter that dared to test its fury: the assault was only beginning. The force of the waves swung the boat around and backward until her bow was pointed north and the stern was roughly 100 feet from the pier. The *Mataafa* was now parallel to the shore. Her rudder was broken away, and her propeller was no longer functional. The waves smashed a lifeboat and life raft and sent another lifeboat splintering against a pier. The crewmen could see dry land but had no way of reaching it. The waves smashed the pilothouse windows, sending shards of broken glass everywhere, cutting the face and hands of wheelsman George McClure, who still clung tightly to the wheel. Humble shouted for more power but was told the engine was dying. The *Mataafa* was dead in the water, totally at the mercy of the waves that seemed to be feasting on her. They split the boat at hatch eight, and the stern began to sag.

Lake water boarded the *Mataafa* at will. It rolled over her decks. It gushed through port holes. It tumbled down the stern steps. It put an ending to any hope of restarting the engine and at least heating the vessel. Humble tried to visit the stern but was driven back to the pilothouse by waves that threatened to wash anyone on deck overboard.

The very lives of the men on the stern were in peril. With water flooding every inch belowdecks, they had no time to consider anything but escaping. That meant only one action on a vessel whose design did not include an aft deckhouse: they had to rush outside, in temperatures hovering at zero, in clothing wet from the boarding water. Once outside, the men tried to hide behind the smokestack or anything else that might shield them from the blustery wind. They would not survive for long in the open.

Rescue would not occur any time soon. After witnessing the grounding of the *England*, Fred Gosford, a resident nearby, had rushed on foot to Duluth. He visited the U.S. Lifesaving Station and reported the accident to Captain Murdoch McLennan, the unit's commander. The *England*'s crew, as far as Gosford knew, was still onboard the stranded boat and might need help. McLennan and his men quickly set out to offer assistance. They were absent from the station when the *Mataafa* ran into the stone piers.

The nine men at the back of the *Mataafa* had no time to wait. Air

The *Mataafa,* stranded and incapacitated, was unable to be helped during the height of the storm.

temperatures were falling steadily, and the sun would be setting within a couple of hours. Carl Carlson, a fireman, desperately attempted to leap from the stern to one of the piers. He failed. He plunged into the lake and drowned.

The only recourse would to be to somehow reach the front of the *Mataafa* and take refuge in the pilothouse or crew quarters. Reaching the bow required a herculean effort. Water and ice covered the spar deck. Waves pummeled the boat, and the fence railing (two boat-length strands of wire about waist high) offered little protection from being washed overboard. The crack in the middle of the freighter was widening as the stern settled on the lake bottom. Still, someone had to risk it.

Second Mate Herbert Emigh went first. Under the usual circumstances, Emigh would have been in the wheelhouse with the captain, mates, wheelsmen, and deck crew. He had gone to the *Mataafa*'s stern to supervise the cutting loose of the *Nasmyth,* and had yet to return to the bow when the *Mataafa* struck the piers and began to fall apart. He had argued with the others that they were all certain to die if they didn't cross over the 200 feet of deck to the front. Emigh half-walked, half-crawled on all fours across the deck. He tried to calculate when the massive waves would wash over the decks. When they did, he hung on to the fence rail, bracing himself against the powerful onslaughts that could drive him overboard. He slipped on ice and fell. The men on the stern watched and shouted encouragement, as did the people onshore, witnesses to a drama they never thought they would see.

Progress was excruciatingly slow, but Emigh eventually reached the front of the boat. One of the *Mataafa* crewmen ventured out, grabbed him, and hauled him, soaking wet and freezing, into the deckhouse.

Porter Fred Saunders, fireman Charles Byrne, and fireman Thomas Woodgate lined up for their turns. The seas knocked them off their feet, hurled debris and driftwood at them, even pushed them overboard. The men clung to the rail and pulled themselves back aboard, back to the slippery challenge of moving forward. Saunders and Byrne succeeded in reaching the bow. Woodgate, after being washed overboard, dangling over the water, and being spared only by his tight grip on the railing, gave up and returned to the stern. No one else would face the dangerous crossing. The *Mataafa* crew was now permanently divided between bow and stern, between those who would survive and those who would not.

Captain Humble couldn't believe that no rescue attempts had been made. He seized a megaphone and shouted for help. He had no way of knowing that the lifesaving station personnel were preoccupied with helping the *England*. It was impossible for Humble and the others to accept that they were stranded, in grave danger so close to shore.

～～～

Darkness was falling on Duluth by the time the U.S. Lifesaving Station team returned from assisting the *England*. No one was in immediate danger on the beached freighter, and when a messenger arrived and relayed all that had happened to the *Mataafa* and how the men in the stern were trapped outside, Murdock McLennan and his crew abandoned any further work on the *England* and hastened to Duluth.

Captain Humble had been busy in their absence. On three occasions, he had tried to get lines to shore, attaching to them a dresser drawer, and, later, doors. He prayed that the seas would carry them ashore. If lines were attached to the shore, they might be able to rig up a makeshift breeches buoy. Unfortunately, all three attempts ended in disappointment. Three pairs of lines never reached their destination; the third pair froze and was rendered useless.

The lifesaving team arrived with professional equipment. The fading daylight worked against them, as they could barely see their target when they fired heavy lines fixed with grappling hooks from a Lyle gun. Humble shouted that the Lyle gun should target the stern. The attempts were futile. One hit the spar deck and could not be retrieved. Others missed the boat entirely. One hit its target, but it was frozen and broke apart. Launching a lifeboat was out of the question. The men would have to wait for sunrise. Only a miracle would spare the men on the stern.

~~~

For the men on the *Mataafa,* each passing hour brought a greater sense of desperation. The men on the stern had probably frozen to death—a thought that Richard Humble preferred to avoid. Those men weren't just coworkers; they were friends. Bill Most, his thirty-six-year-old chief engineer, lived in Cleveland, yet during the shipping season, his wife moved to Chicago and lived with relatives. Most's assistant, Jim Early, lived in Buffalo; his wife had just given birth to a daughter, his first child, only weeks earlier. Chicago resident Carl Carlson, a fireman, had lost his life when he jumped from the boat and drowned; he had signed on the *Mataafa* in Superior, Wisconsin, and was new to the crew. Cook Walter Bush was one of three African Americans working on the boat. The idea of retrieving their frozen bodies saddened him.

The men on the bow stayed as active as the bone-numbing cold allowed. Without heat, they did anything they could think of for minimal warmth. They huddled together for body warmth. They stomped their feet; they danced. They gathered as many kerosene lamps as they could find, with the hope that even a tiny bit of heat might hold them over until morning. They sucked on icicles for moisture. They talked nonstop, keeping their minds hopeful. What they did not do was eat, drink hot liquids, or, most important, sleep. Dozing would have been fatal. "At times it was hard to keep them up, as they became tired and would get anxious to lie down," Humble recalled. "I kept them up, however, until about three o'clock in the morning, when I saw that they were going to freeze on me before daylight."

One by one, the lamps flickered out. With a couple of hours of darkness remaining, Captain Humble knew that he had to do something to manufacture warmth. Acting on his own, he sloshed through

3-feet-deep water belowdecks and hacked wood from rooms and collected oily rags to use as kindling. He had the crew build a small fire in the windlass room.

Outside, on Duluth's shore and beach, thousands of people (one estimate said ten thousand, though that seems unlikely, given the size of the population and the weather conditions) kept an overnight vigil, some as a way of offering encouragement to the *Mataafa* survivors, others out of curiosity. They built bonfires and huddled together, their eyes fixed on the light coming from the silhouette of the broken vessel. The storm, so vicious the previous day, was settling down. The spectators might witness a heroic rescue.

~~~

Men from the lifesaving station assembled at dawn. They had one lifeboat. The seas were still choppy, though they had died down enough for an attempted rescue. The men began the arduous task of rowing out to the *Mataafa* at seven thirty. Waves rocked the lifeboat, nearly upsetting it on numerous occasions. When the lifeboat reached the *Mataafa*, seven crewmen were lowered, cautiously and individually, and rowed to shore. Those gathered gawked at the sight of those men, no more and no less sailors than those they had seen over the years, on boats or in bars and restaurants, on the streets or in houses of worship. Seven souls who had relentlessly fought to stay alive: three were taken by ambulance to the hospital, four to the St. Louis Hotel in downtown Duluth.

While the seven were being transported to safety, those remaining on board the *Mataafa* snacked on lunches and drank brandy sent up in a basket by McLennan and staff. After they had consumed their first meal in more than thirty hours, Captain Humble and First Mate Wally Brown gingerly moved to the back of the *Mataafa* to survey the damage that the storm had wreaked on boat and crew.

"The first mate and myself crawled along aft to see if any of the aft crew were alive," Humble said. "We found four bodies frozen in the ice on deck near the smokestack, and could see that no one could possibly be alive around there." It was a grisly but necessary duty. Nothing about the stern's condition surprised them. It sat much lower in the

The Coast Guard rescued *Mataafa* crew members the morning after the freighter stranded near the mouth of Duluth Harbor on November 28, 1905. Nine crewmen perished, either by drowning or by freezing to death when they were unable to shelter from subzero temperatures.

water than the bow, all but separated from the bow by the water's weight that pulled it downward until it touched down on the bottom of the lake. The *Mataafa* was almost cut in two. Her smokestack wound up at an angle to the deck.

It pained Humble and Brown to see what remained of the crew. Twelve men had sailed as part of the stern crew on this trip. Three had made it safely to the bow; a fourth, Carl Carlson, who had leapt to his death, had washed ashore. That left eight. Three were nowhere to be found and were presumably swept overboard. The other five were found frozen, covered in layers of ice formed from freezing spray and water. All had struggled in vain to shelter themselves from the continuous beating they took from waves and subzero air temperatures. Deckhand Thomas McCloud had climbed into a ventilator shaft and died there, gripping the entrance and staring out at the shore. The others, virtually embalmed in ice, were in the open air, one man so encased in ice that he would have to be chopped from the deck when the bodies were removed from the *Mataafa*.

The broken *Mataafa* after the storm subsided. The vessel was eventually towed, repaired, and placed back into service.

Back in Duluth, some crew members answered reporters' questions about their ordeal. Their concern for their colleagues became an act of mourning. "Nine poor fellows are dead in the stern," Harry Larson, a deckhand from nearby Superior, Wisconsin, told reporter Mary McFadden, the first woman journalist on the *Duluth News Tribune*. "Oh God, it's awful. We knew our nine comrades in the aft part were doomed." Watchman Ernest Dietz, warming in the hotel, also held little hope for those in the back of the boat, though he had yet to hear anything official. "We have heard nothing from the fellows in the back end," he said. "I guess they all perished. It was a dirty shame. They were a nice set of fellows. If you hear anything about them, let us know."

The rescue team returned and removed the rest of the survivors. Richard Humble, by tradition, was the last to leave the *Mataafa*, which would remain where she was, a solemn reminder to Duluth and the shipping world, until the following spring.

～～～

The Pittsburgh Steamship Company, with its fleet of 112 vessels sailing on the Great Lakes, absorbed the greatest loss in terms of lost or damaged boats in the storm. As soon as word spread about the storm and the vessels caught out in it, company president Harry Coulby traveled to Duluth to survey the damage firsthand, talk to the skippers of the boats involved, and take care of any other business at hand.

Coulby was known as a no-nonsense leader. Firm with his beliefs and convictions, he brooked very little criticism or disagreement from those under his command. He was a self-made man, and he demanded nothing but the best from those working under him. Born in England in 1865, he moved to the United States in 1884, and working odd jobs and making his way westward, he eventually landed in Cleveland and found employment with Pickens Mather and Company, a shipping company in the exploding Great Lakes

Harry Coulby.

shipping industry. He latched onto the newly formed U.S. Steel company's Pittsburgh Steamship, and he found his calling. He held an office job in Cleveland, but he learned the essentials of the Great Lakes shipping industry by hitching rides on the freighters. Business was booming. Pittsburgh Steamship was growing exponentially, and Coulby was the company's top dog before he turned forty.

Pittsburgh Steamship provided iron ore to U.S. Steel through a burgeoning Great Lakes trade. The company built boats as fast as they could manufacture them, and the vessels were constantly evolving. Coulby had cut his seafaring teeth on the short-lived whalebacks; in little time, he saw the boats grow in length and carry huge cargoes. This was efficiency that Coulby could appreciate. The bulk carriers in the Pittsburgh Steamship line were called "tin stackers" after their silver-painted smokestacks.

Coulby caught a train from Cleveland to Chicago, and another from Chicago to Duluth. When he and W. W. Smith, Pittsburgh Steamship's marine superintendent, arrived in Duluth, eight hours after the dead sailors had been removed from the *Mataafa*, they heard one alarming story after another. Twelve of the Pittsburgh Steamship vessels had been sunk or grounded in the storm; an equal number of crewmen had lost their lives. The expense of refloating the boats, added to the costs of vessels lost, would be staggering. Coulby's company was no different from the rest of the shipping firms that avoided the high expense of insuring their fleets.

Coulby and Smith didn't have to read the Duluth newspapers or talk to the city's people to know that there would be plenty of finger-pointing over the coming weeks. It was only human nature: somebody had to be blamed for the loss of the *Mataafa* and other vessels. Richard Humble, of course, was near the top of the list. Why had he taken his vessel out into that storm? Had he made the correct decisions when trying to reenter the harbor? Could he have done anything different to save the men trapped on the stern? He was young, but he had been a master long enough to know what actions to take in an emergency of this order.

Corporate greed (and, by extension, Harry Coulby) also entered into the discussion. Big corporations chased profits at every turn. They were especially concerned in the late season, when unpredictable weather could cancel shippings and cost them plenty in profits. This had been the case a week earlier, when the *Mataafa* and other freighters remained tied at the docks during a storm. Had Pittsburgh Steamship pressured its boats and barges into heading out this time, even though a storm had been forecast and red warning flags had been posted? Company officials would always claim, with some justification, that departures were ultimately the captain's decision, and that he was responsible for the safety of boat, cargo, and crew, but young captains like Humble felt the heat to perform. They were vulnerable. They could be—and occasionally were—replaced.

Finally, the U.S. Lifesaving Station was brought under considerable scrutiny in the case of the *Mataafa*. Personnel had been 2 miles away, assisting the *England*, when the *Mataafa* accident occurred. It had taken a lot of invaluable time for them to return to Duluth and set up rescue operations. Could the sailors on the *Mataafa*'s stern have been spared if the lifesaving crew had been in Duluth? After all, those on the *England* were in no danger. More important, the lifesaving group had failed in the day's twilight hours to create a breeches buoy necessary to save those caught in the back of the *Mataafa*.

People demanded answers. . . .

Coulby, Smith, and Augustus Wolvin (the man Coulby had replaced at head of Pittsburgh Steamship, now living in Minnesota) created a headquarters in the Wolvin Building in Duluth. The next day was Thanksgiving, and they wanted minimal answers by then. Reporters, isolated from their room, needed something new to write about, and they weren't going away until they had new information.

The threesome acted decisively. They gathered as much information as available, and they called in four captains from their vessels for questioning: Frank Rice from *Crescent City,* A. J. Talbot from *Edenborn,* Dell Wright from *Lafayette,* and Richard Humble from *Mataafa.* They monitored all developing information about the *Mataafa.* They briefed the press on their findings.

Humble, still exhausted and traumatized by the events of the past two days, met with reporters, patiently answered their questions, and addressed rumors of Pittsburgh Steamship's culpability in the decision to sail into the storm. The decision to sail, he insisted, had been his—and his only. "Never in my experience with the company have I, or any other captain, been urged to put out when he felt that the weather was too great," he said. He was willing to shoulder the blame for the *Mataafa's* being out on the lake when the storm hit: "If there were any error in judgment it was on my own." In making his statement, Humble made certain that the public understood that the weather, though a little rough, was nothing special when he departed from Duluth.

Coulby had heard the rumors about Pittsburgh Steamship ordering their boats to sail. The accusation angered him. He was more than willing to let Humble accept responsibility for the decision to sail. "The company spares no expense to keep its ships seaworthy," he said, adding that "our captains have positive orders that no one of the company would be permitted to give any orders as to when they should leave port or seek shelter."

The lifesaving crew, in general, and Captain McLennan, specifically, had the most abuse heaped on them. It seemed that every Duluth resident had an opinion on the men who had spent the day in the bitter cold helping those on the *England* before tending to the

Mataafa. Their harshest critics called them inept, cowardly, lazy, misguided, incapable of their doing jobs. It didn't matter that Humble and Coulby defended them by stating that they had done everything in their power to assist the men on the *Mataafa*, that no one could have gone up against the forces of nature and won. Kind words by other captains and sailors were waved off, dismissed as cases of shipping folks sticking up for their own.

McLennan was deeply wounded by the criticism. He knew the difficulties his men had faced, how they were exhausted and hungry and cold when they returned to Duluth, only to face another shift of intense work under the worst conditions imaginable. He and his men were being whipped by people who had done nothing for the *Mataafa*; they had no experience in these matters, and they never would. Yet, here they were. . . . McLennan initially refused all interview requests. He was too angry, too depressed, too tired. Explaining himself to critics would bring no resolution. When he eventually backed down, his tormented emotions rose to the surface. The big bear of a man, who had devoted eighteen of his forty-six years to the service of those working on the Great Lakes, broke down in tears. "There is no man

Wreckage of the *Mataafa*.

in Duluth who feels the loss of those men more than I do," he said. He noted that "it was utterly, hopelessly impossible" to land a rescue boat in the seas he found that evening, nor was it possible for a tugboat to have attempted it. Their sole hope was to fire lines at a target that, with the loss of daylight, was difficult to see. "I was powerless when the shot lines failed, and knew it."

Mary McFadden of the *Duluth Herald Tribune* interviewed McLennan—on Thanksgiving Day, no less—and she didn't shy away from asking pointed questions based on criticism she had been hearing. McLennan, who would go on to serve an additional quarter century until his retirement, answered all questions with as much patience as he could muster. Reporters could be tough, but McLennan found an ally in Duluth's *Labor World*. McLennan, the *Labor World* concluded, did everything in his power for those onboard the *Mataafa*. If anything, he was limited by a lack of needed lifesaving equipment.

The debates would not end any time soon. The specter of the tragedy, manifest in the misty air at the end of the pier, would act as fuel for the arguments. The real culprit was mentioned in a shorthand that would last well into the next century. The storm would be called the *Mataafa* blow.

～～～

The *Edna G.*, a coal-powered tugboat based in Two Harbors, was assigned the difficult work of plowing through the remainder of the storm and collecting the crewmen from the *Crescent City, Edenborn, Madeira,* and others.

The cleanup of the storm's damage was going to be prodigious. The high winds and driving seas churned up the kinds of flotsam ordinarily submerged, sometimes for years. Aside from the driftwood and other expected refuse, roiling waters could stir up wreckage from submerged freighters, and on a rare occasion, remains of a sailor lost in a wreck and never recovered. This storm coughed up a headless, skeletal torso, which, some speculated, belonged to one of the missing crewmen from the *Thomas Wilson,* the whaleback brought down three years earlier. He was taken to the coroner's office, but no positive identification was forthcoming.

Another negative aspect of storm damage could be attributed to a small percentage of locals who preyed on grounded vessels. The grounded *Crescent City* was victimized by thieves, who stripped the boat of anything valuable after the crew had abandoned the freighter. They ransacked the crew quarters, yanking open dresser drawers and stealing money and jewelry; they took artifacts from the boat—life preservers, barometers, the captain's megaphone. The turkeys in the cooler, intended for Thanksgiving dinner, were lifted.

The *Edna G.* picked up the crew from the *Crescent City* and delivered them to Duluth, before swinging north and searching the coastline for the missing *Edenborn* and *Madeira*. The tugboat would not find the sunken barge, but it spotted the *Edenborn* perched on the rocks, badly beaten by the wind and waves but still above water. No one was onboard. The tugboat crew knew of the *Edenborn*'s survivors from the word delivered by messenger, and they were aware of the logging camp. When they arrived at the site, they found the surviving crew of both vessels, safe and warm, well fed, eager to get home.

Wreckage of the *Lafayette* was towed into Duluth Harbor.

The storm blew out, as all storms do, and like all serious storms, this one left behind a debris field, part substance, part imagination, the former in the destruction, the latter in the way that cause and effect swirled around the story. More than a century would pass, and the storm would still be graded as the worst in Lake Superior's history. The lives lost, the vessels sunk or crippled—they would linger in memory like a lasting soreness, like the lake itself, freezing in part every winter, then thawing, freezing and thawing.

Other tragedies occurred on Lake Superior during the storm, tragedies removed from Minnesota but looming in history. The *Ira H. Owen*, a 262-foot bulk carrier loaded with 116,500 bushels of barley scheduled to haul from Duluth to Buffalo, another of those last trips of the season, tallied the largest figure in lives lost when she mysteriously disappeared and was never seen again. The eighteen-year-old freighter, carrying a crew of nineteen, slipped out of the Duluth Ship Canal at noon on Monday, November 27. Storm flags had been posted, but like the *Mataafa*, which would sail out of the same harbor a few hours later, the *Owen* had remained docked during the storm of the

All nineteen hands aboard the 262-foot *Ira H. Owen* were lost when the bulk carrier disappeared at the height of the 1905 storm.

previous week. Her captain had used the time to supervise the overhaul of the boat's hatch fastenings, and when the storm moved out of the area, he was ready to move. His first mate, the newly enlisted Thomas Honner, had been brought on board to assist the captain, Joseph Hulligan, who had grown ill. What happened to the *Owen* was never precisely known. The captain of another freighter, the *Harold B. Nye*, reported seeing a twin-stacker similar to the *Owen*, barely visible through the heavy snow, northwest of Outer Island. The vessel was sounding its distress signal. The *Nye*, struggling to stay afloat in the ever-increasing storm, could offer no assistance. The captain thought that the stricken vessel could have been the *Owen*, but visibility had been so poor that he could not be certain. Two days later, another laker spotted wreckage and life preservers marked *Ira H. Owen* but no signs of life or bodies of sailors. The *Owen* had sailed into oblivion.

~~~

The Pittsburgh Steamship Company absorbed the heaviest blows delivered by the storm. Ten of its vessels, none insured, were sunk or damaged. It was going to cost an unprecedented amount to refloat and repair the grounded vessels. As for the total losses . . . the tally for the lost *Madeira, Edenborn,* and *Lafayette* was going to be more than a half-million dollars (in early twentieth-century money) with an added sum of lost cargo to be factored in. Nasty weather had strongly affected the 1905 shipping season throughout the Great Lakes; more than two hundred sailors had perished on the five bodies of water in this single season. Something had to be done, but what?

Harry Coulby made phone calls and crunched numbers. He organized. As head of the company deploying the largest fleet of vessels under one ownership in the world, he wielded great power and influence. Competing firms shared mutual interests, and if they joined forces, the politicians in Washington, D.C., would have no choice but to listen. Under Coulby's direction, a coalition combining the Lake Carriers' Association, vessels' masters, and vessel owners was formed. Coulby and Harvey Goulder, a Cleveland attorney specializing in maritime law, proceeded on to the nation's capital, hoping to secure enough funding to build several lighthouses.

Not that the freighters and barges grounding in the area in the 1905 storm might have been spared by guidance from a new lighthouse: they were being pushed into land by raging seas as much as by masters' confusion over the vessels' exact location. But as far as Coulby was concerned, the drama was effective in gaining the attention and sympathy of a congressional audience.

The strategy worked. The overall process consumed a year to get through the House and Senate, but in March 1907 Congress appropriated $500,000 for the construction of lighthouses throughout the Great Lakes, including $75,000 for the construction of what would become the Split Rock Lighthouse and fog signal.

With no roadway available to the crews building the Split Rock Lighthouse, supplies had to be hoisted up the bare face of the high bluff leading to the construction site.

The early stages of construction of the Split Rock Lighthouse, which was necessitated by the navigational destruction around the north shore during the 1905 storm.

The logistics for creating the lighthouse and surrounding buildings were complex. No roads existed in the wild, sparsely populated area, so all access to the site had to come from the water. That meant designing a means of delivering workers and materials to the top of the sheer 110 feet of rock that had to be scaled to reach the summit of the proposed location for the lighthouse, keepers' quarters, and other buildings. Construction of the octagonal brick lighthouse, designed by Ralph Russell Tinkham, commenced in June 1909.

Prior to that, workers constructed three buildings, eventually used as storage units, to house the supervisors while the lighthouse was being built. Laborers, supplied by Duluth's L. D. Campbell construction firm, lived in tents. To keep the workers content, the construction company hired a chef to serve French delicacies. Men and more than 300 tons of building materials were transported to the top of the cliff on a steam-driven hoist and derrick built specifically for the project. Boats would arrive and onload, and the supplies would be lifted to the site. Production ceased when heavy winds blew in, and no construction occurred during the winter months. Costs for the construction, at $73,000, came in under budget but prevented the installation of the second-order lens as planned. A third-order light was installed instead.

With the lighthouse completed and overlooking Lake Superior, a road leading to the site was completed, and the Split Rock Lighthouse became one of the most visited of the lights around the Great Lakes.

The workmanship evident on the lighthouse's design and construction displayed an astonishing example of splendor in isolation. Fashioned out of yellow brick, the lighthouse rose 54 feet into the sky, sending a beam more than 22 nautical miles. The foghorn could be heard by vessels 5 miles away. Ten buildings—the light, three frame houses for living quarters, and an assortment of storage structures—gave the complex a community feeling. The light shone for the first time on July 31, 1910.

The lighthouse was not only functional: the sight of the structure rising high on the cliff and overlooking the water like a sentinel attracted tourists after a road leading to the site was built in 1924. The accessibility made Split Rock Lighthouse one of the most photographed and visited lighthouses in the United States.

Hurricane on the Lakes, 1913

~~~

The storm came as no surprise. The rough weather had been predicted, the warning flags posted. The 1905 storm that devastated Lake Superior was still fresh in meteorologists' minds. After all, it had been only eight years ago. The storm approaching had the potential to pack a wallop, depending on how the system tracked, but there was no foolproof way of projecting that.

No one could possibly predict the intensity and endurance of what hit the Great Lakes region on November 7–10, 1913. No one had seen anything like it since weather statistics had been recorded, and nothing like this weather event has visited the Great Lakes since then. The 1905 storm ranks as the most severe in Lake Superior history, and this storm would not replace it. Other violent storms have visited the lakes and caused great damage, but historians, backed by numbers, agree that this was the worst to occur on all the lakes.

For four days, nature attacked the region, the first two days on the upper lakes, the next two, on the lower ones. When it departed the area, twelve freighters had been sunk, thirty-one more had been grounded, and dozens had suffered heavy damage. More than 250 sailors lost their lives. Even lightships were torn away from their anchors and tossed about. Snow fell relentlessly, burying cities, most notably Cleveland, in record-shattering totals.

Nothing hinted of a storm capable of producing such numbers. To weather observers, regional and national, this system seemed consistent with the type producing the typical November Great Lakes storm—or, at worst, gale conditions in spots on the lakes. Then again, the Weather Bureau, forty-three years old, was slow and tedious in comparison to today's standard. Weather was measured by temperature, wind velocity and direction, barometric pressure, and precipitation; these measurements were recorded by regional weather stations and forwarded to the national office, which drew up weather maps and sent projections back to the regional offices. This was a painstaking, time-consuming process, but in the case of storms, the national projections no longer applied by the time the regional offices received them. Also noteworthy was the fact that the regional figures might have changed significantly by the time they reached the national office. Wind velocity and direction could change with little warning; barometric pressure could plunge.

The 1913 storm followed the usual pattern for the development of late-season storms. It began in early November in Alaska, dropped to the Pacific Northwest, bringing frigid Canadian air down with it, and moved swiftly along the border between Canada and the United States. It was, in every respect, what the weather watchers referred to as an Alberta clipper.

While this was happening, another system, originating in the southwestern region of the United States, was working its way from west to east, traveling in a northeastern direction, sweeping across the Great Plains and aiming itself at the upper Great Lakes. Nasty, potentially violent weather might be expected if the two systems merged.

They did. On Thursday, November 6, the two systems had created a powerful storm front that had dumped snow on the Dakotas and was moving into western Minnesota. Its path suggested stormy conditions on the southern part of Lake Superior and most of Lake Michigan. Storm flags were posted on those lakes at the ports, and the majority of captains decided to keep their boats in. Those who decided to take their vessels out into the storm were in for a bumpy ride.

~~~

There was an international aura to the *Leafield,* a 248-foot tramp steamer, built and launched in Sunderland, England, in 1896 as part of a three-boat group purchased by the Algoma Central Steamship Lines, all three vessels finding their way to the Great Lakes via the

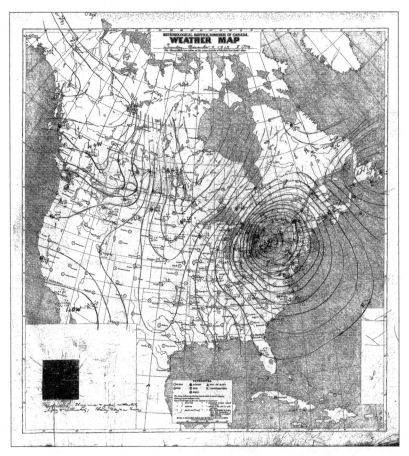

A weather map issued by the Canadian Meteorological Service dated Sunday, November 9, 1913, shows the storm at its peak centered over Lake Huron at 8:00 p.m. At that time the official wind velocity recorded in Port Huron was 56 to 58 miles per hour, but those on the lake claimed it was much higher.

St. Lawrence Seaway. Algoma Central was a Canadian company, and the *Leafield*'s eighteen-man crew hailed from Collinwood, Ontario.

Bad luck seemed to follow all three of the English boats. The *Monkshaven,* four years older than the *Leafield,* was lost in 1905, the first victim of the *Mataafa* blow. She was driven aground, bow first, on Angus Island, near Thunder Bay. Her crew was able to escape, but after being exposed to a relentless battering from the seas, the boat was declared a total loss.

The second of the three boats, the *Theano*, did no better. The year following the loss of the *Monkshaven*, the 255-foot *Theano*, under the command of Captain George Pearson, met her doom on November 17 while fighting through snow and heavy winds in Thunder Bay. She wound up on Trowbridge Island, and after laboring to relaunch her, captain and crew abandoned ship—a fortunate move. Their lifeboats had barely pulled away from the boat before icy water hit the hot boilers and a huge explosion rocked the boat, sending her back into deep water.

The *Leafield* lived her own star-crossed life. On the evening of August 17, 1912, sailing under Andrew "Sandy" McIntyre, the *Leafield* sustained heavy damage as the result of human error. Loaded with iron ore, the *Leafield* was navigating through a passage known for an especially dangerous shoal. McIntyre had supervised the boat's alignment with the range lights before retiring to his quarters, but his wheelsman veered off course and ran the *Leafield* into the shoal, tearing a 140-foot-long and 15-foot-wide gash into the bottom of the boat. The *Leafield* was salvaged and repaired at the cost of two months of dry-dock work. McIntyre was replaced.

Just over a year later, on Sunday, November 9, 1913, the *Leafield* sailed for the last time. The destination was Sault Ste. Marie to Port Arthur, with a cargo of steel rails. The *Leafield*, tossed around by the storm, presented little opposition to the heavy snow and wind. A pas-

The 250-foot *Leafield* disappeared without a trace while carrying a load of railroad rails and trace fastenings during the 1913 storm. Its wreckage has never been located.

senger vessel, the *Hamonic,* piloted by R. D. Foote, barely winning its own contest against the storm, reached Port Arthur in the nick of time. Foote reported spotting the *Leafield,* in great distress, on the rocks and being pounded by waves. Another skipper, W. C. Jordan of the *Franz,* reported seeing the *Leafield* earlier in the day, barely holding her own against the storm, but he lost visual contact with the freighter and grew apprehensive only when his boat, sailing about 20 miles behind the *Leafield,* arrived at Port Arthur and there was no sign of the *Leafield.* Jordan's brother-in-law, Fred Bagley, worked as the *Leafield*'s second mate.

No one would know what exactly happened to the boat. There was speculation that her steel rails might have shifted, causing her to back off the rocks and into the deep water near the shore of Angus Island, where Captain Foote had seen her. Tugboats sent to the scene found nothing—no bodies, no survivors, no wreckage, no indications that the *Leafield* had been anywhere near the site, so near to where the *Monkshaven* had grounded five years earlier. The *Leafield* had disappeared, taking its crew of eighteen, all from Collingwood, Ontario, to their graves. The undiscovered wreckage makes the boat one of the Great Lakes unresolved mysteries.

〜〜〜

Any seasoned Great Lakes captain could lecture about running into a gagger, living through what seemed like an eternity of pitching and rolling in mountainous waves that, at times, seemed to be coming from all directions simultaneously, and wondering if his boat was up to the twisting and turning the hull was enduring over the hours. When it was over, there were always tales to tell. Most of the captains with any seniority required no prodding to talk about what had transpired on Lake Superior just eight years earlier. They had heard the stories, or if luck had been running against them, they had been out in that maelstrom.

Experience and precedence had little to offer when combatting this particular storm in 1913. As time would show, it was the most destructive Great Lakes storm in commercial shipping history. More vessels sank or suffered tremendous damage and more sailors lost their lives than in any other storm in recorded history. Incredibly, the largest of the lakes was spared the worst. That distinction would go to Lake Huron.

Aside from the *Leafield*, only the *William Nottingham*, a 376-foot freighter hauling wheat, suffered fatalities on the western portion of the Lake Superior. The *Nottingham*'s sailing was uneventful until she was blown off course near the Apostle Islands. She grounded, and three crewmen, hoping to get help, lost their lives when they attempted to launch a lifeboat. The rest of the crew stayed onboard for three days until help arrived. They stayed warm by burning wheat when the coal ran out.

Other vessels on Minnesota's north shore and the western portion of Lake Superior fared better. The boats, iced over and worn from their struggles, arrived safely in ports. What meteorologists could not project was how this storm attacked the Great Lakes in a two-pronged assault. The first hit the upper lakes, Superior and Michigan, as the clipper, moving west to east, charged across the region. Then, just when it appeared that the storm was blowing itself out, another system, this one coming from the southeast, turned abruptly and joined forces with the first storm over Lake Huron. What occurred was a freshwater hurricane.

As the storm proceeded across Lake Superior, boats in central and eastern Lake Superior encountered sailing conditions unlike anything they had ever faced. The *L. C. Waldo*, a 472-foot steamer loaded with iron ore, bound for Cleveland from Two Harbors, became the 1913 storm's answer to the *Mataafa* when, after what must have felt like a never-ending confrontation with the elements, the boat grounded on the rocks near the Keweenaw Peninsula. Her rudder was disabled, and the pilothouse was partially blown away; the *Waldo* clung to the rocks while her deck split. Captain John Duddleson, the vessel's sixty-five-year-old skipper and part owner, ordered everyone aft to move forward. The *Waldo* had grounded away from well-traveled shipping lanes, so the crew wondered when the boat's precarious position might be discovered. Another freighter happened by and observed the *Waldo*, shrouded in thick ice, on the rocks. After a couple of tense days the captain and crew were rescued.

The *L. C. Waldo,* stranded and encased in ice during the 1913 storm, broke in two, but captain and crew were rescued when the storm abated.

The onslaught was not limited to the lakes. Minnesota, although racked by heavy wind and snow, escaped the worst of nature's fury, compared to the destruction elsewhere. In Duluth, gale-force winds aided a fire that destroyed one of the loading docks of a coal company. It sent a downtown newsstand flying, leveled fencing, and shot debris in every direction. In Superior, Duluth's sister shipping city on the Wisconsin side of the bay, the tempest blew away three dockside loading rigs.

It was worse to the south and east, at the bottom of Lake Michigan. In Milwaukee, heavy waves mangled a lakeside project, taking out two floating pile drivers and 1,500 feet of construction. In Chicago, people gathered to see the massive waves that flooded Lakeshore Drive and crashed into Lincoln Park, the city's large recreational stretch of land; eight years of expansion and development were wiped out, at a cost of more than $200,000.

After two days of constant pounding, the behemoth storm lessened. Cleanup began. Great Lakes shipping, paralyzed during the storm, prepared to resume its late-season hauling.

High waves and winds pummeled the Great Lakes as far south as Chicago and Cleveland.

This general sense of relief turned out to be tragically premature. Sunday, November 9 dawned with calm waters on Lake Huron. That changed dramatically when a strong weather system turned unexpectedly. Rather than moving up the Atlantic coastline and, eventually, over the ocean, as usual, this system turned westward and charged into the Ohio valley, combined with the storm system that had assaulted Lakes Michigan and Superior, and, ultimately, positioned itself close enough to Lake Huron to churn up the lake's waters into a deadly cauldron by midmorning. The sudden change caught the freighters sailing on the lake—and there were many—by surprise.

The results were historic, never occurring before or since on Lake Huron. Vessels had left their docks with their captains confident in what they figured was a familiar weather pattern: the storm affecting the upper lakes had blown itself out, and sailing would be smooth on the lower lakes. Instead, conditions, terrible by midmorning, deteriorated to the point where no freighter was safe. As the number of sunken, beached, or badly wounded boats grew to breathtaking figures, and the body count of lost sailors was taken, it was apparent that this was an unprecedented storm. By every measure, this was a freshwater hurricane.

The wind velocity held true to hurricane standards. By noon on Sunday, the wind was measured at 40 miles per hour or greater. It would maintain that velocity for the next fourteen hours. Freighter captains maintained that wind velocities on the water exceeded those recorded on land, and, of course, the howling wind, sweeping over the lake, created towering waves that pushed vessels off course, produced deadly troughs between the waves, and threatened to capsize any vessel unfortunate enough to be caught out in the storm. As one observer noted, "The lake was calm as glass" when he attended church services that morning. "By the time church was over," he continued, "it was obvious that no boat could be safe on the waters." Barometric pressures fell every hour, contributing significantly to the sailing conditions, causing meteorologists to hold their breaths and pray for the welfare of any craft facing the storm. Of all the vessels sailing north on Lake Huron, only one reached its intended destination. All of the rest sank, grounded, or sought shelter in the nearest port.

In the weeks following the storm, tales of extraordinary seamanship made the rounds in the lakeside taverns and saloons. Captain Stephen Lyons, guiding the *J. H. Sheadle* through 70 miles per hour winds and seas that boarded his flooded vessel, decided to take a bold approach in addressing the storm: rather than risk his freighter's welfare when he couldn't locate a needed lighthouse beam near the bottom of the lake, Lyons opted to turn the *Sheadle* around and head back up the lake. He kept the *Sheadle* on the lake, repeating the turnarounds throughout the night, and the *Sheadle* was spared when others were not.

Another death-defying drama occurred on Lake Superior when the *Cornell*, a 454-footer owned by the Pittsburgh Steamship Company, traveling light from Conneaut, Ohio, to Duluth–Superior, became trapped in a trough with no way out. The imprisonment lasted a mind-boggling thirteen hours, leading at least one man, Second Assistant Engineer Earl Rattray, to wish the boat would sink and end his misery. Gargantuan waves rolled over the boat, breaking windows, tearing off the overhang of the aft cabin, and entering the engine room. "It was a battle for our very lives," Chief Engineer Charles Lawrence said later. Rattray was convinced the vessel, pitching and rolling heavily in the trough, was going to founder. Somehow, almost miraculously, Lawrence and Captain John Noble kept the *Cornell* afloat while it was being pushed so close to shore that the crew could make out individual trees on land. Noble ordered the anchors dropped. The first two attempts failed: the anchors refused to catch. The anchors caught on the third attempt, and the *Cornell*, in shallower water, came to a stop just as the boat was about to hit land. The vessel survived.

~~~~

To appreciate these success stories, one has only to consider the losses. Eight freighters, some new and powerful, succumbed to the storm with a loss of all crew; another ten were stranded. More than 250 sailors lost their lives. In the weeks following the storm, bodies were collected along the shore of Lake Huron. Wreckage washed up everywhere.

The most perplexing loss could be found at the southern end of the lake, near Port Huron. A freighter had flipped (or turned turtle, as the saying went), and all that could be seen was a section of its inverted bow poking out of the water. The identity of the boat was unknown. There was plenty of speculation over what freighter it might be, but given the abundance of the vessels gone missing, stranded, or taking shelter during the storm, one guess was just as valid as another. It was essential that the boat be identified before the floating bow section filled with water and the boat sank to the bottom of the lake.

This proved to be difficult. The seas were still too choppy for the divers and their rudimentary equipment. Newspapers nationwide capitalized on the mystery, running daily articles on it, and a reward was offered to the first diver to identify it. The weather finally broke, and a diver dropped down, searched in the murky water, and identified the wreck as the *Charles S. Price*, a 524-foot vessel with a reported crew of twenty-eight. The *Price* was assumed to be lost; a few of her crew members had been recovered and positively identified. That the boat was inverted surprised no one: it took little imagination to envision the huge steamer caught in a trough and flipping over.

The *Charles S. Price,* a 524-foot freighter, sank on Lake Huron during the 1913 storm and was found upside down with only a small portion of her bow above water, setting off a rush to identify the boat.

But the mystery didn't end there. One of the boat's recovered victims was wearing a *Regina* life jacket. How had that happened? The *Regina,* a 269-foot package freighter with a crew of twenty, had been observed in the vicinity of the *Price.* Had the two boats collided? Had the *Regina* happened on survivors of the *Price* and rescued them, only to eventually sink and take the survivors with her? No one knew. There were no survivors from either wreck, and the *Regina* was eventually discovered a good distance away from the wreck of the *Price,* on the other side of Lake Huron.

Mysteries and unanswered questions were inevitable at a time when there was no deep-diving equipment, no sonar, no computer projections, no way to track down boats that had gone missing in deep water. The heyday of the shipwreck was in the future, but even then, the discoveries of sunken vessels were often by accident rather than by carefully plotted searches. It was not uncommon for fishermen to latch on to the remnants of a wreck.

Not until May 24, 2013, did shipwreck hunters Jerry Eliason, Ken Merryman, and Kraig Smith find the *Henry B. Smith,* a 525-footer lost with its crew of twenty-five on Lake Superior on November 9. The loss of the *Smith* hit the city of Duluth especially hard. Her captain, Jimmy Owen, was a popular figure around town, and his disappearance led to a front-page story in the *Duluth Herald*. By all indications, the fifty-four-year-old master was easygoing and well liked among his crew.

If he had had his say, he would have waited out the storm in Marquette, Michigan. Loading 10,000 tons of iron ore into the *Smith*'s cargo hold had taken an extremely long time. The ore froze in the loading chutes and had to be knocked loose by sledgehammer. Owen was well behind schedule, and his bosses at the Acme Transit Company in Cleveland were impatient. Owen had come in behind schedule on several occasions during the season, and management balked at Owen's suggestion that the *Smith* remain in during the storm. Lost time meant lost money. Owen was ordered to take the *Smith* on her scheduled run from Marquette to Cleveland—or, as the rumor went, he would be seeking employment elsewhere the following season. Owen, the boat's only master during its seven years on the lakes, reluctantly conceded.

The *Smith* was horribly mismatched in its battle against the wind, waves, and snow. Witnesses to her 5:00 p.m. departure spoke later of the boat's struggle, which began as soon as she cleared the breakwater. Waves crashed over her bow. She pitched so badly that observers wondered how long it might be before she turned back to port. Owen did order his wheelsman to turn, but he unexpectedly turned to port, as if to make a run for shelter at Keweenaw Point. No one would ever know what he intended. The *Smith* disappeared into the snow. A few days later, wreckage from the boat washed ashore, and the remains of two crew members were eventually recovered.

The *Smith*'s demise brought back the discussion of the age-old issue of commerce versus safety. Captains traditionally had the final say about whether to take their vessels out in bad weather, and the heavy-weather captains—those willing to sail their vessels in almost any type of nasty weather—were well known. Jimmy Owen was not one of those skippers. Nor, to be fair, was the shipping company deliberately sending Owen and his crew into a life-threatening situation, although Cleveland would find out, soon enough, how lethal the storm really was.

~~~

Cleveland's Sunday opened in the predawn hours, beginning at 4:30 a.m., with rainfall toasting the end of a warm late-fall period. The early rain, changing to snow, had been predicted. The thirty-five-degree temperatures melted most of the snow before it touched the ground. The wet conditions made for slick sidewalks and roads, but most Clevelanders weren't yet awake to notice.

By midmorning, the rain had changed to snow. The barometer fell as the heavy, wet snow blanketed the city. Wind velocity increased. By two o'clock in the afternoon, William H. Alexander, the Weather Bureau reporter in Cleveland, reported consistent 40 miles per hour winds in the city. That number increased to 74 miles per hour by five o'clock, and for the next nine hours, the wind held at 70 to 72 miles per hour. Cleveland, accustomed to occasional heavy lake-effect snowfall, now faced a full-fledged weather bomb.

The snow piled up, and nearly 22 inches accumulated before it quit falling. The wind blew it into imposing drifts, some measuring 5 feet. The barometer dropped to 28.35, the second lowest measured in the city's history. On Lake Erie, the waves were predictably enormous, but the harbor waters were gravely affected as well. A passenger vessel was torn from its mooring and tossed about the harbor, damaging a number of boats. Several barges, already docked for the winter, broke loose.

Transportation ground to a halt. Trains could not push past the drifts on the tracks. Power lines, sagging from snow and ice, snapped. Downed poles blocked the streets. Communication systems failed. Houses and businesses lost power—and would be without it for a few days. Police, fire, and medical personnel dealt with conditions making their jobs almost inoperable. Cleveland became more and more isolated from the rest of the state.

The people of Cleveland had to address unfamiliar challenges in keeping their homes lit, warm, and supplied. Grocery store shelves ran low. Milk was delivered only to households with infants or very young children, if deliveries could be made at all. Lake Erie, churned into a gloppy mess by rough seas, presented a problem with drinking water: people had to boil water before using it. City health officer

Martin Friedrich warned that Cleveland might experience a spike in typhoid cases as a result of polluted water, while, at the same time, assuring people that the water was safe if certain precautions were taken. "Boil all city water," he cautioned, "but first add a pinch of alum for each pint of water, and let it settle an hour before boiling."

William Alexander understood that his Weather Bureau office was up against a once-in-a-century situation. He had heard the complaining about what people considered to be inadequate warnings and preparations for the storm. This, he tried to convince his critics, was no ordinary November manifestation; it went beyond a major storm. "Take it all in all—the depth of the snowfall, the tremendous wind, the amount of damage done, and the total unpreparedness of the people—I think it is safe to say that the present storm is the worst experienced in Cleveland during the whole forty-three years the Weather Bureau has been established in this city," Alexander said.

The *Cleveland Plain Dealer,* the city's main daily newspaper, weighed in on Tuesday, November 12, the day after the storm subsided. The paper took an almost lyrical approach in its description of the storm. "Cleveland lay in white and mighty solitude, mute and

Damage in Cleveland from the 1913 storm.

deaf to the outside word, a city of lonesome snowiness, storm-swept from end to end, where the violence of the two-day blizzard lessened late yesterday."

The city dug out over the following week. Hotels and taverns allowed the stranded to sleep wherever they could find space. Transportation and communication were restored. Alexander reassured citizens that they had faced the worst, that the cold temperatures would prevent the kind of flooding that struck the state earlier in the year, when the massive meltdown had overwhelmed Johnstown and other cities.

The Great Lakes have yet to see a repeat of a storm of this magnitude.

~~~

The 1913 storm brought the Reid Wrecking Company back from near extinction. Tom Reid, one of the most respected and innovative salvagers on the Great Lakes, had seen his business fade in recent years, due primarily to less work and greater overhead. His business, he knew all too well, depended on the misfortunes of others. He started working for his father, Jim Reid, who had earned a hardscrabble living, much of it in the lumber trade, but Tom's ambitions exceeded those of his father. As his towing and salvaging business expanded, he and his team designed new methods of reaching and raising vessels at a time when diving was still primitive.

Reid Wrecking took on the complicated logistics of raising the *Mataafa* during the spring and summer of 1906. Reid estimated the job would take about ten days to accomplish; it took three months to lift the stern, refloat the *Mataafa,* and bring her into the harbor. The sight might have attracted large crowds dockside in Duluth, but the difficulties of the job, all the trial and error, cut into Reid's profits. The Pittsburgh Steamship Company offered the *Mataafa*'s ore if he removed it from the boat, a fair sum under other circumstances, but Reid estimated that it earned him a mere three dollars a ton. He wound up losing money in the operation.

Reid fared much better after the 1913 storm. He had all the work he could handle on Lake Huron alone. Stranded boats littered the shore,

The *Mataafa,* refloated.

all in need of help. Reid struck a lucrative deal when he removed the *Howard M. Hanna Jr.* from the rocks near the Port Austin lighthouse. The seven-year-old, 480-foot freighter had been hauling 9,120 tons of coal from Lorain, Ohio, to Fort William, Ontario, when, fighting the storm and becoming disoriented, she wound up wedged on the rocks. Her owners agreed to sell Reid the damaged vessel for scrap. Reid paid $13,000 for the *Hanna,* towed it to dry-dock, paid to have it repaired, and resold it for $100,000.

Reid had been one of the first to see the *Charles S. Price* floating upside down while he was assisting other boats near the end of the storm. While the mystery of the vessel's identity continued, Reid told the press that he guessed the wreck was a big freighter, with no survivors, and he proved to be accurate. Reid, intrigued by the prospects of salvaging the boat, sent Louis Meyers, his top diver, to survey the *Price* after she had been identified. After hearing Meyers's analysis of the wreck, Reid decided that the prospects of earning a handsome profit by salvaging the wreck weren't worth the effort.

The inverted *Price* was only one of the bizarre sights witnessed by Reid and his crew during the storm. Farther down Lake Huron, near the mouth of the St. Clair River, *Lightship 26,* an essential vessel warning other boats of the hazards of the area, was torn from its moorings and pushed a short distance away. This had all the earmarks of a disaster when the lightship's commander, a stickler for adhering to the letter of regulations, refused to shut down the light. If a freighter were to see the light and follow its directives, the vessel might be grounded on a nearby shoal.

When he saw *Lightship 26*'s predicament, Tom Reid told its skipper that he would tow the vessel back to its correct placement for twenty-five dollars. The skipper refused. He needed approval from an official before agreeing to the expenditure. Without such agreement he couldn't promise to pay Reid's fee.

Reid sailed on, but before he had gone very far, he spotted a freighter, the 552-foot *Matthew Andrews*, heading in the direction of the lightship. Reid turned his boat around and frantically tried to signal the *Andrews*—to no avail. Following the signal from *Lightship 26*, the *Andrews* plowed into the shoal and was stranded. The cost of refloating her was certainly higher than the towing fee of twenty-five dollars Reid had proposed to those aboard *Lightship 26*.

None of Reid's projects from the 1913 storm carried the burden of tragedy surrounding the loss of *Lightship 82*, the only vessel lost to the storm on Lake Erie. Located at the lake's far eastern point, not far from Buffalo, New York, and the port's expanding traffic, *Lightship 82* was a vital safety precaution. Aside from warning boats of nearby shoals, the lightship also stood guard over a freighter that sank in water shallow enough to pose a hazard to the larger boats sailing over it. Built in Michigan and installed in 1912, *Lightship 82*, at only 95 feet, offered little resistance to the seas battering her during the storm.

Her final hours must have been terrifying. Bits of wreckage, including a life ring, a sailboat, a drawer from the galley, and a cabin door floated to shore, leaving no doubt about the lightship's demise. Despite search efforts from tugboats and cutters, the lightship's wreckage location remained unknown, and the remains of the vessel's six crew members were not recovered until nearly a year later, when the body of the lightship's engineer was found in the Niagara River.

Winter prohibited further search efforts, but in May 1914, a search vessel located the wreckage in 62 feet of water, nearly 2 miles from where *Lightship 82* had been anchored. No victims were found onboard. The wreckage told a story about the lightship's sad confrontation with the storm. Much of the wheelhouse had been beaten away. Windows, doors, hatches, and ventilations were smashed, mute witnesses to the fearsome seas that boarded the boat and drove her to the bottom of the lake. Silt piled up at the wreck site, evidence of the violence that raked the lake bottom.

Tom Reid was contacted after other efforts to raise the boat ended unsuccessfully. It was dangerous to work at that depth at a time before air tanks and Aqua-Lungs, when air was pumped into a diver's helmet by personnel aboard a mother ship floating over the wreckage. One of Reid's divers nearly died from the bends while working on the lightship. The weather in the summer of 1915, when Reid tried to salvage the boat, was brutally hot.

The work took much longer than Reid anticipated when plotting out the job. He approached the elevation of the boat as two distinct tasks. First, he removed all the silt that had settled on the boat and removed debris from inside—anything to lighten the load. Then he rigged four heavy chains to two pontoons used to raise the boat.

The lightship wasn't finished servicing the lakes. She was restored and returned to illuminate the water for years to come.

The storm ripped *Lightship 82* from its moorings, offering testimony of the power that ravaged the Great Lakes. The lightship was recovered and refloated, but its crew was never found.

Armistice Day Blizzard, 1940

~~~

Wet, heavy snow heralded the beginning of the storm. Those remembering it would give their accounts in various ways, some declaring the snowflakes to be as large as they had ever seen, one going so far as to say they were the size of baseballs. The snowflakes filled the sky with a blinding white. They combined and, upon hitting the waters of inland lakes and Lake Superior, created a slush on the surface. The wind kicked in, increasing to gale force. Temperatures plummeted. The combined snow and wind velocity made it difficult to breathe.

The developing storm stood in sharp contrast to the weather Minnesota had been experiencing throughout the fall season. The state was accustomed to wintry weather in early November, especially in the northern and western regions, but in 1940 Minnesotans had enjoyed a prolonged summer, with warmer temperatures extending into autumn. Duck hunters complained that the warm, above-average temperatures were ruining the annual hunt. Cold, Canadian air would signal the beginning of the ducks' southern migration, which usually coincided with the waterfowl hunting season. Not so this year.

The days preceding the storm were gray and damp but warm. Armistice Day (now called Veterans Day, on November 11) fell on a Monday, giving hunters an extra day in the blind. The midwestern headquarters of the Weather Bureau, based in Chicago, forecast light snow with falling temperatures. The *Minneapolis Morning Tribune* called for a day of "occasional snow, and colder, much colder [temperatures]."

Instead, a weather event often referred to as a weather bomb was developing. A powerful, rapidly moving low-pressure system, originating in the Pacific Northwest and sweeping through the Rocky

Mountains in just a couple of hours, dipped to Oklahoma and the Texas Panhandle before taking a northeastern direction though the Plains states. Moisture from the Gulf of Mexico moved north with it, to be greeted by a cold Canadian air mass dropping down to the United States. A book on the storm published four and a half decades later had a title that succinctly described the weather event: *All Hell Broke Loose.*

People were unprepared. They left their homes, for work or school or hunting, wearing thin jackets or sweatshirts; women were bare-legged, some in seasonal sweaters. They stood no chance in confronting the blizzard, which seemed to blow in within a matter of minutes. The predicted snow flurries piled up at a rate of 3 or 4 inches an hour. Duluth recorded its lowest barometric pressure on record.

The blizzard crossed Iowa and the Dakotas first, dumping a snowfall that might have given Minnesota a warning of what to expect, but any such warning came too late. Not that it would have been heeded: the rudimentary forecasting and measuring went largely ignored at that time before radar and GPS tracking, to the extent that even the Weather Bureau office in Chicago, which filed reports midmorning and midevening, had no one on duty during the late evening of November 10.

Jack Meggars, a sixteen-year-old with a future as a game warden, was preparing to duck hunt on an island near Harpers Ferry, Iowa, and witnessed a phenomenon he never forgot: "One of the things I remember most is that, just before the storm hit, the sky turned all orange. It's hard to explain, but I remember thinking that it was really strange."

The approaching storm failed to impress Minnesotans who had seen years of occasionally bad weather. "The day started like any typical late fall morning, with almost balmy breezes reaching well above freezing," recalled Wendolin P. Beckers, a resident of Watkins, a town in central Minnesota. "Mother Nature gave no indication as to the onslaught she was about to unfurl. The serenity and calmness of the morning just caught everyone unprepared, and unless you actually experienced it, it's almost impossible to relate factually."

Beckers would attest to being present in the aftermath of a rare but tragic event when two trains, one a passenger train and the other a freight train, collided head-on near the Watkins train station. The accident occurred when an engineer could not see a track signal through the curtain of snow obscuring the near distance. An engineer and fireman were killed in one of the trains, and many passengers were injured. Dorothy Taylor, a student at the University of Minnesota who was returning to the campus in the Twin Cities after a visit home in Belgrade, Minnesota, was on the passenger train when the trains collided. Her ride had been bumpy, as the train plowed through heavy drifts on the tracks, but the collision was much more serious. She was thrown from her seat, and a piece of luggage stored on an overhead rack fell and struck her in the head. When she managed to escape from the train, she saw injured passengers lying on the ground being attended by emergency personnel. Townspeople had gathered and formed a human chain to assist passengers finding their way to town. Taylor spent the next three days in a bar–restaurant before she was able to return to the university. She later quipped that while a captive of the storm, she learned to play pinochle.

Cars were stranded and buried during the 1940 Armistice Day storm, creating a mess that took days to clear.

The severity of the storm affected virtually everyone in the state. Buses and streetcars were paralyzed by huge snow-blown drifts, and automobiles were stranded in the blizzard. Those attempting to walk home or to safe shelter were blinded by swirling snow that brought visibility to almost zero—and 10 feet at best. Farmers could not find a way to their barns when they left their houses to feed livestock. Cattle in pastures froze to death, while the state's turkey farmers, with turkeys fattened for Thanksgiving, only a couple of weeks away, lost thousands—some reports said millions—of their birds. Motorists got stuck and abandoned their vehicles where they were; many returned days later to find their engines frozen because they had used alcohol, rather than the much more expensive antifreeze, in their cars. Every household had a story about the blizzard.

For all the accounts of misery, suffering, and death, the Armistice Day storm of 1940 would forever be known as "The Day the Duck Hunters Died." Usually inclement weather did not deter a duck hunter. If anything, rain or snow was ideal. "A prediction of bad weather not only fires up the hunter, it moves the hunted," journalist Larry L. Reid observed. The moving hunted were ducks flying in advance of the weather system. Those out hunting on November 11, their memories fresh even after the passing of decades, recalled flocks of ducks blackening the skies and lifting sore spirits who had thus far endured a disappointing season.

"It seemed that all the waterfowl in North America were on the move and riding ahead of the storm," stated Donald F. Henkel of Duluth. "Never before [and] not since have I seen as many millions of waterfowl at the same time. The air was packed full of hurtling bodies and the sound of their wings was a steady whistling roar."

Norman Roloff, a nineteen-year-old hunting with his friend Sonny Ehlers near the Mississippi River, expressed his amazement at the sheer numbers of ducks flying in the intensifying wind. "The ducks just kept coming," he remembered. "It was fabulous . . . you could hear the shooting everywhere."

Milwaukee Journal outdoors editor Gordon MacQuarrie, covering the hunting in Minnesota, filed his report from the same area in which Roloff and Ehlers were hunting. Those outdoors, MacQuarrie wrote,

The Armistice Day storm assaulted Minnesota at incredible power and speed, devastating everything in its path.

paid a steep price for their enthusiasm: "Mother Nature . . . promised ducks in the wind. They came all right, but by that time the duck hunters were playing a bigger game with the wind, and their lives were the stake."

Hunters had never encountered such malevolent conditions. Rain turned into sleet, which turned into snow driven by wind that held steady at 35 miles per hour, gusting as high as 50 miles per hour. Air temperature fell throughout the day, dropping forty to fifty degrees.

At first, hunters took little notice: they were too focused on trying to bag their day's limit. They had started their day before dawn, driving to their favorite spot, guiding their wooden duck boats to small islands on the Mississippi River or elsewhere, setting their decoys, and properly preparing their blinds. By the time the weather had deteriorated to a dangerous level, it was too late for those caught unprepared. The wind had whipped up waves that made navigating boats back to the mainland treacherous. Boats were swamped or tossed over. Men drowned while seeking safety. Others became confused when trying to see through the curtains of snow.

Future Minnesota Vikings coach Bud Grant, fourteen years old at the time, was hunting with a friend when the harsh weather blew in. Like so many others, he ignored the initial warnings because the hunting was so sensational. By the time Grant and his friend were ready to call it quits, the wind was so heavy that they couldn't launch their boat. "It was snowing so hard that we could barely see," Grant said of his futile attempt to leave the island.

Hunters switched to survival mode. Those marooned on islands, particularly those wearing lightweight clothing, busied themselves preparing for what was certain to be a perilous night ahead. Some built fires, using their decoys for wood; others shot down tree branches. Many hid beneath their boats to stay out of the elements; far too many were unlucky when their boats were then buried in drifts. Men stomped in the snow, pounded on each other, ran in place—anything to generate minimal warmth.

On Tuesday, November 12, the blizzard had greatly diminished. The snow quit falling, and the wind, while still strong, had died down. It was time to assess the damage. Max Conrad, owner of a Piper Cub aircraft, fought nasty headwinds in his search for survivors. He left his home in Winona and flew to the Mississippi River, where he scoured the riverbanks and island shores. He witnessed the tolls exacted by the storm, evidenced by the living and the dead. According to the official count, forty-nine hunters perished; unofficial totals were higher. When he found a half-frozen survivor, Conrad would briefly cut his plane's engine and shout that help was on the way; he would then circle back and drop a parcel containing sandwiches, whisky, matches, and cigarettes. He would circle the area until a rescue boat arrived. Conrad searched until ten o'clock that evening and resumed the next day, "Dozens of hunters would later acknowledge that they owed their lives to him," one report stated.

The blizzard united the state against a common enemy. Hundreds of acts of kindness and assistance aided those cut off from their families. Homeowners invited strangers to stay with them until they could return home—and that sometimes amounted to days of feeding and sheltering those trapped by the storm. Hotels, restaurants, taverns, and retail stores allowed stranded people to sleep wherever they could find a space. An American Legion outpost served strangers two hundred holiday dinners that had been reserved for members.

~~~

For as much damage as it did on land, the 1940 Armistice Day storm did relatively little on Lake Superior; the lake escaped the worst of the storm, to the relief of those on the water. Captains, warned that an intense weather system was heading into the area, kept their vessels at port. There was to be no redux of boats heading into the sort of sailing conditions that badly damaged or destroyed freighters in the past. Weather prognostication had markedly improved with the development of radar and a better understanding of upper air patterns, even though jet streams would not be part of weather forecasting until after the 1940 storm. Posting of warnings at ports had advanced well beyond the use of flags and lights, and warnings were based more on local or regional weather forecasts than in the past. The lake was battered by high seas and heavy winds, but the vessels fought through the storm and found safe haven in Minnesota ports. Fatalities were limited to those onshore.

Still, the Armistice Day storm served an invaluable function: while inclement weather had been predicted, no one foresaw the incredible speed at which the system moved. The warmer than average autumn morning had drastically changed to plunging temperatures and blizzard conditions in just a few hours as the storm front ripped through Minnesota and presented life-threatening conditions. The water on Lake Superior was whipped into a frenzy, which might have gravely affected vessels battling the conditions. Had duck hunters heeded the call for foul weather and not acted only on the current conditions they were experiencing, the casualty numbers would have been much lower.

By 1940, fewer vessels were lost in stormy weather—but not none. The *Henry Steinbrenner* succumbed to wicked weather conditions, and the largest boat lost in Great Lakes history, the *Edmund Fitzgerald* in 1975, sank in a fierce storm, though Captain Bernie Cooper, an acknowledged authority on Great Lakes weather who was piloting a freighter not far behind the *Fitzgerald*, would testify that he had been in rougher storms than the one that claimed the *Fitz*. It is noteworthy that both boats departed in warmer than usual weather, and both Cooper and Captain Ernest McSorley of the *Fitz* encountered stormy weather earlier than had been projected, right about the time they were nearing Isle Royale on their individual journeys.

The *Fitzgerald* could boast of one advantage over the *Steinbrenner*: she was constructed after 1948, when shipbuilders began using stronger, more flexible metal in their hulls. In the beginning, of course, builders used wood, which not only broke apart more easily, but also caught fire. By 1940, fires sinking boats had all but disappeared on freighters and passenger vessels. Metal eventually replaced wood in boat construction, and though it was a major improvement, it could be especially problematic early and late in the shipping season, when frigid water would test the flexibility and brittleness of materials used on bulk carriers. The three survivors of the *Carl D. Bradley* and *Daniel J. Morrell,* two enormous freighters built prior to 1948, both boats that broke in two in late November storms, witnessed the horrors of the fracturing and sinkings. Fortunately, the shipping companies slowly but surely began to retire their older vessels when builders started using the new metals.

Shipping companies and sailors both resisted some of the changes recommended by the Coast Guard after hearings that followed shipwrecks. Change did not come easily, particularly in the implementation of safety measures such as survival suits and enclosed life rafts. Other measures were more readily adopted and made work in the shipping industry safer.

Human error, obviously, could not be anticipated. As we have seen in stories in this book, human error played a significant role in some of the losses on the lake. That might be expected, but it is difficult to understand the arrogance displayed over nearly two centuries of commercial shipping. Companies, shipping offices, officials, and captains and crews, in pursuit of late-season profits and bonuses, believed their vessels to be indestructible in a confrontation with nature's forces. Most sailors will tell you that they feel as safe on their vessels as they feel on land. But nature, with heavy seas, overwhelming winds, thick fog, ice, and other dangerous conditions, can prevail. Heavy-weather captains, although skilled in handling almost anything they encounter, are becoming an extinct species.

Safety, stormy weather, danger, and human error rarely became a topic or issue of concern to those occupying large, heavily loaded boats moving smoothly across gently undulating water. To a sailor working through a lengthy season keeping them from their families and friends for inordinate stretches of time, the vessel may have seemed like a temporary home. They could drop by a harborside watering hole, drink beer, play cards or cribbage, and repeat stories or gossip, and forget that they had told the same stories at the last port in another bar with a seafaring motif. They knew the anecdotes of disaster. The details were imprinted in each sailor, regardless of rank, who had logged any measurable time on the Great Lakes. But these accounts had an almost mystical aura. The sailors were aware of what was possible—what had happened—though they knew nature's fury can be something to be admired.

It's a magnificent power.

Acknowledgments

A book like this doesn't just magically happen. A number of people contribute, some in large ways, others in small, but all in important ways. Each contribution is a piece of the overall mosaic, and each adds color to the overall picture. This has been the case with all my previous shipwreck books, and it was true here as well.

Laura Jacobs, an archivist at the University of Wisconsin–Superior, was invaluable during the research for this book. She provided me with clippings dating back over one hundred years, as well as transcripts of the hearings between freighters' masters and crew after the losses. Thanks so much, Laura.

Thom Holden, authority on all things Isle Royale and major contributor to the seminal *Lake Superior Shipwrecks,* was generous with his time and knowledge, as was C. Patrick Labadie, whose book *Pride of the Inland Seas* was a crucial guide to my understanding of the Port of Duluth, so important to many of the stories told here.

Books consulted in my research are listed in my bibliography, but three merit special mention. Julius F. Wolff Jr.'s *Lake Superior Shipwrecks* is the beginning, middle, and end of all discussion concerning losses on this Great Lake. Impeccably researched and written in a brisk, easy-to-follow pace, the book is essential to any library on Great Lakes shipping disasters. The same could be said about Mark L. Thompson's *Graveyard of the Lakes,* a well-documented volume that has become one of my go-to books on Great Lakes disasters. Finally—and far from least—is *Shipwrecks of Isle Royale National Park,* the text edited by Daniel J. Lenihan, on the stories behind many of the shipwrecks I have written about. Lavishly illustrated with drawings and photographs, the book can serve as a diver's guide as well as great reading for the casual Great Lakes aficionado.

To my friends at the University of Minnesota Press, Erik Anderson, Kristian Tvedten, Heather Skinner, and Mary Keirstead: my appreciation for the hard work and friendship.

Special thanks to Adam, Emily Joy, Jack Henry, Susan, Ken and Karen, Jim, Chris and Bethany, Steve, Dave, and my other friends at Franks Diner. You helped me in more ways than you know. Writing is a lonely, self-centered adventure. These folks keep me grounded.

Glossary

aft (or afterdeck) back, or stern, section of a vessel

ballast added weight, usually lake water, to lower a boat in the water and add stability

ballast pumps pumps that remove water from a boat's ballast tanks

ballast tanks large, watertight storage tanks below the cargo hold, on the starboard and port sides of the boat, in which ballast is stored

barge a vessel, usually without power, that carries and is towed by another vessel

beam width of a vessel at its widest point

boat Great Lakes vessels are usually referred to as "boats"; ocean-going vessels are referred to as "ships."

boatswain (or bos'n) crew member in charge of a vessel's anchors and rigging

boiler large, steam-generating machine in the engine room

bow front, or forward section, of a boat

breakwall a human-made stone wall designed to protect a harbor from heavy seas

bulkhead partition that divides sections of a boat's hull

buoy a cautionary marker warning boats of shallow water, objects in the water, or other obstacles

capsize to roll on a side or turn over

captain (or master) commander, or chief officer, of a boat

Chadburn a communication device, connecting the pilothouse with the engine room

chief engineer crew member in charge of a boat's engine

deck flat exterior surface of a vessel

draft depth of a boat's hull beneath the waterline

fantail overhang of a vessel's stern

fathom a measurement of depth equal to 6 feet

first mate second in command of a boat, after the captain

flotsam floating debris or wreckage

fore (or foredeck) forward, or bow, section of a boat

founder to fill with water and sink

freeboard height of a boat's hull above the water

galley a vessel's kitchen

green water solid water, rather than spray, that washes over a boat's deck

grounding a vessel striking bottom or running completely aground

hatch coamings raised rims around the hatch openings on which the hatch covers are fitted

hatch covers large, flat sheets of steel (or wood, in older boats) that cover the hatch coamings and prevent water from entering the cargo hold

hatches openings in a boat's spar deck, through which cargo is loaded

hawse pipe the anchor chain passage

hold large section below the decks where cargo is stored

hull main body of a boat, on which the decks and superstructures are built

keel backbone of a boat (running the entire length of a boat), on which the framework of a vessel is built

keelson reinforced "ribs" of a boat, attached to the keel

light A vessel is sailing "light" if not carrying cargo.

lightship small vessel, equipped with warning lights and anchored to the floor of the lake, designed to be a floating lighthouse

list a boat's tipping or leaning to one side

master (or skipper) captain or commander of a vessel

pilothouse (or wheelhouse) enclosed, uppermost deck of a boat, where the wheel and map room are located

poop deck highest deck at the stern, where lifeboats are stored

port left side of a boat when facing the bow

reef shallow area of shore with rocky bottom

screw a boat's propeller

shoal shallow area of water, usually marked by a sandbar, reef, or rising lake floor

shoaling striking, or bottoming out, against the bottom of a shallow area of water

Soo common term for the locks at Sault Ste. Marie, Michigan

spar (or weather) deck deck where the hatches are located

starboard right side of a boat when facing the bow

stern back, or after section, of a boat

steward (or stewardess) a boat's cook

texas the deck just beneath or behind the pilothouse, which contains the captain's and mates' quarters

trough a low, depressed area between two large waves

wheelsman crew member who steers a boat

windlass machine to lift anchors

working a boat's twisting, springing, and flexing in heavy seas

Notes

Stranger

Page 4, "When the whalebacks . . .": Walter Havighurst, *The Long Ships Passing* (New York: Macmillan, 1942; reprint, Minneapolis: University of Minnesota Press, 1975), 74.

Page 5, "he was considered . . .": "Wrecked," *Superior Times*, December 28, 1875.

Page 5, "hurricane": ibid.

Stranger accident: Howard Sivertson, *Schooners, Skiffs, and Steamships* (Duluth: Lake Superior Port Cities, 2001), 48–49; Julius F. Wolff Jr., *Lake Superior Shipwrecks* (Duluth: Lake Superior Port Cities, 1979, 1990), 25.

Page 8, "Few sailing vessels . . .": Havighurst, *The Long Ships Passing.*

Page 8, "They continued . . .": ibid.

Thomas Wilson

Alexander McDougall: Bill Beck and C. Patrick Labadie, *Pride of the Inland Seas* (Afton, Minn.: Afton Historical Society Press, 2004), 112–17; Mark Bourrie, *Many a Midnight Ship* (Ann Arbor: University of Michigan Press, 2005), 157–58, 159–60; Mark L. Thompson, *Queen of the Lakes* (Detroit: Wayne State University Press, 1994), 47–48; George Barrington Mason, "McDougall's Dream: The Whaleback," *Inland Seas,* Spring 1953 (reprinted online); Ric Mixter, "McDougall's Dream," *Michigan History,* May/June 2013.

Whaleback history: Bourrie, *Many a Midnight Ship,* 156–69; Wes Oleszewski, *Ghost Ships, Gales, and Forgotten Tales* (Marquette, Mich.: Avery Color Studios, 1995), 4–7; Mason, "McDougall's Dream," *Inland Seas*; Mixter, "McDougall's Dream."

Christopher Columbus: Thompson, *Queen of the Lakes,* 49–51; Bourrie, *Many a Midnight Ship,* 160–61; Mason, "McDougall's Dream," *Inland Seas*; Mixter, "McDougall's Dream."

Thomas Wilson: Oleszewski, *Ghost Ships, Gales, and Forgotten Tales,* 6–8; Wolff, *Lake Superior Shipwrecks,* 96–97.

Wilson–Hadley collision: Bourrie, *Many a Midnight Ship,* 162; James R. Marshall, *Shipwrecks of Lake Superior,* 2nd ed. (Duluth: Lake Superior Port Cities, 2005), 92–96; Al Miller, *Tin Stackers* (Detroit: Wayne State University Press, 1999), 45–46; Oleszewski, *Ghost Ships, Gales, and Forgotten Tales,* 12–19; Wolff, *Lake Superior Shipwrecks,* 97; "Steamer Wilson Sunk," *Duluth Evening Herald,* June 7, 1902; "Nine Lost in Collision of Steamers Handley and Wilson," *Duluth News Tribune,* June 8, 1902; "Annual Report of the United States Life-Saving Service, 1902"; M. C. Cameron, statement given at St. Louis Hotel, Duluth, Minnesota, undated; Neil McGilvray, statement given at St. Louis Hotel, Duluth, Minnesota, undated.

Page 16, "The watchman said . . .": "Steamer Wilson Sunk," *Duluth Evening Herald.*

Page 16, "One moment the two . . .": ibid.

Page 17, "While some tried . . .": "Annual Report."

Page 17, "Just before she sank . . .": McGilvray, statement given at St. Louis Hotel.

Page 17, "When I went down . . .": Cameron, statement given at St. Louis Hotel.

Benjamin Noble

Noble background: Dwight Boyer, *Ghost Ships of the Great Lakes* (New York: Dodd, Meade, 1968), 29–30; Frederick Stonehouse, *Went Missing* (AuTrain, Mich.: Avery Color Studios, 1977), 76.

Page 22, "Captain Johnny": "Lost Captain Popular," *Duluth Herald,* May 1, 1914.

Page 23, "Hell, he ain't . . .": Boyer, *Ghost Ships of the Great Lakes,* 33.

Storm: "Fierce Storm Sweeps Lake," *Duluth Herald,* April 28, 1914.

Page 23, "one of the worst . . .": "Fierce Gale," *Duluth Herald,* n.d.

Noble accident: Boyer, *Ghost Ships of the Great Lakes,* 32–39; Stonehouse, *Went Missing,* 76–79; Wolff, *Lake Superior Shipwrecks,* 152–53; "Steamer Benjamin Noble Carrying Crew of Twenty Founders in Lake Superior," *Duluth Herald,* April 29, 1914; "Believes She Saw the Benjamin Noble Founder in the Lake," *Duluth Herald,* April 30, 1914; "Noble Only Vessel Lost," *Duluth Herald,* April 30, 1914; "Saw the Noble Pass Lakeside," *Duluth Herald,* April 30, 1914; "Search for Noble Is Discontinued," *Duluth Herald,* May 1, 1914.

Page 26, "well-known": "Believes She Saw the Benjamin Noble Founder in the Lake."

Page 26, "all hope . . .": ibid.

Duluth Harbor lights: "Lighthouse Was Dark during the Big Storm," *Duluth Herald,* April 29, 1914; "Oil Lamp Is Only Light," *Duluth Herald,* May 1, 1914; "Would Know the Reason," *Duluth Herald,* May 1, 1914; "Lack of Light Not the Cause," *Duluth Herald,* May 4, 1914.

Discovery of wreckage: Ken Merryman, interview by author.

Page 27, "near the top . . .": ibid.

Page 28, "It was like . . .": ibid.

Onoko

Onoko: Dwight Boyer, *Great Stories of the Great Lakes* (Cleveland: Freshwater Press, 1966), 63–66; Havighurst, *The Long Ships Passing*, 221–22; Thompson, *Queen of the Lakes*, 31–38.

Page 29, "A monstrosity": Thompson, *Queen of the Lakes*, 34.

Page 29, "An eye-sore . . .": "Onoko: Construction and Career," Minnesota Historical Society, online edition, https//mnhs.org/places.

Page 32, "*Onoko* has proven . . .": ibid.

Western Reserve: Boyer, *Great Stories of the Great Lakes*, 55–61; Mark L. Thompson, *Graveyard of the Lakes* (Detroit: Wayne State University Press, 2000), 218–25; Maritime History of the Great Lakes, "Western Reserve (Propeller) US1294, sunk, 30 Aug 1892," online edition. (This site features excerpts of newspaper articles written about the *Western Reserve* accident.)

Western Reserve dropping anchor: In *Graveyard of the Lakes*, his detailed and annotated volume about scores of shipwrecks, Great Lakes maritime historian Mark L. Thompson disputes the widely accepted idea of the *Western Reserve*'s dropping anchor and taking shelter, even if briefly, during the storm. The timeline of the sinking, Thompson argues, does not allow for it, and, perhaps as important, Harry Stewart, the accident's sole survivor, does not mention it in his accounts of the voyage and sinking.

Page 34, "While we were . . .": "Western Reserve (Propeller) US1294, sunk, 30 Aug 1892."

Page 34, "The sea was . . .": Boyer, *Great Stories of the Great Lakes*, 58.

Henry Steinbrenner

Steinbrenner background: "Steinbrenner Had Rocky History; Sank Once Before," *Cleveland Plain Dealer*, May 12, 1953; "As We See It," editorial, *Detroit Free Press*, May 13, 1953; "Disaster Marked Steinbrenner's Life," *Duluth News Tribune*, May 17, 1953; J. P. Furst, "Memories Surface of Earlier Ship Sinkings," *Duluth News Tribune*, November 10, 1990.

Steinbrenner family: The Steinbrenner family became nationally known when George and Hal Steinbrenner bought the New York Yankees.

Collision on St. Marys: Thompson, *Graveyard of the Lakes*, 273–75.

Page 42, "going up and down . . .": "Sanduskians Tell of Storm on Lake," *Sandusky (Ohio) Register-Star-News*, May 16, 1953.

Steinbrenner final trip and foundering: Frederick Stonehouse, *Isle Royale Shipwrecks* (AuTrain, Mich.: Avery Color Studios, 1983), 158–63; Frederick

Stonehouse, *Steel on the Bottom* (Gwinn, Mich.: Avery Color Studios, 2006), 68–73; Thompson, *Graveyard of the Lakes*, 288–94; Wolff, *Lake Superior Shipwrecks*, 202–3; Richard D. Bibby, "Donation Recalls 1953 Steinbrenner Tragedy," *The Nor'Easter*, September-October 1983; "Ore Freighter Henry Steinbrenner Strikes Rocks, Sinks in Seas off Isle Royale," *Sandusky (Ohio) Register-Star-News*, May 11, 1953; Louis Cook, "The Great Lakes Claim Another," *Detroit Free Press*, May 12, 1953; Shinto Wessman, "They Saw Men Die," *Duluth Herald*, May 12, 1953; "Rough Sea Too Much for Jinx Freighter: 6 Men Still Missing," *Toronto Evening Telegram*, May 12, 1953; "10 Killed, 7 Missing in Lake Wreck," *Detroit Free Press*, May 12, 1953; "3 Duluth Men, on Sunken Boat, Missing," *Duluth Herald*, May 12, 1953; Geoffrey Howes, "10 Minutes and She Was Gone," *Detroit Free Press*, May 12, 1953; Marine Board of Investigation Report, U.S. Coast Guard, filed on July 10, 1953; "Record of Proceedings of a Marine Board of Investigation Convened at Sault Ste. Marie, Michigan, and Cleveland, Ohio, to Inquire and Investigate the Foundering of the SS HENRY STEINBRENNER, with Loss of Life on 11 May 1953" (transcript of Coast Guard Board of Investigation hearings, hereafter referred to as "Coast Guard testimony" when quoting from the proceedings).

Page 43, "The wave ...": Thomas Wells, Coast Guard testimony.

Page 43, "We pulled ...": Norman Bragg, Coast Guard testimony.

Page 43, "I thought ...": Albert Stiglin, Coast Guard testimony.

Page 44, "They were scattered ...": ibid.

Page 44, "Everybody was scared ...": Bernard Oberoski, Coast Guard testimony.

Page 44, "The watchman ...": Kenneth Kumm, Coast Guard testimony.

Page 45, "I was frightened ...": ibid.

Page 46, "We had difficulty ...": David Autin, Coast Guard testimony.

Page 46, "So long, boys ...": ibid.

Page 46, "I was trying ...": Frank Jozapaitis, Coast Guard testimony.

Page 47, "The suction took me ...": Oberoski, Coast Guard testimony.

Page 47, "It was cold ...": Kumm, Coast Guard testimony.

Page 47, "I looked around ...": Oberoski, Coast Guard testimony.

Page 47, "Our wheelsman ...": Stiglin, Coast Guard testimony.

Page 50, "He was coming ...": ibid.

Page 50, "We informed them ...": ibid.

Page 52, "I was afraid ...": Bragg, Coast Guard testimony.

Rescue efforts: Miller, *Tin Stackers*, 180–82; Thompson, *Graveyard of the Lakes*, 291–95; Wolfe, *Lake Superior Shipwrecks*, 202–3; "The Work of

Rescue Vessels Keeps Superior Death Toll Down," *The Bulletin,* n.d.; "Rescuers Spot 8 Aboard Raft," *Detroit News,* May 11, 1953; "Rescue Ship Men Hailed for Deeds," *Cleveland Plain Dealer,* May 19, 1953.

Page 53, "We ran into . . .": newspaper clipping of article by Geoffrey Howes, *Detroit Free Press,* May 12, 1953.

Page 54, "nothing worked . . .": Jack D. Strohm, "Bitter Survivors Call the Ship Too Old," *Detroit Free Press,* May 16, 1953.

Page 54, "just too old": ibid.

Coast Guard hearings: "CG Opens Inquiry in Ore Ship Sinking," *Sandusky (Ohio) Register-Star-News,* May 12, 1953; "Coast Guard Quiz in Shipwreck," *Detroit News,* May 12, 1953; "Coast Guard Plans Inquiry in Wreck," *Detroit Free Press,* May 13, 1953; "Skipper Discounts Gale Theory," *Detroit Free Press,* May 14, 1953; Stoddard White, "Coast Guard Inquiry Moves to Cleveland for Hearings," *Detroit News,* May 15, 1953; Strohm, "Bitter Survivors Call the Ship Too Old"; "CG Board Prepares Report on Sinking of Steinbrenner," *Sandusky (Ohio) Register-Star-News,* May 20, 1953; "Asks Prosecution of Steinbrenner Captain for Sinking," *Sandusky (Ohio) Register-Star-News,* August 5, 1953; "Blame Lake Skipper in Sinking," *Detroit Free Press,* August 7, 1953.

Page 55, "the adverse weather . . .": "Coast Guard testimony," 7.

Page 55, "The board concluded . . .": ibid., 8.

Page 56, "Such record . . .": Thompson, *Graveyard of the Lakes,* 297.

Page 57, "very largely . . .": "Asks Prosecution of Steinbrenner Captain for Sinking,"

Cumberland

Cumberland background: Daniel J. Lenihan, *Shipwrecks of Isle Royale National Park: The Archeological Survey* (Duluth: Lake Superior Port Cities, 1994), 37–39; Frederick Stonehouse, *Isle Royale Shipwrecks* (AuTrain, Mich.: Avery Color Studios, 1983), 12–14; Wolff, *Lake Superior Shipwrecks,* 27–28.

Page 65, "a trim . . .": *Duluth Tribune,* August 3, 1877, reprinted in Lenihan, *Shipwrecks of Isle Royale National Park,* 40.

Cumberland accident: Lenihan, *Shipwrecks of Isle Royale National Park,* 39–40; Stonehouse, *Isle Royale Shipwrecks,* 14.

Henry Chisholm: Lenihan, *Shipwrecks of Isle Royale National Park,* 41–45; Stonehouse, *Isle Royale Shipwrecks,* 38–42; Wolff, *Lake Superior Shipwrecks,* 81–82; Thom Holden, interview by author.

Algoma

Algoma background: Dana Thomas Bowen, *Shipwrecks of the Lakes* (Cleveland: Freshwater Press, 1952, 1991), 122–25; Lenihan, *Shipwrecks of Isle Royale National Park*, 45–50; Wolff, *Shipwrecks of Lake Superior;* Daniel J. Lenihan, ed., with Toni Carrell, Thom Holden, C. Patrick Labadie, Larry Murphy, and Ken Vrana, *Submerged Cultural Resources Study: Isle Royale National Park* (Santa Fe, N.Mex.: Southwest Cultural Resources Center Professional Papers, 1987), 80–87.

Page 69, "She is certainly . . .": Lenihan, *Submerged Cultural Resources Study*, 86.

Page 69, "of the highest . . .": ibid., 84.

Page 71, "There is a screw loose . . .": *Duluth Tribune*, August 8, 1884, reprinted in Lenihan, *Shipwrecks of Isle Royale National Park*, 50.

Algoma accident: Bowen, *Shipwrecks of the Lakes*, 125–32; Lenihan, *Shipwrecks of Isle Royale Park*, 50–56; William Ratigan, *Great Lakes Shipwrecks and Survivals*, rev. ed. (Grand Rapids, Mich.: William V. Ferdmans, 1977), 266–68; Stonehouse, *Isle Royale Shipwrecks*, 20–25; Wolff, *Shipwrecks of Lake Superior*, 43–45; Lenihan, *Submerged Cultural Resources Study*, 87–98.

Page 72, "tossed around . . .": Lenihan, *Shipwrecks of Isle Royale National Park*, 51.

Page 73, "The captain alone . . .": statement reprinted in "SS Algoma: Wreck Event and Survivor Accounts," National Park Service, Isle Royale National Park, online edition.

Page 74, "We all owe . . .": ibid.

Monarch

Monarch background: Lenihan, *Shipwrecks of Isle Royale National Park*, 58–61; Stonehouse, *Isle Royale Shipwrecks*, 62–63; "Monarch's Experience," *Duluth Evening Herald*, November 27, 1896; "A Beautiful Ship," *Duluth Evening Herald*, October 22, 1890.

Page 79, "the finest running . . .": "A Beautiful Ship."

Page 79, "On her first . . .": ibid.

Thanksgiving trip to Duluth: "Monarch's Experience."

Grounding: Lenihan, *Shipwrecks of Isle Royale National Park*, 61–62; Stonehouse, *Isle Royale Shipwrecks*, 37–59; Thompson, *Graveyard of the Lakes*, 43–46; Wolff, *Lake Superior Shipwrecks*, 121–22.

Survivors' ordeal: Lenihan, *Shipwrecks of Isle Royale National Park*, 62–64; Stonehouse, *Isle Royale Shipwrecks*, 59–62; Thompson, *Graveyard of the Lakes*, 46–48; Wolff, *Lake Superior Shipwrecks*, 122.

Attempts to salvage *Monarch*: Mary Frances Doner, *The Salvager: The Life of Captain Tom Reid on the Great Lakes* (Ross and Haines, 1958; reprint ed., Minneapolis: University of Minnesota Press, 2017), 124–26; Lenihan, *Shipwrecks of Isle Royale National Park*, 65–66.

Page 87, "with the channel . . .": Doner, *The Salvager*, 122.

Page 89, "The *Savona* . . .": ibid., 126.

Chester A. Congdon

Congdon background: Lenihan, *Shipwrecks of Isle Royale National Park*, 93–94; "Hawgood's New Boat," *Toledo Blade*, August 29, 1907; "Chester A. Congdon," *The Bulletin*, Lake Carriers' Association 1, no. 3 (November 1912); "Chester A. Congdon," *The Bulletin*, Lake Carriers' Association 4, no. 7 (November 1915).

Page 92, "on stopping . . .": Lake Carriers' Association Annual Report, 1918.

Congdon accident: Lenihan, *Shipwrecks of Isle Royale National Park*, 94–97; Stonehouse, *Isle Royale Shipwrecks*, 85–87; Thompson, *Graveyard of the Lakes*, 49–51; Wolff, *Lake Superior Shipwrecks*, 159–60; "Congdon Strands on Canoe Rocks," *Detroit Free Press*, November 8, 1918; "Steamer Congdon Grounds in Storm," *Duluth Herald*, November 8, 1918; "Steamer Said to Be Total Loss," *Duluth Herald*, November 9, 1918; "Wreck of Steamer Congdon Bought," *Duluth Herald*, December 4, 1918; "Report of Casualty," U.S. Coast Guard, December 11, 1918.

Kamloops

Kamloops: Boyer, *Ghost Ships of the Great Lakes*, 126–29; Anna Lardinois, *Shipwrecks of the Great Lakes* (Guilford, Conn.: Globe Pequot, 2021), 171–73; Lenihan, *Shipwrecks of Isle Royale National Park*, 104–7; Stonehouse, *Isle Royale Shipwrecks*, 100–101; Lenihan, *Submerged Cultural Resources Study*, 187–91.

Page 96, "big, harmonious family": Boyer, *Ghost Ships of the Great Lakes*, 128.

Kamloops wreck and search: Boyer, *Ghost Ships of the Great Lakes*, 129–38; Lenihan, *Shipwrecks of Isle Royale National Park*, 107–11; Stonehouse, *Isle Royale Shipwrecks*, 101–11; "Canadian Ship, Crew of 22 Lost in Lake Superior," *Detroit Free Press*, December 14, 1927; "Whereabouts of Kamloops Remains Marine Mystery," *Detroit Free Press*, December 15, 1927; "Port Arthur Tug Takes Up Search for Kamloops," *Detroit Free Press*, December 17, 1927; "Urge Search of Isle for Kamloops Crew," *Detroit Free Press*, December 17, 1927; "Tug Fails to Find Missing Kamloops," *Detroit Free*

Press, December 22, 1927; "Search for Missing Lake Ship Abandoned," *Erie (PA) Dispatch,* December 24, 1927; "Bodies Identified as Kamloops Crew," *Detroit Free Press,* May 29, 1928; "Bodies of Two on Reef Found," *Detroit Free Press,* May 31, 1928; "6 More Kamloops Victims Are Found," *Detroit Free Press,* June 5, 1928; "Crew Perished on Isle, Belief," *Detroit Free Press,* June 14, 1928; "Search Is Abandoned for Kamloops Captain," *Detroit Free Press,* June 15, 1928; Lake Carriers' Association Annual Report, 1927.

Page 98, "Rocks . . .": Boyer, *Ghost Ships of the Great Lakes,* 140.

Page 99, "It was blowing . . .": ibid., 141.

Page 101, "I am the last . . .": "A Shipwreck, a Young Woman, and a Message in a Bottle," *Soo Today,* May 26, 2019, online edition. See also "Bottle Tells Lake Tragedy," *Detroit Free Press,* January 22, 1929.

Discovery of wreckage: Lenihan, *Shipwrecks of Isle Royale National Park,* 199–201; Stonehouse, *Isle Royale Shipwrecks,* 112; Ken Merryman, interview by author.

Page 102, "The wreck site . . .": Lenihan, *Shipwrecks of Isle Royale National Park,* 198–99.

Page 103, "You learn . . .": Merryman, interview.

Page 103, "When you first . . .": ibid.

America

Page 105, "Boat day was huge . . .": Karen Sunderman, "Looking for America: The Life, Death, and Afterlife of a Storied Vessel," *Lake Superior Magazine,* February 1, 2016.

Page 105, "It was the *America* . . .": as reprinted in Thom Holden, "The *America,*" in *Shipwrecks of Lake Superior,* ed. James R. Marshall, 2nd ed. (Duluth: Lake Superior Port Cities, 2005), 70.

Page 107, "In each of these . . .": Sivertson, *Schooners, Skiffs, and Steamships,* 56.

Page 108, "despite numerous . . .": Holden, "The *America,*" 69.

Page 108, "smell his way . . .": ibid.

America accident and sinking: Wolff, *Lake Superior Shipwrecks,* 83; "SS America," Isle Royale National Park, National Park Service, online edition; Holden, "The *America*"; Lenihan, *Submerged Cultural Resources Study,* 137–41.

Page 109, "Beach her . . .": "SS America."

Page 109, "The boat started . . .": "SS America."

Page 109, "The ship began to settle . . .": ibid.

Page 114, "Our plan . . .": James R. Marshall, "The *America* Salvage Attempt," in *Shipwrecks of Lake Superior*, 72.

Page 114, "pump the *America* . . .": ibid., 73.

George M. Cox

Cox background: Bowen, *Shipwrecks of the Lakes*, 308–9; Lenihan, *Shipwrecks of Isle Royale National Park*, 85–89; Lenihan, *Submerged Cultural Resources Study*, 153–58.

Page 117, "The boats are . . .": *Manistee News Advocate*, May 25, 1933, reprinted in Lenihan, *Shipwrecks of Isle Royale National Park*, 69.

Cox grounding: Bowen, *Shipwrecks of the Lakes*, 309–12; Lardinois, *Shipwrecks of the Great Lakes*, 177–99; Lenihan, *Shipwrecks of Isle Royale National Park*, 89–91; Lenihan, *Submerged Cultural Resources Study*, 158–63; Stonehouse, *Isle Royale Shipwrecks*, 134–38; Thompson, *Graveyard of the Lakes*, 51–53; Wolfe, *Lake Superior Shipwrecks*, 192.

Page 122, "The sounding of . . .": Lenihan, *Shipwrecks of Isle Royale National Park*, 168.

Page 123, "framed by . . .": Stonehouse, *Isle Royale Shipwrecks*, 139.

Page 123, "reckless navigation . . .": Lenihan, *Submerged Cultural Resources Study*.

Emperor

Emperor accident: Lenihan, *Shipwrecks of Isle Royale National Park*, 97–102; Thompson, *Graveyard of the Lakes*, 76–77, 79; Wolff, *Shipwrecks of Lake Superior*, 199–200; Lenihan, *Submerged Cultural Resources Study*; "Steamer Emperor of Canada S. S. Lines Sinks Off Isle Royale," *Duluth Herald*, June 5, 1947; "Tell How 12 Died in Lake," *Toronto Evening Telegram*, June 4, 1947; "12 Perish in Sinking of Lake Ship," *Detroit Free Press*, June 5, 1947; "Renew Search for 10 Bodies Lost with Ship," *Toronto Evening Telegram*, June 5, 1947; "Steamer Emperor of CSL Wrecked Off Isle Royale," *Great Lakes Review*, June 1947; "Vessel Losses in 1947," Lake Carriers' Association Annual Report, 1947.

Page 128, "She was capsized . . .": "SS Emperor," Isle Royale National Park, National Park Service, online edition.

Page 129, "I neither believe . . .": Frederick Stonehouse, *Haunted Lakes* (Duluth: Lake Superior Port Cities, 1991), iv.

Page 129, "an eerie experience . . .": ibid., 130.

Lake Superior's Toughest Storm

1905 storm: Curt Brown, *So Terrible a Storm: A Tale of Fury on Lake Superior* (Minneapolis: Vanguard Press, 2008), 202–4; "Disastrous Storm Sweeps Duluth," *Duluth Evening Herald*, November 28, 1905; "19 Ships Wrecked by Lake Storm," *Duluth News Tribune*, November 29, 1903; "Superior Is First in Storm's Grasp," *Duluth News Tribune*, November 29, 1905; "Terrific Storm on Three Lakes," *Duluth News Tribune*, November 29, 1905; "The Worst in History," *Duluth Evening Herald*, November 29, 1905; "Wind and Sea Combine to Destroy at Two Harbors," *Duluth News Tribune*, November 29, 1905; "A Big Storm," *Cleveland Gazette*, December 2, 1905; "Many Union Sailors Are Lost in Storm," *Duluth News Tribune*, December 2, 1905; "Ore Shipments Will Continue," *Duluth News Tribune*, December 2, 1905; "Some Stories of Wrecks," *Duluth News Tribune*, December 2, 1905; "Gale on Lake Superior Exacts More Than Tolls," *Duluth News Tribune*, December 3, 1905; "Services for Sailors Dead," *Duluth News Tribune*, December 3, 1905; "Losses from Lake Tragedy," *Duluth News Tribune*, December 4, 1905; "Masters Talk about Storm," *Duluth News Tribune*, December 4, 1905; "Storm Had Bad Effect on November End Trade," *Duluth News Tribune*, December 4, 1905; "Repair Work Rushes Yard," *Duluth News Tribune*, December 5, 1905.

Crescent City: Robert W. Abrahamson, *Luck of the Draw* (self-published, 2014), 172–82; Brown, *So Terrible a Storm*, 66–74, 88–93, 162–64; "Big Freighter Crescent City Driven on Rocks at Lakewood and Will Probably Be Total Wreck," *Duluth Evening Herald*, November 28, 1905; "Crescent City Not in Pieces," *Duluth Evening Herald*, November 29, 1905; "Views of the Crescent City," *Duluth Evening Herald*, November 29, 1905; "Veteran in Shipwreck," *Duluth Evening Herald*, December 1, 1905; sworn statement, Frank Rice (*Crescent City* master), December 1, 1905; sworn statement, Thomas P. Thompson (*Crescent City* first mate), December 1, 1905; sworn statement, Harry J. Stephens (*Crescent City* second mate), December 1, 1905; sworn statement, Andrew E. Buddameyer (*Crescent City* chief engineer), December 2, 1905.

Page 136, "I have sailed . . .": Brown, *So a Terrible Storm*, 66.

Page 136, "It was blowing . . .": sworn statement, Frank Rice.

Page 137, "My mate reported . . .": ibid.

Arizona: Abrahamson, *Luck of the Draw*, 160; Brown, *So a Terrible Storm*, 85–86; "Boat Spun like a Top," *Duluth Evening Herald*, November 28, 1905.

Edenborn and *Madeira*: Abrahamson, *Luck of the Draw*, 39–47; Brown, *So a Terrible Storm*, 74–82; Miller, *Tin Stackers*, 70–72; "The William Edenborn Is a Total Loss," *Duluth Evening Herald*, November 29, 1905; "Another

Wreck Is Reported by the Captain of an Incoming Ship," *Duluth Evening Herald*, November 29, 1905; "Madeira Is Broken Up," *Duluth Evening Herald*, December 1, 1905; "Boat to Stay at Split Rock," *Duluth News Tribune*, December 3, 1905; sworn statement, A. J. Talbot (*Edenborn* master), December 11, 1905; sworn statement, William F. Hornig (*Edenborn* first mate), December 11, 1905; sworn statement, Henry Roach (*Edenborn* second mate); sworn statement, Silas H. Hunter (*Edenborn* chief engineer), December 11, 1905; sworn statement, Lester L. Hineline (*Edenborn* first assistant engineer), December 11, 1905; sworn statement, John Dissette (master *Madeira*), December 1, 1905.

Page 143, "Everything proceeded as usual . . .": sworn statement, A. J. Talbot.

Page 143, "The stern would . . .": sworn statement, Lester L. Hineline.

Page 143, "I was in . . .": sworn statement, Silas H. Hunter.

Page 143, "I saw nothing more . . .": sworn statement, John Dissette.

Page 144, "He had a habit . . .": sworn statement, A. J. Talbot.

Lafayette and *Manila*: Abrahamson, *Luck of the Draw*, 20–33; James P. Barry, *Wrecks and Rescues of the Great Lakes* (Holt, Mich.: Thunder Bay Press, 1994), 54–56; Miller, *Tin Stackers*, 66–69; "The Steamer Lafayette and Barge Madeira Go Ashore Near Encampment Island in Spectacular Fashion," *Duluth Evening Herald*, November 30, 1905; "Crew Tells the Story," *Duluth Evening Herald*, December 1, 1905; "Wright's Men on Their Way Home," *Duluth News Tribune*, December 3, 1905; "Lafayette Is Badly Wrecked," *Duluth News Tribune*, December 5, 1905; sworn statement, D. P. Wright (*Lafayette* master), December 2, 1905; sworn statement, F. D. Selee (*Lafayette* first mate), December 2, 1905; sworn statement, George J. Belfour (*Manila* master), December 1, 1905.

Page 146, "By this time . . .": sworn statement, D. P. Wright.

Page 147, "The captain of . . .": sworn statement, George J. Belfour.

Page 151, "Owing to the fact . . .": sworn statement, John Dissette.

Mataafa and *Nasmyth*: Abrahamson, *Luck of the Draw*, 57–58, 60–54; Barry, *Wrecks and Rescues of the Great Lakes*, 49–53; Brown, *So a Terrible Storm*, 118–83, 197–201, 208–15; Miller, *Tin Stackers*, 75–82; Michael Schumacher, *November's Fury* (Minneapolis: University of Minnesota Press, 2008), 21–28; Thompson, *Graveyard of the Lakes*, 233–40; "Crew on Steamer Mataafa, Pounded by Waves at Entrance of Harbor, Is Facing Awful Death," *Duluth News Tribune*, November 29, 1905; "Deaths in Storm," *Washington Post*, November 29, 1905; "Nasmyth Rides Out the Storm," *Duluth Evening Herald*, November 29, 1905; "Sailors Die in Fearful Storm," *Lincoln (NE) Daily Star*, November 29, 1905; "The Lifesavers Reach Mataafa," *Duluth Evening Herald*, November 29, 1905; "Washed Up

on Beach," *Duluth Evening Herald,* November 29, 1905; "Diver to Search
Vessel for Victims," *Duluth News Tribune,* November 30, 1905; "Forty May
Be Dead in Storm," *New York Times,* November 30, 1905; "More Vessels
Lost," *Daily Telegram* (Eau Claire, Wis.), November 30, 1905; "Nine Men
Perish in Mataafa Wreck; Fifteen Are Saved; Captain Humble Tells the
Story," *Duluth News Tribune,* November 30, 1905; "Will Hold an Inquest,"
Duluth Evening Herald, December 1, 1905; "Report by the Master," *Duluth
Evening Herald,* December 2, 1905; "Believes the Men Perished in Night,"
Duluth News Tribune, December 3, 1905; "Searchers Unable to Find
Bodies in Quarters of Wrecked Mataafa," *Duluth News Tribune,* Decem-
ber 3, 1905; "Life Losses on Mataafa Probed by Lieut. Winrun," *Duluth
News Tribune,* December 5, 1905; "Crew of Vessel Frozen to Death,"
Grand Rapids (WI) Tribune, December 6, 1905.

Page 153, "The weather conditions...": sworn statement, Richard Humble
   (*Mataafa* master), December 1, 1905.

Page 155, "The sea had gotten...": ibid.

Page 155, "A great many...": ibid.

Page 157, "We remained...": sworn statement, Thomas Treleaven.

Page 158, "Two sections...": sworn statement, Alex S. Brown.

Page 158, "When we were...": sworn statement, C. H. Cummings.

Page 159, "It sheered to...": sworn statement, Richard Humble.

Page 163, "At times...": ibid.

Page 164, "The first mate...": ibid.

Richard Humble: Brown, *So Terrible a Storm,* 57, 116; "Capt. Humble Tells
   Tale of Mataafa's Fatal Trip," *Duluth News Tribune,* December 2, 1905;
   "Report by the Master," *Duluth Evening Herald,* December 2, 1905; sworn
   statement, Richard Humble.

Harry Coulby: Abrahamson, *Luck of the Draw,* 35–36, 142–43; Brown, *So a
   Terrible Storm,* 94–104, 184–92, 250–54; Miller, *Tin Stackers,* 51–54, 63–64,
   80–83; "Coulby Is in the City," *Duluth Evening Herald,* November 30, 1905;
   "Statement of Losses," *Duluth Evening Herald,* December 1, 1905; "Wrecking Has Begun," *Duluth Evening Herald,* December 2, 1905; "Coulby Back
   from Islands," *Duluth News Tribune,* December 5, 1905.

Spencer and *Amboy*: "Spencer and Amboy Lost," *Duluth Evening Herald,*
   December 1, 1905.

R. W. England: Abrahamson, *Luck of the Draw,* 160–61, 184–86; Brown, *So a
   Terrible Storm,* 136–38; "Steamer Is Up on Beach," *Duluth Evening Herald,*
   November 29, 1905; "Str. England Strikes Point," *Duluth News Tribune,*
   November 29, 1905; "To Pull the R. W. England," *Duluth Evening Herald,*
   November 29, 1905; "Str. R. W. England Released by Tugs," *Duluth News
   Tribune,* December 2, 1905.

Ellwood: Abrahamson, *Luck of the Draw*, 161–63, 188–89; Brown, *So a Terrible Storm*, 170–73; Miller, *Tin Stackers*, 73–74; "Ellwood Sinks after Battle," *Duluth News Tribune*, November 29, 1905; sworn statement, C. H. Cummings (*Ellwood* master), December 2, 1905; sworn statement, Alex S. Brown (*Ellwood* first mate), December 2, 1905; sworn statement, Harvey J. Bonnah (*Ellwood* second mate), December 3, 1905; sworn statement, Thomas Treleaven (*Ellwood* chief engineer), December 2, 1905.

Page 169, "The company spares . . .": "Statement of Losses."

Page 170, "There is no man . . .": Brown, *So a Terrible Storm*, 208.

Owen: Brown, *So a Terrible Storm*, 54–55, 236–48; "Every Member of Owen Crew Believed to Be Lost," *Duluth Evening Herald*, December 2, 1905; "Owners of Str. Owen Abandon Hope; Daring Heroism Saves Umbria and Crew," *Duluth News Tribune*, December 2, 1905.

Split Rock Lighthouse: Abrahamson, *Luck of the Draw*, 215–17; Brown, *So a Terrible Storm*, 256–60; Lee Radzak, "Split Rock Lighthouse Was an Early-20th Century Engineering Marvel," *Minnpost*, December 17, 2013.

Hurricane on the Lakes

1913 storm: Frank Barcus, *Freshwater Fury* (Detroit: Wayne State University Press, 1986); David G. Brown, *White Hurricane* (Camden, Maine: International Marine/McGraw-Hill, 2002); Schumacher, *November's Fury*; "Big Area Is Stormswept," *Duluth Herald*, November 10, 1913; "Fierce Gale over Lakes," *Duluth Herald*, November 10, 1913; "Traffic Tied Up on Lakes," *Duluth Herald*, November 10, 1913; "Big Storm Is Recalled," *Duluth Herald*, November 11, 1913; "Cleveland Paralyzed as Result of Storm," *Duluth Herald*, November 11, 1913; "Last Trips This Week," *Duluth Herald*, November 11, 1913; "Appalling List of Deaths, Strandings and Wrecks in Big Storm Is Growing Every Hour," *Duluth Herald*, November 12, 1913; "Huron Still Stormswept," *Duluth Herald*, November 12, 1913; "Believed Two Fierce Storms Met on Lakes," *Duluth Herald*, November 13, 1913.

Lost vessels: Barcus, *Freshwater Fury*; Brown, *White Hurricane*; Schumacher, *November's Fury*; Wolff, *Shipwrecks of Lake Superior*; "Ship Pounds on Manitou," *Duluth Herald*, November 10, 1913; "Unknown Steamer Said to Be Pounding on Manitou," *Duluth Herald*, November 10, 1913; "Seventeen Lake Vessels Missing or Ashore," *Duluth Herald*, November 11, 1913; "Two Vessels Reported Ashore on Isle Royale," *Duluth Herald*, November 11, 1913; "Capsized Vessel Still a Mystery," *Duluth Herald*, November 12, 1913; "Experience Most Harrowing," *Duluth Herald*, November 12, 1913; "Ice-Coated Steamers Arrive at Port after Weathering Terrific Gale,"

Duluth Herald, November 12, 1913; "Lake Captains Tell of Battle for Life," *Duluth Herald,* November 12, 1913; "Fear Barge and Crew Are Lost," *Duluth Herald,* November 12, 1913; "More Loss of Life and Property," *Duluth Herald,* November 12, 1913; "Nottingham Is in Bad Shape," *Duluth Herald,* November 12, 1913; "Six Men Perish on Lightship," *Duluth Herald,* November 12, 1913; "Turret Chief on the Beach," *Duluth Herald,* November 12, 1913; "Two Pittsburg Boats Are Lost," *Duluth Herald,* November 12, 1913; "Waldo Hopeless; May Save Chief," *Duluth Herald,* November 12, 1913; "Wreckers Are Hard at Work," *Duluth Herald,* November 12, 1913; "Estimate the Loss of Life in Big Storm at 167," *Duluth Herald,* November 13, 1913; "Given Up for Lost," *Duluth Herald,* November 13, 1913; "List of Vessels Wrecked in the Great Storm Is Not Yet Complete," *Duluth Herald,* November 13, 1913; "Looking for More Wreckage," *Duluth Herald,* November 13, 1913; "Lost with All of Her Crew," *Duluth Herald,* November 13, 1913; "More Seamen's Bodies Have Been Identified," *Duluth Herald,* November 13, 1913; "Name of Capsized Boat Not Learned," *Duluth Herald,* November 13, 1913; "Search for Boats," *Duluth Herald,* November 13, 1913; "Steamer High and Dry," *Duluth Herald,* November 13, 1913; "Estimate Death List at More Than 250," *Duluth Herald,* November 14, 1913; "Few Duluthians in the List of Storm Victims," *Duluth Herald,* November 14, 1913; "List of Losses in Great Lakes Storm Corrected Up to 2 P.M. Friday," *Duluth Herald,* November 14, 1913; "More Bodies Found," *Duluth Herald,* November 14, 1913; "Steamer Major Abandoned," *Duluth Herald,* November 14, 1913; "Captain James L. Owens Mourned by Many Friends in Duluth," *Duluth Herald,* November 15, 1913; "Mysterious Derelict in Lake Huron Identified as the Steamer C. S. Price," *Duluth Herald,* November 15, 1913; "Steamer List in Lake Huron," *Duluth Herald,* November 15, 1913.

Leafield: "Leafield May Have Foundered," *Duluth Herald,* November 12, 1913.
Page 187, "The lake was calm": Schumacher, *November's Fury,* 64.
Page 226, "It was a battle . . .": ibid., 47.

Armistice Day Blizzard

Page 198, "One of the things . . .": Lowell Washburn, "The Armistice Day Blizzard of 1940," *Iowa Outdoors,* September/October 2008.
Page 198, "Mother Nature . . .": William H. Hull, *All Hell Broke Loose* (Holt, Mich.: Thunder Bay Press, 1985), 20.
Page 200, "A prediction . . .": Larry L. Reid, "A Look Back: Armistice Day Blizzard of 1940," *Waterfowl,* February 4, 2011.

Page 200, "It seemed . . .": Hull, *All Hell Broke Loose,* 96, 97.

Page 200, "The ducks . . .": Mary Divine, "Armistice Day Blizzard Killed 49 in Minnesota," *St. Paul Pioneer Press,* November 2012 (updated November 9, 2015).

Page 201, "Mother Nature . . . promised . . .": Gordon MacQuarrie, "Icy Death Rides Gale on Duck Hunt Trail," *Milwaukee Journal,* November 13, 1940.

Page 202, "It was snowing . . .": "Storm on Armistice Day Was a Killer," *Post Bulletin* (Rochester, MN), November 10, 1990.

Page 202, "Dozens of hunters . . .": Tom Davis, "The Day the Duck Hunters Died," *Sporting Classics Daily,* December 22, 2020.

Bibliography

Abrahamson, Robert M. *Luck of the Draw: The Mataafa Story*. Self-published, 2014.

Barcus, Frank. *Freshwater Fury*. Detroit: Wayne State University Press, 1960.

Barry, James P. *Wrecks and Rescues of the Great Lakes*. 2nd ed. Holt, Mich.: Thunder Bay Press, 1994.

Beck, Bill, and C. Patrick Labadie. *Pride of the Inland Seas: An Illustrated History of the Port of Duluth–Superior*. Afton, Minn.: Afton Historical Society Press, 2004.

Bourrie, Mark. *Many a Midnight Ship*. Ann Arbor: University of Michigan Press, 2005.

Bowen, Dana Thomas. *Shipwrecks of the Lakes*. Cleveland: Freshwater Press, 1952, 1991.

Boyer, Dwight. *Ghost Ships of the Great Lakes*. New York: Dodd, Meade, 1968.

Boyer, Dwight. *Great Stories of the Great Lakes*. Cleveland: Freshwater Press, 1966.

Brown, Curt. *So Terrible a Storm: A Tale of Fury on Lake Superior*. Minneapolis: Voyager Press, 2008.

Brown, David G. *White Hurricane*. Camden, Maine: International Marine/McGraw-Hill, 2002.

Devendorf, John F. *Great Lakes Bulk Carriers 1869–1985*. Self-published, 1995.

Doner, Mary Frances. *The Salvager: The Life of Captain Tom Reid on the Great Lakes*. Minneapolis: University of Minnesota Press, 2017.

Havighurst, Walter. *The Long Ships Passing: The Story of the Great Lakes*. New York: Macmillan, 1942; updated ed., New York: Macmillan, 1975; reprint ed., Minneapolis: University of Minnesota Press, 2002.

Hemming, Robert J. *Ships Gone Missing*. Chicago: Contemporary Books, 1992.

Hull, William H. *All Hell Broke Loose*. Holt, Mich.: Thunder Bay Press, 1985.

Lardinois, Anna. *Shipwrecks of the Great Lakes: Tragedies and Legacies from the Inland Seas*. Guilford, Conn.: Globe Pequot, 2021.

Lenihan, Daniel J. *Shipwrecks of Isle Royale National Park: The Archeological Survey*. Duluth, Minn.: Lake Superior Port Cities, 1994.

Marshall, James R., ed. *Shipwrecks of Lake Superior*. Duluth, Minn.: Lake Superior Port Cities, 1987, 2005.

Miller, Al. *Tin Stackers: The History of the Pittsburgh Steamship Company*. Detroit: Wayne State University Press, 1999.

Oleszewski, Wes. *Ghost Ships, Gales, and Forgotten Tales: True Adventures of the Great Lakes*. Marquette, Mich.: Avery Color Studios, 1995.

Ratigan, William. *Great Lakes Shipwrecks and Survivals*. Grand Rapids, Mich.: William B. Eerdmans Publishing Company, 1960.

Schumacher, Michael. *November's Fury: The Deadly Great Lakes Hurricane of 1913*. Minneapolis: University of Minnesota Press, 2013.

Sivertson, Howard. *Schooners, Skiffs, and Steamships*. Duluth, Minn.: Lake Superior Port Cities, 2001.

Stonehouse, Frederick. *Isle Royale Shipwrecks*. AuTrain, Mich.: Avery Color Studios, 1983.

Stonehouse, Frederick. *Lake Superior's Shipwreck Coast*. Marquette, Mich.: Avery Color Studios, 1985.

Stonehouse, Frederick. *Steel on the Bottom: Great Lakes Shipwrecks*. Gwinn, Mich.: Avery Color Studios, 2006.

Stonehouse, Frederick. *Went Missing*. AuTrain, Mich.: Avery Color Studios, 1977.

Thompson, Mark L. *Graveyard of the Lakes*. Detroit: Wayne State University Press, 2000.

Thompson, Mark L. *Queen of the Lakes*. Detroit: Wayne State University Press, 1994.

Wilterding, John H. *McDougall's Dream: The American Whaleback*. Duluth, Minn.: Lakeside Publications, 1969.

Wolff, Julius F., Jr. *Lake Superior Shipwrecks*. Duluth, Minn.: Lake Superior Port Cities, 1979, 1990.

Illustration Credits

The University of Minnesota Press gratefully acknowledges the following institutions and individuals who provided permission to reproduce the illustrations in this book.

Page 4: Duluth Public Library.

Page 7: The *Superior Times* [6] (Superior, Wisconsin), December 23, 1875. Chronicling America: Historic American Newspapers. Library of Congress. https://chroniclingamerica.loc.gov/lccn/sn85040344/1875-12-23/ed-1/seq-4/.

Pages 11, 51, 52, 151, 159, 161, 165, 166, 170: Lake Superior Maritime Collections, University of Wisconsin–Superior.

Pages 12, 14, 15, 30, 31, 63, 67, 78, 87, 88, 106, 107, 116, 136, 137, 142, 173: C. Patrick Labadie Collection, Thunder Bay National Marine Sanctuary, Alpena, Michigan.

Pages 19, 49, 50, 70, 91, 93, 94, 146, 172, 189: Kenneth Thro Collection, University Wisconsin–Superior.

Pages 22, 24, 39, 42, 96, 125: Alpena County George N. Fletcher Public Library, Alpena, Michigan.

Pages 37, 182, 185: Historical Collections of the Great Lakes, Bowling Green State University.

Page 40: Archives of Michigan (Reid raising the sunken steamer *Steinbrenner,* MS 77-27, Box 1, AOM#001568).

Pages 62, 91, 139, 157, 177: Minnesota Historical Society.

Page 75: Courtesy of City of Thunder Bay Archives (Wreck of Str. *Algoma* on Greenstone Island; Accession 1991-01, Item 160).

Pages 82 and 120: Michigan Technological University Archives and Copper Country Historical Collections, MTU Negative Collection.

Page 110: National Park Service, Isle Royale National Park (IRNP RMR, 003.35.04-004, Isle Royale Photo Archive [*America* in port], circa 1925).

Page 111: National Park Service, Isle Royale National Park (IRNP RMR, 003.35.04-002, Wolbrink Photos, #003 [*America* sinking], circa 1930).

Page 113: Courtesy of National Park Service Submerged Resources Center.

Page 119: National Park Service, Isle Royale National Park (IRNP RMR 003.35.02.01-021 #019 Rock of Ages Light Station [Under Construction], July 1, 1908).

Page 122: National Park Service, Isle Royale National Park (Larsen Album 1 #063 [wreck of the SS *George M. Cox*] 5.28.33).

Page 134: Minnesota Historical Society—Charles P. Gibson.

Page 140: The Northeast Minnesota Historical Collections, housed in the Kathryn A. Martin Library, on permanent loan from the St. Louis County Historical Society.

Pages 142 and 150: Fr. Edward J. Dowling, S.J., Marine Historical Collection, University of Detroit Mercy.

Pages 152, 153, 194: Great Lakes Marine Collection/Milwaukee Public Library.

Page 156: Detroit Publishing Company, copyright claimant and publisher. Str. *R. W. England* on the ways, Great Lakes Engineering Company, i.e., Engineering Works, May 5. Photograph retrieved from the Library of Congress. www.loc.gov/item/2016805104/.

Page 167: Courtesy of Hagley Museum and Library (Harry Coulby, *Nation's Business* 5, no. 4 [April 1917]; "Here's What Coulby Discovered," by James Morrow, 35; Haley ID: nationsbiz041917).

Page 175 and 176: Minnesota Historical Society—L. D. Campbell.

Page 181: Meteorological Service of Canada, Environment Canada.

Page 186: *Chicago Daily News* collection, Chicago History Museum (DN-0061476).

Page 192: Library of Congress, Prints and Photographs Division (LC-B2- 2903-9 [P&P] Lot 10882).

Page 196: U.S. Coast Guard photograph. Courtesy National Archives [26 LS 82-1].

Pages 199 and 201: Minnesota Historical Society—*Minneapolis Star-Journal.*

Index

Michael Schumacher has written six books about Great Lakes ship-wrecks and twenty-five narratives about Great Lakes shipwrecks and lighthouses. He is the author of *Mighty Fitz: The Sinking of the* Edmund Fitzgerald; *November's Fury: The Deadly Great Lakes Hurricane of 1913; Torn in Two: The Sinking of the* Daniel J. Morrell *and One Man's Survival on the Open Sea;* and *The Trial of the* Edmund Fitzgerald: *Eyewitness Accounts from the U.S. Coast Guard Hearings,* all published by the University of Minnesota Press. He lives in Wisconsin.